FREUD'S JAW AND OTHER
LOST OBJECTS

Freud's Jaw and Other Lost Objects

FRACTURED SUBJECTIVITY IN THE FACE OF CANCER

LANA LIN

FORDHAM UNIVERSITY PRESS
New York 2017

Fordham University Press has no responsibility for the
persistence or accuracy of URLs for external or third-party
Internet websites referred to in this publication and does not
guarantee that any content on such websites is, or will
remain, accurate or appropriate.

Fordham University Press also publishes its books in a
variety of electronic formats. Some content that appears in
print may not be available in electronic books.

Visit us online at www.fordhampress.com.

Library of Congress Cataloging-in-Publication Data
available online at http://catalog.loc.gov.

Printed in the United States of America

19 18 17   5 4 3 2 1

First edition

for LT

CONTENTS

Caring for myself is not self-indulgence,
it is self-preservation, and that is an act
of political warfare.

—AUDRE LORDE

Introduction

Every text poses itself as a demand for survival . . .

—AVITAL RONELL

In his autobiography, Roland Barthes relates that a piece of his rib was removed during an operation and subsequently returned to him by his doctor.[1] This bone was a remnant of many years of ill health, treatment, and recurrence. Between 1935, when he was nineteen, until 1947, Barthes tolerated extended stays in hospitals and sanatoriums, which altered his conception of his bodily being as well as the expected trajectory of his life. Barthes's relationship to objects is constructed through the effects of disease, one of the three words that he tells us comprise a life.[2] He stored his body fragment, a keepsake from a time when his body and its debilitated state must have been pressing upon his mind, in a drawer with other objects, such as old keys, his student report card, and his grandmother's dance program. He enshrines these "precious" objects in order to come to terms with the "death of objects."[3]

Freud's Jaw and Other Lost Objects examines loss and bodily disruption through a psychoanalytic lens. I track three exemplary figures who, like Barthes, grappled with life-threatening illness that is fundamentally destabilizing. Psychoanalyst Sigmund Freud battled oral cancer for sixteen years; poet Audre Lorde endured breast cancer for fourteen years; and literary theorist Eve Kosofsky Sedgwick suffered from breast cancer for eighteen years. With Freud, Lorde, and Sedgwick as my points of departure, I consider the ways in which cancer exposes a person to the vulnerability of her perceived bodily integrity and agency, rupturing her sense of wholeness as a human being with a degree of control over her body parts and the presumed continuities of life. Cancer not only complicates the ideal of wholeness in which people are physically and psychically invested, but it also unveils the unwanted knowledge that from the outset we have never been entirely whole, a knowledge that most of us repress in order to function from day to day. In short, cancer shows the hole in the whole.[4] It lays bare the illusory aspects of our feelings of bodily stability and the unconscious assumption that our bodies and psyches are and will remain invulnerable to disrepair. The subjects I investigate are in the process of devolving into fragmented partial objects and must devise means to reinstate, at least temporarily, their physical and psychic unity. This, I propose, is accomplished through creative reparative projects such as love or writing.

In the following chapters, I scrutinize theoretical, literary, and artistic texts that chronicle the psychic life and "death of objects." Each chapter focuses on a different type of object, which bears a relation to the psychoanalytic lost object: the prosthetic object, the breast—which is considered the "first object" according to psychoanalytic theory, love objects, and reparative objects. I will explain more fully in what follows what I take to be a lost object, but for now I emphasize its multiplicity, that it can be a lost loved person, a lost part of oneself, both physical or psychic, as well as a lost thing. Barthes shelters his severed rib much as one might stow away fears, anxieties, unwanted or outgrown parts of the self in the recesses of the unconscious. In hanging onto his partial body object, he attempts to retain this part of himself that may have signified a prior felt wholeness. When he comes to terms with his mortality, he is able to relinquish the fetish object that had protected his illusions, flinging it out the window. Like Barthes's enigmatic tale, the stories I narrate take the form of atypical autopathographies. Over the course of their slow acting but ultimately fatal affliction, Freud, Lorde, and Sedgwick were in many ways undone. Even as it confirmed their human embodiment, cancer was dehumanizing and objectifying, rendering them into objects at odds with themselves. Moreover, being the object of recurrent threats to their life forced into disturbing consciousness what people ordinarily repress, namely the heightened awareness of death's immanence in life. As Lorde phrases it, "death is the fractured border that runs through the center of my days."[5] The unwelcome knowledge of death and one's susceptibility to it is a knowledge that once released cannot be put back into the drawer. This is what makes cancer's intrusion irreparable, even as organs are replaced and tissues healed. The realization of self-difference cannot be put back, which may be why Barthes casts his bone away.

The figures I study illuminate some of the features of a subjectivity of survival. Survival for Freud meant maintenance and adjustment of his oral prostheses, addiction to smoking cigars, and the collection of thousands of antiquities. Survival for Lorde was bound up with a politics of self-preservation that involved mobilizing the mothering instincts of comrades with shared oppressions. Survival for Sedgwick was explicitly a reparative project composed of disseminating love through creative works and pedagogy. I draw on the theories of psychoanalyst Melanie Klein for the concept of "reparation," which she proposes as the creative and constructive forces that one harnesses to repair damage to one's internal psychic objects. For Klein, reparation is a means of countering the psychic fragmentation of sadistic aggression, and thereby establishing a relationship to whole objects (e.g., "mother,") as opposed to partial objects (e.g., "breast"). I discuss the ways that Freud, Lorde, and Sedgwick attempt to "make good" on the losses that cancer produces, but I want to stress that this does not equate to a reintegration or a making whole. Reparation implies that something is repaired to the extent that life can go on. For Lorde and Sedgwick, at least, community secures an always "contingent whole."[6] As will become evident especially through Sedgwick's work, reparation may indeed be something that cannot be completed by the individual but remains only partial. Through her study of Buddhism, Sedgwick comes to realize that living is a collaborative project. The Freud Museums in London and Vienna take up the collaborative project of sustaining the Freudian legacy. The Freud Museums mobilize reparative objects to compensate for the loss of "the Father" to cancer and exile. These efforts at restitution show that the nonhuman object has a privileged relation to reparation; it may even be a vital form that reparation takes. Recall that while Barthes disposed of his bony part-object, he could not be parted with the other souvenirs of his childhood. He memorializes these love objects as a museum conservator might. Similarly, the Sigmund Freud Museum in Vienna consecrates photos of Freud's residence as it appeared in 1938, before his forced departure, and the Freud Museum in London fetishizes Freud's couch and antiquities, which trailed the ailing psychoanalyst to his adopted home. These endeavors to restore a sense of untroubled intactness indicate how the psychic life of things can function ultimately as a mediation of death that helps one endure loss and enables continued survival.[7]

Freud's prolonged cohabitation with what he referred to as "my dear old cancer" qualifies him for what Arthur Frank calls "remission society."[8] According to Frank, advanced medical technologies have allowed masses of people to survive illnesses and disabilities in a state where they are "effectively well but could never be considered cured."[9] More recently, Eric Cazdyn has named the ever-growing population of those who subsist in a chronic state of neither crisis nor wellness the "already dead."[10] Beset by such temporal, physical, and hence psychic instability, Lorde and Sedgwick also join the ranks of contemporary zombies who suffer the mainte- nance of life as a death continuously and unceremoniously deferred. My project concerns the ways in which members of this "society" survive the entanglements between cancer and the other violences that they are com- pelled to endure. As Lorde states in her essay, "A Burst of Light: Living with Cancer": "Racism. Cancer. In both cases, to win the aggressor must conquer, but the resisters need only survive. How do I define that survival and on whose terms?"[11] This is a question I probe throughout the follow- ing chapters. A cancer diagnosis, psychoanalyst Mavis Himes argues, "demands a response. . . . It is impossible to remain neutral in the face of a potentially life-threatening illness."[12] *Freud's Jaw* thus applies Avital Ronell's provocation in the epigraph to Freud, Lorde, and Sedgwick's can- cer responses, suggesting that cancer performs like a text in "[posing] itself as a demand for survival."[13]

Psychoanalysis and the Cancerous Object

Cancer, as Siddhartha Mukherjee notes, is the emperor of all maladies, but it might also reasonably hold the title of the emperor of metaphor.[14] It signifies uncertainty, chronicity, unknowability. Much as Susan Sontag would have us divorce cancer from its metaphorical meanings, cancer so easily and powerfully slides into metaphor that S. Lochlann Jain argues that it is as much comprised of its metaphors as its statistics, cellular struc- ture, biomedical bureaucracy, and biotechnologies.[15] Cancer is inseparable from metaphors of invasion, in particular of an enemy from within, an enemy composed of one's own internal body parts. In Sherwin Nuland's *How We Die*, the "Malevolence of Cancer" is described as immortal, amoral, and immoral. Cancer cells are lawless, asocial nonconformists, invading their law abiding, conforming neighbors.[16] Cancer tends to rhyme with the prevailing cultural climate such that its unceasing accumu- lation can be seen as a mirror to neoliberal capitalism. The very antithesis of containment, cancer is defined as malignancy, profusion, proliferation.

The treatment of this too-muchness often entails enforcing absence upon an excessive presence.

There have been innumerable studies on cancer from medical, sociological, anthropological, historical, cultural, and psychological perspectives. What does psychoanalysis offer that so many of these other studies do not? While previous studies have tended to concentrate upon cancer's conscious effects, one of the hallmarks of psychoanalysis is that it attends to the unconscious dimension of human experience. Psychoanalytic intervention can clarify the problems that cancer stages across the tenuous divide between the conscious and unconscious. Cancer can be seen as doing the work of psychoanalysis in making conscious what was once unconscious. Affliction has the capacity to uncover knowledge that is typically repressed in order for humans to carry on quotidian existence, for instance, our susceptibility to damage, the awareness of one's mortality, and death's immanence in life. What is fundamentally lost as a result of a cancer diagnosis is the reassuring sense of wholeness that comes from feeling at one with oneself. This is related to what Freud, referencing Romain Rolland, has called "oceanic feeling." Freud and Rolland described the feeling of being at one with the universe.[17] Although Freud insisted that he was not subject to the religious sentiments that Rolland associated with this feeling, he acknowledged that before being able to distinguish itself from the external world, the infant experiences itself and its universe as one. Gradually the infant learns that some sensations are stimulated from sources outside itself, and in this way it comes to perceive itself as an ego and objects as originating outside of its own ego.[18] Upon differentiation between self and world, the oceanic feeling with regard to the ego and its objects may for the most part be discontinued (though Freud notes that it continues without pathology when one is in love); however, it is carried on in relation to one's own ego.[19] That is to say, the mature ego is experienced as coincident with itself. One's sense of wholeness derives from the feeling that I and myself are "one." Psychoanalysis provides concepts that elucidate the disruption of the oceanic feeling as it pertains to one's own ego. Cancer could be said to be ego-dystonic in the sense that it works against the ideally integrated, totalizing ego, opposing Ernest Jones's definition of ego-syntonic tendencies as those that are "consonant, compatible and consistent with the standards of the self."[20] Trauma, such as cancer, can unmoor ego and self-object, producing the disconcerting feeling that a foreign object has intruded upon the ego.

Physical calamity shatters the sensation of unity with oneself, resulting in the experience of an alien version of oneself intruding upon oneself. In an essay titled "The Intruder," Jean-Luc Nancy describes his heart transplant whose follow-up treatment caused cancer. He observes that a "gentle sliding separated me from myself."[21] Nancy is afflicted by a "strangeness of my own identity," and experiences the discontinuity "between me and me" where "I" can no longer be expressed by the simple equation "I" = "I."[22] Grave illness produces divisions in the bodily ego that give rise to the feeling that I am not myself. Felix Deutsch, once Freud's physician, called Freud's cancer an "uninvited, unwished intruder," and Sharon Romm, a plastic surgeon who compiled Freud's case history, titled her book *The Unwelcome Intruder*.[23] For Nancy it is not so much cancer or a transplanted heart that intrudes, but the self that becomes an intruder upon itself. Freud has identified this intruder as the uncanny. He tells the anecdote that during a train trip the car in which he was riding made a sudden jolt, and the washing cabinet door swung open to reveal a stranger in his compartment.[24] Jumping to his feet, he realized that the intruder was none other than his own reflection in the mirror of the open door. Part of the unconscious that is dredged up with cancer is expressed as an uncanniness in which one is estranged from oneself.[25] Less to do with bodily impairments that can be repaired, cancer can awaken core primal fears: doubt, dread, anxiety. The self no longer feels at home with itself. The ailing subject loses its relationship to itself. Psychoanalysis can get at this particular species of subjectivity because it has dealt with it with regard to infantile psychic life as well as psychotic episodes. In Melanie Klein's language, the infant feels itself and its environment to be made up of disconnected partial objects. Recognizing and interacting with whole objects (both internal and external) is a developmental achievement that may not be secured in the case of psychosis or may be derailed through trauma that thrusts the sufferer back to an infantile stage when the self as a coherent bodily and psychic entity was not yet established.

Cancer has a psychoanalytic meaning. Cancer has meaning for the body of psychoanalysis. It bears repeating that it is not any disease that has cast its shadow upon psychoanalytic history and theory. It is specifically cancer that plagues psychoanalysis as "unwelcome intruder." While both psychoanalysis and oncology are uneasy with the notion of cure, like cancer treatment, psychoanalysis induces an illness (the transference neurosis) as part of its "cure." Furthermore, the cancer metaphor infects and proliferates in psychoanalytic discourse. Lacan uses it to describe the powerful, even treacherous effects of language: "speech is an overlay, a parasite, the form of cancer with which human beings are afflicted."[26] Kristeva following upon Lacan defines the symptom as a "language that gives up . . . a non-assimilable alien, a monster, a tumor, a cancer that the listening devices of the unconscious do not hear."[27] Ernst Simmel claimed that civilization produces anti-Semitism, which he diagnosed as a pathological symptom-formation that, like cancer, destroys its host: "Anti-Semitism is a malignant growth on the body of civilization."[28] While Erich Fromm coined the term "malignant narcissism," Michael Balint designates regression as either malignant or benign.[29] In his speech on the tenth anniversary of Freud's death, Felix Deutsch connects cancerous proliferation to an innate dread of death: "Any person carries within him . . . the fantasy of the infantile past, in which he wished and feared the fulfillment of a procreative growth."[30] Paul Schilder observes that it is quite common to fear cancers, which eat away from inside: "The idea of rotting and losing the inside or the outside of one's body is one of the deepest and most primitive fears."[31] These apprehensions relate not only to the menace of cancer cells but also to their toxic treatment. The combined threat of a "rotting" disease such as cancer and its draconian treatments may be responsible for touching off deep-seated fears in many, not only cancer patients. Klein refers to a patient who "had phantasies that a tapeworm was eating its way through his body and a strong anxiety of cancer came to the fore."[32] The Kleinian internalized love object is reduced to "dangerous fragments" that are reminiscent of malignant cells.[33] These key psychoanalytic thinkers indicate how psycho-analysis conceptualizes not only metastatic disease, but also the idea of recurrence, the absence of cure, the presence of death or proximity to one's mortality. In addition, they deploy cancer and its vicissitudes as a metaphor for the fantasy of immortality, recognition of self and other, and the rejection of not-self or the foreign object. On a figurative level, cancer helps to explain multiple concepts that constitute the subjectivity of survival.

Cancer's delayed effect, the fact that one might harbor cancerous cells long before any symptoms manifest themselves, can also be thought of in psychoanalytic terms, according to the temporality of *Nachträglichkeit*. The concept of deferred action presumes that a prior trauma is the cause of a present day event the effect of which is belatedly experienced. Cancer's peculiar temporal threat is one of both prediction and postponement. With a cancer diagnosis one is always looking both backward for a cause, to a genetic predisposition, an exposure to toxins, or to lifestyle choices, and forward to a potential recurrence or a metastasis. Applying the concept of *Nachträglichkeit* to the cancer situation, the present state is continually rein-terpreted based upon revised understandings of the past. A cancer diagnosis casts doubt and suspicion upon the familiar recall of a life, rescripting its predicted narrative.

Cancer provides a dramatic example of how a person can occupy the position of subject and object at the same time. Moreover, cancer itself can seem to become an object in its own right. When a doctor finds a lump in her breast, journalist Joyce Wadler feels it is "as much a presence in the room as another human being," though the physician has yet to even mention it by name.[34] During her cancer treatment, anthropologist S. Lochlann Jain is confounded by "being an object in other people's daily work lives."[35] As an immune disorder, the cancerous body literally betrays the self, seeming to turn itself into its own malignant object. Cancer cells perform their treason through over productivity. In 1951, unbeknownst to her, cells from Henrietta Lacks's cancerous cervix were cultured for biomedical research and still survive today as the first human immortal cell line.[36] Lacks's aggressive tumor cells, named HeLa cells, continue to reproduce themselves although their host has long since passed away. This has led Mukherjee to judge cancer successful in the very goal that humanity has eternally sought, that of immortality, though it achieves it at the expense of its subject.[37]

Cancer's striving for an immortality exacted from one's mortality mirrors the contradictions of Freud's death drive. Freud proposes his radical and speculative theory of the death drive in *Beyond the Pleasure Principle*. He turns to cancer for evidence of narcissistic behavior on the cellular level, meaning that the cells conserve their energy for their own preservation rather than for external objects: "The cells of the malignant neoplasms which destroy the organism should also perhaps be described as narcissistic."[38] To characterize cancer cells as narcissistic is paradoxically to link the destructive forces of malignancy with love of self, as seen through the need and desire to survive. Cancer epitomizes the workings of the death drive in its aim of returning the organism to a state of inertia, while also demonstrating the strivings of the life drives toward immortality. Cancer cells refuse to comply with the "internal necessity of dying."[39] They multiply wildly, and can thus be seen as carriers of the life drives. This is why I propose and will elaborate in Chapter 1 that the death drive, with cancer as its avatar, is more about "not-death," that is, the process of entanglement of the life and death drives, than it is about death itself.[40] Cancer is emblematic of this condition of not-death.

Psychoanalysis and Death

If psychoanalysis has not hitherto been commonly associated with cancer, it has been represented variously as lethal and as itself dying or already dead.[41] The specter of death haunts psychoanalysis in several ways. There are at least two important reasons for this. One is that Freud, the founder of psychoanalysis, tolerated a life threatening illness for a decade and a half, and was already predisposed to thoughts of death prior to his cancer diagnosis, as I will bring out in Chapter 1. Second, the impact of the wars during the formative years of psychoanalysis should not be underestimated. In the late nineteenth century, the early period of the psychoanalytic movement, Jews comprised psychoanalytic society to such an extent that many consider it a Jewish science. As racialized targets of persecution, many of the important voices in psychoanalytic history suffered displacement and exile, some were exterminated, others committed suicide.[42] The horrors of such a history validate psychoanalysis's chief characteristic of existential unhappiness, the discontent (*Unbehagen*) that Freud seeks to yet cannot fully explain in *Civilization and its Discontents*. The American poet H.D. recounts a remark that Freud made to her that reveals the extent to which death is tied to psychoanalysis: "In analysis, the person is dead after the analysis is over," to which H.D., Freud's former analysand, asked, "Which person?"[43] Not only is there confusion as to which person Freud is speaking about (the analysand, the analyst, the parental figures are all viable options), as H.D. points out, there is also an ambiguity about the meaning of death. The "impossibility" of psychoanalysis, as Janet Malcolm appraises the profession, is bound up with its death obsession, its veritable death-inducing practice.[44] Malcolm compares the morbidity of psychoanalysis to the morbidity of the body and its rejection of foreign matter:

> All analyses end badly. Each "termination" leaves the participants with the taste of ashes in their mouths . . . each is a small, pointless death. Psychoanalysis cannot tolerate happy endings; it casts them off the way the body's immunological system casts off transplanted organs. Throughout its history, attempts have been made to change the tragic character of psychoanalysis, and all have failed.[45]

Freud came to believe that all organisms unconsciously desire a return to their origins that can be equated with death. If nothing else, Freud's complicated formulation that all organic life is oriented toward its own destruction while at the same time seeking self-preservation could be said to give death agency in life. In his theory of the death drive he argued that every organism "wishes to die only in its own fashion."[46] Consistent with his theory, in his last years he confirmed the wish to die in his own fashion, securing a promise from his physician not to let him die in agony.[47]

Following Freud, Lorde, also, contrived to die only in her own fashion, turning self-care and self-preservation into "an act of political warfare."[48]

When death takes on an active presence in life, such as for inhabitants of war zones and areas of chronic crime, or those harboring incurable illness, it can be channeled into action. This is the tactic Lorde employs when tackling unjustifiable deaths from poverty, race riots, and environmental disaster. She is determined to find a way "to integrate death into living, neither ignoring it nor giving in to it."[49] Referring to Lorde's poem "Today is Not the Day," about embracing but postponing death, Lisa Diedrich writes: "According to Lorde, dying isn't simply something that happens to a person: dying is something one does."[50] Sedgwick likewise found the prospect of death to be galvanizing, propelling her AIDS and cancer activism, pedagogy, and publication. Drawing upon Buddhism, she teaches that we must come to *realize*—which is to comprehend mentally, emotionally, and affectively—the death that we know we will bear. Through their protracted illnesses, Freud, Lorde, and Sedgwick were each made to realize the role of death in life, and each constructed a response to it that enabled them to survive with the imbrication of death and life.

Key Psychoanalytic Concepts

Central to my argument is an analysis of the power of and affective investments in objects. I must therefore ask what work an object does, particularly under conditions of debility and precarity. To begin with, then, what is an object, according to psychoanalysis? Freud introduced the term "object" in relation to sexual instincts.[51] At the outset of *Three Essays on Sexuality* he states: "Let us call the person from whom sexual attraction proceeds the *sexual object*."[52] This begs the question of what an instinct is, which is no small matter. I do not wish to go into an overly technical explanation of the concept of the instinct and its vicissitudes, which would detract from my aim of setting the stage for a psychoanalytic discussion of objects. For my purposes, it is sufficient to understand an instinct as Freud perhaps most succinctly puts it in *Instincts and their Vicissitudes*, as "a concept on the frontier between the mental and the somatic."[53] One can think of it as a psychical urge that is bound up with somatic impulses, and the object is that toward which the instinct is directed. It is important to note that an object can be a thing or a person or even a part of a person, and that it can be either external to or constitutive of the subject, for instance, it can be a part of an external body such as the maternal breast or it can be part of the subject's own body such as one's jaw.[54] The psychoanalytic school of object-relations theory focuses upon the interrelation between subjects and objects. A subject from an object-relations point of view is constituted by and through objects. With her concept of internal objects, Klein goes further to situate objects within the realm of unconscious phantasy.[55] According to Klein, psychic life begins with phantasies involving part-objects. Part-objects dominate during the infantile stage of human development. A "part-object" is typically defined as a part of a whole anatomical object of desire, but it is "firstly an emotional object, having a function rather than a material existence."[56] The maternal breast is both the original part-object and the prototypical lost loved object. It is the first object toward which love and hatred is directed. The psychoanalytic study of child development sheds light upon the psychic effects of physical trauma because, as Klein understands it, trauma later in life can revive the infantile destruction and reparation of part-objects.

The psychoanalytic study of psychosis can also lend some concepts that elucidate the psychic depletion and decomposition that people with organic illness experience. Psychoanalyst Wilfred Bion described a splitting of the ego in schizophrenic patients whose perceptual apparatuses are "cut up, split into minute fragments."[57] This psychic procedure leaves the patient in a state "which is felt to be neither alive nor dead," a condition that Nancy and Sedgwick describe in very similar terms.[58] Nancy's youngest son called him "one of the living-dead," and when Sedgwick tries to devise a substitute for the term "cancer survivor," she rolls out a long list of alternatives, settling on "undead" as her favorite.[59] Bion calls the eviscerated ejecta of the split ego "bizarre objects," which are a monstrous hybrid of evacuated bits of psychic material and a real external object.[60] Bion recognized an affinity between the "bizarre object" and technology in citing the example of a gramophone that spies on his patient. Most of the objects that I deal with could be considered in some sense "bizarre." Freud's prosthetic jaw and Sedgwick's prosthetic breasts, for instance, both force a reconception of self as fragmented, fabricated, and foreign to themselves. Exhausted from the pain of years of prosthetic maladjustment, Freud is made into a mechanical object: "I detest my mechanical jaw because the struggle with the mechanism consumes so much precious strength. Yet I prefer a mechanical jaw to no jaw at all. I prefer existence to extinction."[61]

Freud's dependence upon prosthetic objects demonstrates the degree to which humans are composed and decomposed by technology. His objectification proceeds by technology even as he repudiates becoming an object. And Sedgwick contemplates how to align her bodily image with physical reality, suggesting a discontinuity that requires her to make reparations in order to find herself recognizable. "Just getting dressed in the morning means deciding how many breasts I will be able to recognize myself [*sic*] if I am wearing (a voice in me keeps whispering, *three*)."[62] Day-to-day survival requires both to deploy their bizarre objects to reconstitute themselves, but doing so can be felt as a technologization of the body. Nancy confirms this experience of a technologized existence when his disconcerted "I" "always finds itself tightly squeezed in a wedge of technical possibilities."[63]

The notion of attachment and dependency recurs throughout this book in both its literal and psychoanalytic senses. I begin with Freud's literal attachment to his prosthetic jaw, which was installed to prop up the tissues of his mouth and even his eyeball, and allow him to eat. I then turn to other types of attachment necessary to his survival, including his addiction to smoking cigars, his devotion to his dogs, and his almost complete dependence upon his daughter and caregiver, Anna. Anaclisis, from the Greek *anaklino*, to rest upon or to lean on, refers to an attachment of dependency.[64] Jean Laplanche and J. B. Pontalis point out that the relation of the object to instinct is intimately tied to the concept of anaclisis (*Anlehnung*), which Freud introduced in 1905. The sexual instincts *lean upon* the self-preservative instincts, initially depending on those vital functions to supply them with their source, orientation, and object. Freud consequently designates two types of object-choice, the anaclitic and narcissistic. The narcissistic choice is modeled on the subject's own self. Cancer is a fundamentally narcissistic wound because, as I have been arguing, it injures the subject's relationship to herself. The anaclitic object-choice is modeled on parental care, those figures upon whom the infant leaned for self-preservation. In Chapter 1, I elaborate on how Freud's instinct for survival leans upon and is propped up by his prosthesis, that is, how he has an anaclitic relationship to his prostheses. Chapters 2 and 3 center on Lorde's anaclitic relationship to her politics and community, and Sedgwick's anaclitic relationship to her therapist as well as how she herself serves as an anaclitic object for her readers.

Attachments for Freud, and within the school of object relations, are always conditioned by loss. Through his definition of mourning and melancholia, Freud shows how loss and attachment implicate each other.[65] Mourning is the psychic process by which libido is gradually detached and withdrawn from a lost loved object. With melancholia the object is lost in one sense, yet preserved in another. The melancholic incorporates the lost object into her own ego and identifies with it. In this way she maintains an attachment that is, however, toxic. But prior to his 1917 essay on mourning and melancholia, Freud had already outlined a theory of sexuality that is founded upon loss. In his *Three Essays*, he emphasizes that finding the first sexual object is really a refinding of it, following the original loss of the maternal breast.[66] The sexual instinct begins with the maternal breast as its object, then it loses its object and turns to itself, becoming autoerotic, and finally it rediscovers object choices outside of itself. The prototype for the love object is therefore lost before any object relation is established, pointing to an originary loss at the heart of all object relations.

In their anthology *Loss: The Politics of Mourning*, which unpacks the sociocultural and political meanings of loss, David Eng and David Kazanjian observe that loss is "inseparable from what remains, for what is lost is known only by what remains of it, by how these remains are produced, read, and sustained."[67] My research highlights the manner in which remains can be material or immaterial. Prostheses, for instance, literally take the shape of what is lost, but what remains of the first object? *Freud's Jaw* suggests that "what remains" can take the form of representations, body parts, memories, writing, photography, architecture, legend. I argue that the way in which lost objects are negotiated (incorporated, repudiated, hallucinated, etc.) is a way of mediating death (physical and psychic). Rather than propound a passive hopelessness that is typically associated with melancholia, I mean to follow Eng and Kazanian's counterintuitive reading of loss, which "encourages us to understand the melancholic ego's death drive as the precondition for living and for living on."[68] Ultimately, my aim aligns with their recuperation of melancholia for a politics of creativity. Only by attending to, rather than disavowing, perennial loss can we as a culture and as a collection of lost objects ourselves, refind ourselves, love one another, and labor toward physical, emotional, and political reparations.

In addition to part-objects, anaclitic objects, and lost objects, I rely upon the psychoanalytic concept of the fetish object. The fetish is a sexual fixation to a part-object. For Freud it is installed as a substitute for the maternal penis in its absence.[69] As a memorial to a treasured belief that the fetishist refuses to abandon, it shares with melancholia a defiant attachment to a lost object. As such, the fetish is a useful concept with which to understand the psychic and material solutions to problems of loss. The threatening danger of loss drives the fetishist to conjure substitutes. A fetish can alleviate the fear that one will no longer be whole, or it can compensate for a feeling of not being whole. Fetishism performs a creative misidentification or inventive identification with something that is not present. In contrast to melancholia, it is characterized by a lack of ambivalence. A fetishist has no qualms about her fetish.[70] Fetishism, then, may be a mode of mourning, a way of dealing with the ambivalence toward one's morbidity and finitude. The constructive impulse behind fetishism explains why it is deployed in traumatic situations. In dialogue with Lorde's critique of breast prostheses, I read contemporary breast reconstruction in terms of a fetishism in which the reconstructed breast defends against the terror of absence that is associated with the loss of the first part-object. Additionally, in Chapter 4 I analyze the collection of thousands of antiquities that Freud amassed as his own fetish idols to appease the pain of his ordeal with cancer and political exile. After his death, Freud was himself fetishized by Anna Freud, who preserved her father's study as a memorial to her lost love object, one that now serves as the centerpiece of the London Freud Museum. Since all of Freud's significant possessions were transported from his home and offices in Vienna and are currently on view in the London Freud Museum, the Sigmund Freud Museum in Vienna has a more complicated relation to fetishism than its rival. Armed with little more than absence, the Vienna Museum fetishizes its literal lost objects by way of photographs that memorialize and substitute for them, and, I argue, are displayed in the Museum as a partial remedy for its deprivation of the authentic Freudian artifacts.

Psychic Life of Objects

One of the goals of this book is to broaden the scope of what "counts" as an object in the theory of psychoanalytic object relations. In this aim I am influenced by Bill Brown's proposal of an expanded field of object relations that takes into account the constitution of the human through nonhuman objects.[71] An expanded notion of object relations contends with objects that are not "properly" psychoanalytic, namely the psychic life of things as opposed to persons. Conventionally psychoanalytic objects correspond to human beings, parts of human beings, or their psychic equivalents. But human survival entails encounters with foreign objects, be they human or nonhuman. In showing how morbidity is negotiated through nonhuman objects, I intend to give psychoanalytically informed criticism a more nuanced discussion around material culture. To these ends I intentionally conflate what psychoanalysis has tended to hold apart, drawing attention to the unstable boundaries between the human and nonhuman, the immaterial and material. Challenging fixed notions of what constitutes an object and the psychic work that objects can do, I assert that moments of rupture blur the clear distinctions between subjects and objects, human and nonhuman, and the physical and psychic. Confrontation with the foreignness of mortality reveals the fragility and vulnerability of the contours of our selves and our worlds. Presumed binaries, such as the distinction between the animate and inanimate, and between life and death, are put into question.

People suffering affliction are often perceived by others and themselves as objects, of either the animate or inanimate variety. Objectification is also a brutal effect of social violences such as racism, sexism, homophobia, and transphobia. Freud and Lorde uncannily illustrate the predicament of self-objectification, and its entwinement with social objectification, with essentially the same metaphor. Following a heart attack, Freud wrote to his friend and colleague Sandor Ferenczi about feeling like a fox that bites off its leg to free itself from a snare.[72] Later Freud returns to this same metaphor to describe his escape from Nazi-controlled Austria.[73] More than once, in the context of racial and sexual oppression as well as health crisis, Lorde compares herself to the she-wolf who likewise destroys a part of herself to survive. It is significant that in each of these cases, whether medical or social, a threat to life transforms the subject into an object of self-aggression. But this self-destructive impulse paradoxically serves the subject's survival. For Melanie Klein, destruction sets the scene for reparation. The subject wishes to repair what has been destroyed. Reparation is a creative, constructive impulse that expresses love for the damaged object. Psychoanalyst D. W. Winnicott theorizes that destroying the love object is actually a precondition for the capacity to love.[74] Drawing on Winnicott, my study suggests that when the subject must answer to the demand for survival, acceptance of destruction coincides with sustenance of the love object. Destruction is necessary for the subject to experience love for itself and others, which in turn makes survival possible.

My research seeks to cast the categories of both the human and nonhuman into new light, indicating the ways in which humans are dehumanized while also highlighting the animate quality of things. Prosthetic and fetish objects are material objects that are endowed with powers of agency that put them on par with or at least in dialogue with their human owners. I follow Diana Fuss in "treating objects as viable philosophical subjects, and subjects as tenable material objects."[75] I take Fuss to mean that objects, whether human or nonhuman, are worthy of philosophical inspection and that subjects always possess a degree of brute materiality that entails examination. It is with this in mind that I analyze the vitalizing purpose of a panoply of material objects: Freud's prostheses, cigars, and antiquities, Lorde's mother's mortar, reconstructed breasts, Sedgwick's therapist's business card, magazines, photographs, and books. An anecdote about how Freud bought himself a consolation gift of an antique vase following one of his many surgeries demonstrates how nonhuman objects can become infused with psychic force. In a letter to a friend he described the effect of acquiring the vase as a revitalization or enlivening comfort (*Erquickung*).[76]

His jaw prosthesis and art collection—although the former was experienced as monstrous and the latter almost divine—functioned analogously in mediating the painful process of facing his mortality.

Freud's Jaw wants to think about *matters* of life and death, and the stress on matter comes in the wake of a "nonhuman turn" in contemporary scholarship, as Richard Grusin has put it.[77] This attention to the nonhuman intersects with a vast array of literatures that take objects as philosophical subject, including actor-network theory, speculative realism, object-oriented philosophy, new materialism, vital materialism, agential realism, animal studies, affect theory, assemblage theory, systems theory, thing theory, and posthumanism.[78] *Freud's Jaw* joins these studies to the extent that it views the human as an imbrication of rather than a distinction between human and nonhuman, however, it diverges significantly from this heterogeneous scholarship. My primary purpose is not to examine things in themselves, as is the aim of object-oriented ontologies that advance new metaphysics about the nature of objects. Certainly Freud's prosthesis qualifies as a tool in its most basic sense. Exceeding its brute quality and usefulness, as an extension of its user, it exhibits what Graham Harman calls "tool-being" in his expansion of Heidegger's concept of "readiness-to-hand."[79] The horror story of Freud's multiplying prostheses exemplifies an excessive presence that Harman ultimately rejects yet speculative realist Steven Shaviro embraces wherein the tool "stands forth *too* actively and aggressively. . . . That is to say, the tool, or the thing, becomes *alive.*"[80] The prosthetic assemblage treads in that intermediate area between life and nonlife where vital materialists gather. But *Freud's Jaw* is fundamentally a psychoanalytically informed study that pursues the involvement of subjects and objects (physical and psychic, human and nonhuman) in order to gain insight into human conditions. While it attends to the relations between subjects and objects, its emphasis is on a psychoanalytic understanding of objects, which is to say, it asks how human and nonhuman objects interact and impinge upon one another on the level of the conscious and unconscious. I admit to a remnant of binary thinking between "subject" and "object" because so much of psychoanalytic theory rests upon this distinction. However, the terminological divide between "subject" and "object" does not mean that a body may not be both or that it must be human. In this sense, my thinking is closer to Sara Ahmed's queer phenomenology, which wishes to *queer* and reorient the ways in which bodies are oriented toward and away from others, than it is to the aforementioned literature.[81]

As with object-oriented ontologists or speculative realists, political theorist Jane Bennett is motivated by an urge to foreground the nonhuman animal, thing or assemblage. She concisely describes her book *Vibrant Matter* as "highlight[ing] what is typically cast in the shadow."[82] By this she means the vital materiality of nonhuman, not quite human, or not entirely human actants. Bennett's investigation of the creative power of things has an affinity to mine, however, within my psychoanalytically guided framework, the shadow that falls upon the object is the shadow of a lost object, typically a lost loved person, but also an ideal.[83] For my purposes, this embodied loss arrives at the impetus of illness, but I also cast my eye upon the shadow on the floor at Freud's former home in Vienna, in the empty space that remains after his exile. In doing so my goal is to use psychoanalytic terms to stretch the ways in which psychic life is thought about and discussed, whereas Bennett strives to contribute to a political ecology of vibrant materialism. As an example of nonhuman agency, Bennett turns to Charles Darwin's study of earthworms. Psychoanalyst Adam Phillips also elects Darwin's observations on worms as exemplary, but for him, the worms provide the occasion to discover what they mean to Darwin.[84] The meaning of worms for Darwin leads Phillips to ask what it means for humans to live with transience. My reflections upon the human and nonhuman are more akin to Phillips, which is to say that I examine the nonhuman arena in order to contemplate the psychic problem of how to endure the ephemerality of life, one's own and others.

In her seminal "Cyborg Manifesto," feminist science and technology scholar Donna Haraway selects the woman of color as her prototypical cyborg figure. Audre Lorde is her representative of "a cyborg identity, a potent subjectivity synthesized from fusions of outsider identities."[85] Within my reading, Lorde is indeed a cyborg, and I would suggest that to some extent what I am calling the technological predicament of illness renders its hybrid subjects/objects into cyborg identities, including Freud and Sedgwick. Consistent with Haraway's description, within the context of *Freud's Jaw*, Lorde, Freud, and Sedgwick show how "cyborg writing is about the power to survive."[86] As feminist philosopher Rosi Braidotti narrates it, "[Haraway] wants to invent a new discourse for the unconscious," and she uses the becoming-animal, the cyborg, the trickster, and the oncomouse [*sic*] as her revolutionary figures, or her "structures of otherness."[87] This new discourse for the unconscious is precisely what I aspire to when I examine a relative of the OncoMouse™, the reconstructed postmastectomy woman. Whereas Haraway opposes the Oedipalized unconscious, and the binary structures that descend from the Oedipal family romance, this book contends that there is more to psychoanalysis than Oedipalization, and hence, is not fundamentally at odds with many psychoanalytic naysayers. My analysis of cyborg bodies shares with Braidotti's critical posthuman theory an interest in the politics of subjectivity. As Braidotti opines, "One needs at least *some* subject position: this need not be either unitary or exclusively anthropocentric, but it must be the site for political and ethical accountability, for collective imaginaries and shared aspirations."[88] Along with Braidotti, I believe there is still much to collectively learn about human subjectivity, and I remain invested in probing its complexities, among which I count its persistent ambivalence, its obscurity (i.e., that it is largely unconscious), and its impingements by human and nonhuman external objects. I continue to be drawn back to the question Barbara Johnson poses, how do we treat persons as persons and not as things?[89] In the end, Johnson concedes that we do not yet know what a person is. Objects are everywhere she says. We know all too well how to treat persons as objects. We often cannot escape treating ourselves as objects. But we have not done learning about the psychic life of persons. To this end, she quotes Paul de Man, Sedgwick's teacher, who claimed that there is something inhuman at the heart of language, and since language is a human invention, this may mean that there is something inhuman within our very humanity.[90]

Sedgwick, like Lorde, Haraway, and many fellow feminists and activists, was critical of the ways in which Freudian psychoanalysis and often Freud himself reduced what she called its "lush plurality."[91] However, this criticism did not equate to dismissing psychoanalysis, for she embraced Kleinian theory. In Sedgwick's hands, due to the influence of psychologist Silvan Tomkins, Klein's psychoanalysis becomes a theory of affect.[92] If we accept, as Richard Grusin suggests, that affect theory is always object-oriented, one could trace a relation between Sedgwick's interests and object-oriented ontologies that highlight autonomous affect.[93] As Sedgwick and Adam Frank make clear in their introduction to *Shame and Its Sisters: A Silvan Tomkins Reader*, Tomkins's affect theory was informed by cybernetics and systems theory. Tomkins conceived of the human as a layering of the biological and machinic. Tomkins's human is, in this sense, if not a cyborg, a precursor to a cyborg. Sedgwick and Frank situate Tomkins's theories within what they deem the "cybernetic fold," a time period characterized by imaginative creativity, especially in regard to the potential of computers, and likely motivated by the technological incapacity to realize those fantasies.[94] One might say, therefore, that Sedgwick and Frank place Tomkins within a psychoanalytic framework of fantasy, despite Tomkins's own rejection of psychoanalysis. Sedgwick and Frank's enthusiasm for Tomkins's affective model has since popularized it for contemporary scholars. Elizabeth A. Wilson, for instance, relying on Tomkins's taxonomy of affects, locates the synergies between affect and artificial intelligence within the "cybernetic fold" and points out that psychoanalysts sat with mathematicians at the historic Macy conferences (1946–53) where the new science of cybernetics was debated.[95] Today such a dialogue would be unheard of, but history reveals that at one time it was at least hoped that psychoanalysis and computer science could have something to say to one another. Because I am focused on a psychoanalytic, as opposed to an affective, account of survival under the threat of malignant disease, I merely note here Tomkins's significance within a lineage of affect studies. It is also worth knowing that amongst the "scripts" that Tomkins defined as consisting of "the scene as a basic element in life as it is lived," "nuclear scripts" are described as cancerous.[96] In attempting to defensively turn bad scenes that threaten our idealizations back into idealized good scenes, nuclear scripts involve a kind of malignant growth because they must be chronically replayed. Tomkins states: "Nuclear scripts arrive from the unwillingness to renounce or mourn what has become irresistibly seductive and the inability to recover what has been lost."[97] Tomkins's nuclear scripts are bound up with the mourning, loss, and desire for reparation that I am associating with the onset of cancer. Expanding upon and beyond the focus of this book, a history of affect might be written in which cancer's losses and reparations play a part.

Methodologies: Psychoanalysis and Pathography

While I chiefly deploy psychoanalytic concepts to investigate how people suffer their entanglements with the object world, specifically within the realm of life-threatening illness, I also make use of literary theory, and gender, visual culture, and disability studies. Relying on the public and private writing of Freud, Lorde, and Sedgwick, I engage in textual analysis and enact the type of close readings that are associated with literary criticism. My objects of study include Freud's theoretical writing, letters, diary, and doctor's case notes; Lorde's published essays and poems as well as letters and excerpts from unpublished journals; and Sedgwick's breast cancer journalism and poetic memoir, which contains her therapist's notes. I also draw on site visits to the London and Vienna Freud Museums to make phenomenological observations of their spaces and holdings. I strive to lead the reader toward greater insight through associations, interpretations, and constructions that mimic the psychoanalytic method.

Directing my attention to the ways in which illness is inscribed on the page, within culture, and onto the body has involved me in a study of pathography. Pathography originally referred to the description of disease, but has come to mean the study of an individual or community's life and history with regard to the influence of a disease.[98] Anne Hunsaker Hawkins defines pathography simply as an autobiography or biography that describes personal experiences with illness and treatment.[99] I choose to analyze Freud's, Lorde's, and Sedgwick's cancer narratives because as atypical pathographies, they testify to the vulnerability and unpredictability of our corporeal materiality, refusing to serve up hope, closure, and coherence in the encounter with bodily disintegrity. Lorde's *The Cancer Journals*, published amid the early wave of modern pathographies, offers a more radical critique and politics than typical pathographies, but consistent with the genre is recognized as empowering to those afflicted. Lorde may not have intended a correlation between her breast cancer narrative and slave narrative, but G. Thomas Couser argues that they have an affinity in sharing "the hope of abolishing a threatening condition that their narrators were fortunate enough to escape."[100]

If it is not autopathography, psychoanalysis clearly bears some relation to autobiography, if only because its primary material derives from the stories of people's lives. The autobiographical basis of psychoanalysis, combined with its preoccupation with death, has motivated Derrida to designate psychoanalysis *autothanatography*.[101] Actually for Derrida all writing is autothanatography, a writing of one's own death, because to write is to sign oneself to a text that survives after one's death. Psychoanalysis is autothanatography to Derrida because it brings together Freud's obsessions with his own family drama and with death. Psychoanalysis and autopathography share the narration of one's own process of dying, at greater or lesser speeds. Death is what binds the analysand to the analyst, and the pathographer to the reader, the viewer, the listener, the witness, because it is what everyone has in common—mortality.

Mel Y. Chen's *Animacies* contains an autopathographic account of the cultural and biopolitical construals of life and death within the regimes of race and sexuality.[102] Chen deploys toxicity as a methodology to track the queer capacities and mobilities of animacies, a plural concept deriving from linguistics that connotes liveness, and whose contradictions and complications problematize the very notion of "life" and "death," exposing their instability. Poisoned by mercury, Chen must navigate daily existence and the intimacies of public engagement with a sensitivity toward survival. In this, Chen resembles the figures that guide *Freud's Jaw*, pressured by multiple and conflicting practices of survival.[103] Chen's sensitized cells demand an avoidance of offending bodies that impinge upon their own bodily stability through perfume, smoke, or sunscreen, while a history of internalized racist glances and disdain for their gender-nonconforming appearance has trained Chen to refuse the self-monitoring that such encounters call for. In contrast to Sedgwick's expulsion of toxic queer shame, and José Esteban Muñoz's disidentificatory absorption of toxic desire, Chen's toxicity is neither simply exterior nor interior; it is a sociality in which bodies ingest the cells of their surround.[104] Similar to my conception of "not-death," introduced in Chapter 1, toxicity for Chen intervenes between the binary of "life" and "death," disrupting this illusory boundary. While they may be repelled by animate objects, Chen has discovered an intimacy, even a "communing" with inanimate objects such as their couch.[105] Their notion of interanimacy strikingly demonstrates the extension of the psyche that Freud pondered a year before his death, a problem that I cannot help but imagine he contemplated in communion with the single sheet of paper on which his final musings appear and remain.[106] Chen proceeds to ask what is lost when a person attains a condition resembling an inanimate object, a question that comes to the fore in the interanimate relation between Freud and his prostheses. Further, Chen prods, "what is lost when we say that couches must be cathected differently from humans?"[107] I side with a psychoanalysis that poses the question as to what cathecting a couch can mean, and devote a chapter on the Freud Museums to reflecting upon the literal loss of a highly cathected couch. Although Chen urges a move beyond fetishism, to my mind fetishism remains a compelling analytic with which to at least partially explain desire, anxiety, and fear of loss, and deserves a place in the new materialist discourse that Chen advocates. Such new materialisms "not only diagnose the 'facts' by which humans are not animals are not things (or by which humans cannot be animals cannot be things), [but also] simultaneously reveal such 'facts' to be the real uncanny permeating the world we know."[108] Indeed, I take to heart the uncanny ways in which Freud is and is not his prostheses (his living and not living prostheses, for I count his daughter Anna and dogs amongst his prosthetic others,) and the ways that today Freud is and is not the psychoanalytic couch, his treasured artifacts, or even the photographs of his loved and hated Viennese home.

Joining Chen in the autopathographic impulse, I punctuate *Freud's Jaw* with observations collected from my own experience with breast cancer.

Upon diagnosis I initially underwent a nipple-sparing mastectomy, whose name, although not commonly known, ought to be self-explanatory. When the pathology report indicated that the margins were not clear, that is, that the knife that presumably drew a line between cancer and not-cancer came too close to the cancerous side for everyone to feel comfortable, I was ultimately advised to have what is called a "completion mastectomy." This term confirms the counterintuitive, or what Sedgwick deems the "ass backwards" terminology of cancer world.[109] Only the surgeon could fail to see the irony in a term that suggests one would become more complete as a consequence of the further removal of parts of oneself. But having already undergone a mastectomy, I could not sensibly submit myself to another on the same side, and so a qualifier was required. Nonetheless, I couldn't help but question the very idea of what constitutes completion. Completion may consist of the feeling—whether it is illusory or fantasy—of wholeness, a kind of psychic completion wherein body and psyche are for the most part aligned. A cancer diagnosis can sever this reassurance and calls for a creative response that mitigates both the reality and prospect of destruction.

In her collaborative autothanatography, Stephanie Byram's response to her cancer diagnosis conveys this psychic and corporeal fracture as a betrayal: "My body . . . could no longer be trusted. . . . I was no longer whole."[110] I delve more deeply into this subjectivity-in-dissolution in the following chapters, and discover, as Byram did, that "reconstructing her private and public selves" requires a constructive "effort to 'piece together a new self.'"[111] To the question of how a body broken by sexual, environmental, political, and biological abuses can "live with so much fracturing, so much loss," in her foreword to Eli Clare's classic *Exile and Pride*, Aurora Levins Morales responds: *"The story of what is broken . . . is something whole."*[112] Words may loosely hold together disrupted tissues and fragmented part-objects into a semblance of something whole. This "unsingular, fractured and whole" body can undergo a process of reparation in which it might be "reclaimed," as Clare avows, to the extent that it can demand to be counted amongst the stories told of our precarious lives.[113] Pieced together from a wide-ranging and wild interdisciplinarity, an interdisciplinarity like what Chen calls "feral," the constructive labor of this book attempts such reparative work.[114]

Overview of Chapters

In Chapter 1, I take Freud's trial with oral cancer, which resulted in him being outfitted with a prosthetic jaw, as the departure point for investigating the psychic impact of long-term survival in proximity to one's mortality. Freud's endurance test exposes the ambivalence of survival in the face of ongoing loss. While he underwent painful refittings of his prostheses, Freud proclaimed that through technological advancement humans had attained the status of "prosthetic gods," though we had not overcome our misery.[115] The contradiction between the promise of technology and its potential to fail is implicit in his claim. The prosthesis paradoxically represents both illness and its cure. From this view, affliction can be seen as a technological predicament. Freud's corpus devolves into incongruous parts—part fleshy subject, part foreign object, evidencing an increasing technologization of the body. While it can injure, technology can also be deployed for the reparative work of mourning, not only in the mechanical form of a prosthesis but also through the creative process of writing. Creative strategies for wrestling with embodied loss may seek to close a gap that is felt between one's human and inhuman parts. Freud depends on alternate prostheses—his cigars, his dogs, and his "mouthpiece,"[116] his daughter Anna—in an effort to control what his jaw prosthesis deprives him of, and to die in his own fashion. Through a close reading of Freud's medical case alongside his theories and relevant personal narrative, I assess Freud's survival as a condition that I term "not-death," which is a persistent entanglement of the life and death drives.

In Chapter 2, I analyze the ways in which Lorde's absent breast conjures phantasied attachments and anxieties, in contrast to the focus of Chapter 1 on Freud's literal attachments. I draw on Melanie Klein's theories of the maternal breast as the first part-object, the original lost object that initiates a cycle of destruction and reparation. I consider the psychic consequences of losing the breast through the process of weaning as well as the traumatic circumstance of cancer. Indicating how destruction can play a part in reparation, Lorde described her own breast amputation as breaking off a piece to make her whole, a process she felt was at least as painful as leaving her mother and home. Lorde's experience of cancer and racial injury correlates to the oral stage, the psychic stage of sadistic aggression dominated by an urge to incorporate and eject part-objects. For Lorde, illness, racism, and sexism are conjoined as objectifying forces. I ask how psychoanalytic object-relations theory contends with objectification—becoming the object of a fatal disease, racial hatred, or sexist assault. Lorde rejects the breast prosthesis on the grounds that it enforces gendered norms. Conformity to those conventions renders the postmastectomy woman invisible to others, denying her agency and depriving her of the solidarity of her sisters in survival. Lorde's critique of the "prosthetic pretense" remains relevant to contemporary breast cancer culture.[117] I propose that one of the unconscious motivations behind the social pressure to reconstruct the breast stems from a fetishism of the first object. I conclude Chapter 2 with a reflection on how the first object is mourned. According to Klein, damaged internal objects must be tended to and psychically repaired, which occurs during a period of mourning. I suggest that Lorde offers herself up as an object that can facilitate this repair, "like a drug or a chisel," as she says.[118] She fashions herself as an instrument for her community's use, which makes her available for fetishization.

As in the case of Lorde, Sedgwick's cancer supplied the occasion to reflect upon how one survives in the face of continual loss. It is not commonly known that from 1998 to 2003 Sedgwick wrote a breast cancer advice column called "Off My Chest" for *MAMM*, a women's magazine for "women, cancer, and community." Simultaneously, in 1999 she published *A Dialogue on Love*, a memoir of her therapy that records her struggle with her cancer diagnosis and metastasis. In Chapter 3, I argue that Sedgwick's journalistic and experimental writing circulates a public discourse of love that mediates her relationship to her own mortality. Sedgwick sets herself up as an object for collective identification. By disseminating pieces of herself in published works she strives to serve as an instrument for "good pedagogy" to counter the "bad pedagogy" of the cancer establishment. For Sedgwick, the assaults of cancer reveal that identity can never be naturalized into a stable whole object, but is woven through with loved and hated part-objects moving "across the ontological crack between the living and the dead."[119] She learns to loosen her grip on a desire for wholeness by embracing her own dissolution. Influenced by Klein's concept of reparation, which she regards as another word for love, she offers a Buddhist-inflected teaching that recognizes life as an ongoing collaborative project sustained through the anonymous and impersonal love of readers she has never met, but who survive her death. She mobilizes the destruction of cancer and its treatment into a process of collective reparative work—with her therapist and with her readers.

Chapter 4 returns to the Freudian narrative of loss, specifically to sites of his memorialization in the two Freud Museums. I contemplate the meaning of reparative objects that facilitated Freud's survival and that survive him. Forced into exile after living in Vienna for seventy-eight years, Freud escaped to London where most of his material objects followed him. I examine the reconstruction of Freud's Viennese study and consulting room at what is now the Freud Museum in Hampstead, London where Freud died in the presence of his massive collection of antiquities. I analyze Freud's passion for collecting idols as fetishized objects that helped him mediate his suffering, which was heightened through the combined effects of a degenerative illness and traumatic displacement. Whereas the Freud Museum in London now houses all the "good" Freudian artifacts, the museum that occupies Freud's former residence in Vienna compensates for his expulsion and the evacuation of his prized possessions through a fetishizing and melancholic reliance upon photographs taken prior to the objects' displacement. I interpret Freud's former home and offices at Berggasse 19, now the Sigmund Freud Museum, Vienna, as a space of irremediable loss where Freud's missing objects—his couch, books, and antiquities—take on the character of phantasied partial objects enlisted to perform the work of mourning.

Freud, Lorde, and Sedgwick undertake different forms of reparation to mitigate the burdens of mortality and approaching death. While such creative constructions make survival possible, they are, according to Freud's formulation of the psychoanalytic technique of construction, "only a preliminary labour."[120] They cannot render a life whole but can only mark its necessary incompletion. I select these figures because, much as they might seem "celebrities" of cancer survival, the ways in which cancer occupied them literalizes in their bodies the dynamics of loss, mourning, creativity and reparation that were arguably already present within their respective intellectual projects.[121] Their responses to the destabilization of malignancy shows how we, as human assemblages, are constituted in our vulnerability. Vulnerability is not a crisis that we endure temporarily, but rather an ongoing "crisis ordinary," as Lauren Berlant has described persistent conditions of precarity and precariousness that are transformed through media and rhetoric into crisis situations.[122] Vulnerability to life-altering loss is a chronicity from which no one is immune. As subjects who suffer as objects, we are often lost to ourselves, and we must strain to repair what holds us together both within and between ourselves.

CHAPTER I

Prosthetic Objects

On Sigmund Freud's
Ambivalent Attachments

Following the surgical removal of much of his jaw at the age of sixty-seven, Sigmund Freud endured the implementation of multiple prostheses for the remainder of his life. Freud's sixteen-year cancer burden and drama of prosthetic adjustment demonstrates the way in which cancer and its treatment destabilizes its sufferer's experience of corporeal and psychic cohesion.[1] Cancer and its treatment render survival a product of relentless maintenance and adjustment. Freud's prolonged cohabitation with what he referred to as "my dear old cancer" is characterized by a state of persistent ambivalence resulting from dependency upon an object that both preserves and impairs his bodily and psychic integrity.[2] His affectionate moniker, intended with sarcasm, nonetheless highlights the ongoing conflict generated when one becomes attached to objects that simultaneously sustain and work against one's life. Psychically, these prosthetic attachments are to Freud horrific monsters at once loved and hated, despised yet needed.

Prosthetic objects substitute for the objects Freud lost to cancer, and the prosthetic condition can be understood as a technological predicament in which technology both repairs and dehumanizes the body. Because of its capacity to disturb the boundaries between the human and nonhuman, the prosthesis introduces questions as to how one determines self from what is foreign to the self. Freud's prostheses strikingly and painfully materialize David Wills's concept of "dorsality" as that which turns the human into a technological thing.[3] Dorsality presumes that technology and humanity are utterly imbricated. Technology is brought into being at the moment a human comes into the world such that the human could itself be considered technology, "a technology that defines and so produces the human."[4] Wills's description of this technology resembles the work of cancer; it "proliferates or mutates."[5] Freud's cancer-ridden body models a "mutual dependence between the flesh and machine" that comes to characterize contemporary posthuman techno-bodies in which, as Braidotti affirms, the "technological construct now mingles with the flesh in unprecedented degrees of intrusiveness."[6]

Freud's case also shows how the prosthesis resembles the *pharmakon*, which Derrida explains is a drug or medicine that acts as both poison and remedy.[7] For Derrida, the *pharmakon* presents a fundamental ambivalence that intrudes upon the body of discourse. Freud's "chemical prosthesis," the nicotine to which he was addicted, exemplifies the paradox of needing and gaining pleasure from that which endangers one's life. Smoking, which imperiled his health, fueled Freud's creative production, allowing him to psychically resist the destructive forces of cancer and death. According to Freud's formulations, the life drives that impel creativity and integration are pitted against the death drives. Within Freud's "autothanatography," his public and private writing of his own death, the disintegrating effects of cancer manifest in the death drives.[8] I argue that cancer and psychoanalysis can be productively thought together to detect the work of "not-death," my reading of Freud's concept of the death drive. "Not-death," as I conceive of it, is a paradoxical entanglement of the life and death drives and a mode of survival. Freud proposed that one's own death is unrepresentable to oneself. As if to compensate for this unconscious negation, Freud's embattled struggle with prosthetic attachments can be seen as mediating his relationship to his mortality, both representing death and warding against it.

The Prosthetic Contest Between Human and Nonhuman

In April 1923, Sigmund Freud detected a lesion in his mouth. When it worsened, he consulted two friends, Felix Deutsch, an internist, and Maxim Steiner, a dermatologist. Although malignancy was already evident, both physicians hid this from Freud, diagnosing it as "leukoplakia," a premalignant lesion. After a botched and inadequate surgery performed by Marcus

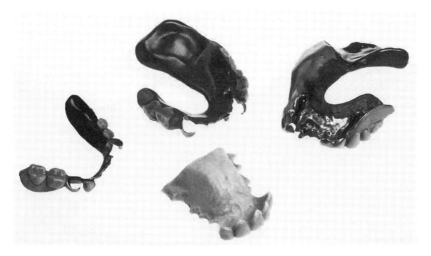

Figure 1. Freud's prostheses, Freud Museum London, 2013. Photograph by Ardon Bar Hama.

Hajek, yet another doctor who failed to inform Freud of the malignancy of his tumor, Freud suffered a severe hemorrhage from his mouth on a night train to Rome. When he returned to Vienna, he was finally put in the hands of a surgeon who would unflinchingly perform the radical surgery required for the gravity of the situation. Hans Pichler removed so much tissue and bone that he left a gaping hole in Freud's mouth, necessitating a prosthesis for the most fundamental activities that sustain life: eating, speaking, and, perhaps most important for Freud, smoking. The pathological results were squamous cell carcinoma of the hard palate, a cancer associated with a low survival rate.[9] Had Pichler been more conservative, as his predecessor had been, Freud would likely not have survived as long as he did. Freud's prolonged survival from his diagnosis at the age of sixty-seven to his death at eighty-three is impressive even by contemporary standards, and it resulted from an unusually vigilant surveillance on the part of Pichler, Max Schur, who was to become Freud's personal physician, and his primary caregiver, his daughter Anna. Together they succeeded in keeping Freud cancer-free for the next decade and a half.

In 1924, Pichler consulted with Freud seventy-four times; in 1932 he saw him ninety-two times.[10] Over the course of thirty-three surgeries, ten prostheses, and countless examinations, Pichler took exacting surgical and consulting notes.[11] These notes convey an overwhelming feeling of exhaustion, of the arduousness of maintaining life, of the chronicity of adjustment. To this point, Freud's biographer, Ernest Jones, provides a rationale for relegating excerpts from Pichler's notes to the appendix of his mammoth three-volume biography: "Even for faithful admirers the repetition about the prosthesis must become boring."[12] Indeed much of the chronicle of Freud's lengthy illness consists of an extended embattlement with what Jones describes as a *"a sort of magnified denture or obturator . . . a horror; it was labelled 'the monster.'"*[13] "Horror" aptly names the genre that befits Freud's grueling saga, the genre that Christina Crosby likewise selects following her catastrophic accident when she compares living with disabling incapacity to a horror story that excites fear beyond reason.[14] In Freud's story, the prosthesis is the horror that incites fear and pain, yet it also delivers him from starvation and silence. Crosby and Freud must adapt to horror that becomes mundane, horrors whose constant recurrence is both diabolical and enervating. The prosthetic maneuvers in defiance of cancer's potential recurrence are deadening in their repetition, arousing uncanny conflicts in Freud's state of mind. After nearly four years of unrelenting procedures, Pichler succinctly comments on Freud's ambivalence: "Patient reports some interesting self-observations on the ingratitude of patients and rebellion against dependence."[15]

Pichler initiated his treatment notes on September 26, 1923, describing the first major and most extensive operation that he was to perform to extricate the cancer from Freud's mouth. It was to be a radical operation in two stages, removing much of the upper right hard palate, right jawbone, submandibular lymph nodes, right soft palate, cheek, and tongue mucous membranes. The operation required weakening the mandible to permit it to be removed, along with the upper jawbone.[16] The ghastly violence of the procedure was accentuated by its being rehearsed on a corpse in order to test its feasibility. The manipulation of an inanimate body serves as evidence for the surgical possibilities of the animate body; the knowledge gained from the inanimate informs the surgeon about the workings of the animate.

This preparatory investigation indicates a codependence between the animate and inanimate that persists throughout the course of a human life and its aftermath. Life-threatening illness compels the afflicted subject to confront the necessary entanglement between what one considers one's own body and foreign "others." The illusion of the independent unified body is exposed as the sufferer is thrown back to her psychic prehistory when she was nothing but an amalgam of disconnected partial objects, those psychic equivalents of anatomical parts, such as a mouth, a breast, a thumb. This process of disunification characterizes not only the experience of the patient but can be perceived in, and is perhaps even provoked by, the attitude of the attending doctor. Pichler writes in the traditional detached manner of a surgeon, as if he were talking about a collection of anatomical parts rather than an integrated human being: "Cut through the middle of the upper lip, then around the nose till half height. . . . Then opened the jaws."[17] As paternal as the doctor might seem to be, he is better likened to the mother in Lacan's mirror stage scenario. In Lacan's description the mother or some other prosthetic support holds the infant up to the mirror and in recognizing the unity of her child might be said to hold her child together.[18] In contrast to this "good mother" (in Melanie Klein's terms), the surgeon is experienced as akin to Klein's "bad mother," whose persecutions fragment the intact body into an assortment of parts—lip, nose, jaw.[19]

A prosthesis exemplifies the powerful attachments humans have to material objects that are not strictly human. Used to replace a lost anatomical part, a prosthesis serves as a kind of material memory. Freud's jaw prosthesis was a material trace of the presence and absence of his mouth, made from an impression of his teeth and mouth cavity. What is most striking in reading through the two-hundred-page transcription of his medical case history is the chronic adjustment required of the prosthesis because of the changing conditions of his mouth. The impossibility of a prosthesis to ever fully substitute for a lost part is due to the fact that the prosthesis cannot itself adjust to changing conditions in the way that human tissue can. Living tissue is characterized by its adaptability and constant change, that it can never be static unless it dies. This is of course what makes living substance vital and animate, and a prosthesis, at least as of the twentieth century, is inanimate. Yet a prosthesis is not a thing like any other thing. It tends to be made by hand, rather than mass-produced. Its nonuniversality is the result of the fabrication skills of a prostheticist in ongoing rapport with a surgeon and a patient. It might be more accurate to consider the prosthesis a process or even a condition as opposed to a contained, inanimate thing.

While Freud's prostheticist was also his surgeon, his prosthetic management involved mutuality amongst many bodies besides his own, including numerous specialists and caregivers. The singularity and hybridity of the prosthetic object arises from this set of relations. The prosthesis participates in a reciprocal relation of care—it cares for its owner and must in turn be cared for. Perhaps this is one reason that the prosthesis seems to exercise a kind of agency that sets it apart from other inanimate things. The owner of a prosthesis becomes intimate with it through physical and emotional attachment. It is frequently indispensable because it performs a function necessary to everyday life. The owner obtains a familiarity with it through habitual use. It is usually worn in a relation of physical proximity that needs to be managed.[20] Biophysicist and engineer Hugh Herr reports, "The connection between the artificial limb and my body isn't that secure."[21] That Herr uses the word "secure" underscores not only a physical but also an emotional connection.

With the prosthesis, as with love objects, one seeks a secure attachment, and yet it cannot be too close. One requires a "good enough" attachment, to use D. W. Winnicott's lexicon, as in a "good enough mother."[22] For Freud this meant that his prosthesis should close enough so that he could speak but open enough to allow him to eat and smoke. Furthermore, it not only served these essential activities but provided support for his other organs and bodily appearance: "The prosthesis was designed so that it could support the eye, if necessary, and provide a full contour for the cheek."[23] It is at these sites of attachment that questions emerge as to the nature of what separates humans from the nonhuman and what constitutes the human. The intimacy of the prosthesis with its wearer and its participation in a network of human relations has the effect of animating it with human character, and this is what makes it something of a hybrid object. John C. Davenport's brief history of Freud's prostheses reflects the sense that they have been endowed with a certain life force: "On several occasions old prostheses were *resurrected* to be worn alternatively with the newer ones" (my emphasis).[24]

The miscegenation of the nonhuman and the human propagates from the prosthetic site. It is not known when Freud's biological body merged with the artificial substances introduced to fills its gaps. But when Pichler finds a loose piece of guttapercha embedded in the mucous membrane of Freud's mouth he records that it "may have been there any length of time."[25] Guttapercha (also gutta-percha and gutta percha) is a natural rubber that is biologically inert. It was popular in the nineteenth century for use in marine cables, dentistry and surgical procedures, mourning jewelry, and furniture. Pichler relined rough spots on the prostheses with guttapercha to prevent abrasion.[26] He frequently used it to stop up gaps in hopes that the perennially ill-fitting prostheses could be made more comfortable. Guttapercha is one of the most recurrent words in Freud's medical record. The substance is emblematic of the prosthetic condition as a *condition* because it is key to the process yet does not itself constitute the prosthesis—it is an agent in the process of manipulation. Guttapercha can mold to human tissue and resembles living substance in its malleability when it is warmed, but hardens when returned to room temperature.[27] Guttapercha lubricates the entire prosthetic process but is not in the least apparent to anyone outside of the process.

It is noteworthy in my characterization of the prosthetic condition as a *technological* predicament that guttapercha was employed extensively for underwater telegraphy cable insulation, and was thus fundamental to early efforts at globalization. The nineteenth-century colonial and imperial projects resulting in industrialization and modernization of the Western world involved massive harvesting of guttapercha in Southeast Asia.[28] The irrational manner in which guttapercha was collected, by felling an entire tree for a mere eleven ounces of latex per tree, mirrors the irrational treatment of cancer, which similarly involves a process of cutting and extraction that far exceeds its miniscule rewards, simultaneously brutalizing the surrounding environment in which the sought after object grows.[29] Guttapercha was therefore ultimately unsustainable for long-term industry, which moved from the discovery and harvesting of natural resources to manmade production.[30] This transition from the natural to the artificial propelled the proliferation of environmental toxins, which, as we know, foster cancer. By the time Pichler was using guttapercha its mass production had been scaled back. But it was and is still selectively used in dentistry and golfing, so it is in the individualized realms of medicine and recreational sport that the substance survives. John M. Picker suggests that the guttapercha that insulated the electric cables crucial to the Victorian colonial economy allowed Victorians to sublimate their unconscious guilt over their exploitative industrial progress.[31] He argues that this ill-gotten product protected the telegraph wires that transmitted erotically charged signals and thereby insulated the Victorians from their own otherwise uncontainable desires, both in terms of their economic and sexual exploits. This is one means by which eroticism is embedded in the material manipulation of the prosthetic relation.

The prosthetic relation can be "tinged with erotism," bringing it under the rubric of Freud's antagonism between the life and death instincts, of Eros striving toward its inanimate nature, as I will discuss further.[32] The level of intimacy that characterizes the prosthetic condition is not unlike a sexual relationship wherein antagonism brings both distress and relief. Freud's cycle of prosthetic abuse resembles a frustrated lover's rotation of sexual partners. He accumulates a full retinue of prostheses, his partners in health, and new partners/prostheses are introduced when old ones prove unsuitable. He is reunited with old prostheses when new ones become intolerable. Like a sexual relationship, the coupling of an individual and his prosthesis requires privacy, and even demands a kind of monogamy—no amount of meddling even from an expert will do. Pichler complains at one point that only Freud can put in and take out his prosthesis: "If somebody else tries, a position of mandible is adopted involuntarily which prevents insertion."[33]

Entry after entry of Pichler's notes documents the trials and tribulations of soft living tissue at odds with the inanimate devices meant to aid its continued vitality. On June 10, 1925, he writes: "Prosthesis 3 more comfortable when hinge open, therefore knob loosened by one whole turn."[34] And later in 1925, "Prosthesis 3 fits incomparably better now with altered hinge-clasp."[35] But then a screw can no longer be tightened because the teeth upon which the screw rests have loosened.[36] When numerous alterations have been effected on the prostheses to no avail, it is the human subject that must be adapted to its object. Pichler comments, still notably dissecting his patient into parts: "Unmistakable new bite on tongue. Therefore plan to re-arrange teeth right side above and below."[37] The stubborn constancy of the prosthesis meets up against the malleable weaknesses of the human body. It frequently exerts unbearable pressure or mere annoyances like squeaking. S. H. Foulkes recalls a sound emitted from Freud's mouth that could be produced only by a mechanical apparatus in contrast to the voice one would anticipate issuing from the orifice: "From time to time [Freud] adjusted his prosthesis, which each time made a kind of rattling noise."[38] Human vulnerability extends from ever-evolving pliable substance, setting it apart from the essential stasis of the inanimate object.

Yet the prosthesis is not invulnerable to disrepair. In 1927 Freud's lower prosthesis breaks, though "specially manufactured from stainless-steel wire."[39] A year later, prosthesis 4 cannot be used because of "imperfect action of spring."[40] A decade later the "upper prosthesis [is] impossible to remove still."[41] I have chosen selective examples from the voluminous case study to convey the exhaustion of the "whole prosthesis-business" as an enforced and often conflicted partnership between the human and nonhuman.[42] In their constant entanglement, the distinction between the human and nonhuman often appears to defy detection, yet a gap remains that marks the limits of what is recognized as human. Pichler appeals to Freud's human capabilities after he had endured a prolonged bout with his prosthesis, which he had "regrettably" removed and once again found impossible to reinsert. The doctor urges him to use his lower prosthesis "as soon as *humanly* possible" (my emphasis).[43] In other words, he needs to coax Freud to put his human capacities at the service of his nonhuman parts, which will allow him in turn to reclaim his humanity.

The Prosthetic Condition as Technological Predicament

Like the *pharmakon*, that "dangerous supplement" that Derrida so carefully unpacks, the prosthesis paradoxically represents both illness/injury and its cure or restoration.[44] Freud confirms this when he writes of his ambivalence: "I detest my mechanical jaw because the struggle with the mechanism consumes so much precious strength. Yet I prefer a mechanical jaw to no jaw at all. I prefer existence to extinction."[45] In *La peau de chagrin* (*The Magic Skin*, also translated as *The Fatal Skin* and *The Wild Ass's Skin*), the last book Freud read before he died, Honoré Balzac describes a similar trade-off between human life and technicity. His protagonist "wanted life at any price, and so he led the life of a machine."[46] While Freud underwent painful refittings of his prosthetic jaw, he famously proclaimed in *Civilization and Its Discontents* that through the advancements of science and technology humans had attained the status of "prosthetic gods."[47] Nevertheless, according to Freud, we had not risen above our misery. The prosthesis epitomized for him the discomfort and unhappiness that seem to necessarily accompany the benefits of civilization. The contradiction between the promise of technology and its potential to fail and/or injure is implicit in Freud's claim.[48]

The person who uses a prosthesis engages in a process of technological affiliation that involves adaptation of the body to the prosthesis and manipulation of the prosthesis to the body. For Baudrillard, the prosthesis represents an automatically reproducible, technologically homogenized posthuman, a condition he couples with and crystallizes in a cancer metaphor: "Every body is now nothing but an invariant reproduction of the prosthesis: this point means the end of the body. . . . It means that the individual is now nothing but a cancerous metastasis of his basic formula."[49] Medical prostheses, which technologically extend the human through a painstaking, often faulty process of accommodation, urge a rethinking of the human in regard to the supports and extensions that sustain life. The predicament in encountering one's mortality can be felt as a contest between one's animate and inanimate parts with the technological instruments upon which one depends winning out. For instance, when I declined breast reconstruction following my mastectomy, I explained to my surgeon that I was uncomfortable with housing a foreign object inside my body. He replied, nonplussed, "You have fillings don't you?" Silicone breasts, dental fillings, pacemakers, and neural chips can blend seamlessly with embodied daily existence, but when something goes wrong, the struggle that ensues can be felt as a process of technological dehumanization. To adapt Wills's assertion, to be human is to also be in some way dehumanized or technologized. For Wills, existence is fraught with ruptures to "self-enclosed intact human identity [each of which] opens the space of the technological or even the inanimate."[50]

In its dehumanizing effect, illness confuses and erodes the relationship between human and nonhuman. Psychoanalyst Harold Searles contends that "the processes and products of technology tend to cause [humans] to lose sight of the basic kinship between human and nonhuman."[51] If technology blinds humans to their nonhuman dependencies, illness reorients the human relation to technology. Years prior to his cancer diagnosis, Freud confirms that the dehumanization of illness can have positive and negative effects. He tells Princess Marie Bonaparte: "I decided not to have sciatica any more, to become human again, and to abandon the luxury of being ill."[52] During the course of his ravaging illness, the technical instruments to which he was once so attached become defamiliarized. His relationship to once familiar tools is altered. He confides to Bonaparte: "I have not written to you for quite some time. . . . I assume you know why, and will also recognize the reason from my handwriting. (Not even the pen is the same any more.)"[53]

In the novel that captivated Freud at the end of his life, Balzac details the progressive dehumanization of his protagonist, Raphael, who comes into possession of an animal skin that has the magical power to grant his every wish at the cost of his remaining life. With every wish granted, the skin, a materialization of Raphael's diminishing days of life, visibly shrinks, which is cause for simultaneous celebration and mourning. Raphael invests in the skin, which is his *pharmakon*, his enabling and disabling prosthesis, with a morbid pleasure. "He had given up all the rights of life in order to live; he . . . almost rejoiced at thus becoming a sort of automaton."[54] I read Raphael's plight as parallel to Freud's. He is bound to an inanimate object that represents his mortality, the workings of Thanatos. His enslavement to the skin takes on a compulsive character akin to what Freud, deploying a cancer metaphor, observes in those who give the impression "of being pursued by a malignant fate or possessed by some 'daemonic' power."[55] Raphael's fate can be viewed as having been overtaken by a demonic contract with technology. I refer to technology in the senses that Heidegger specifies when he turns to the Greek origins of technology as *techne*: as modern technology it can instrumentalize the human body, and as *poesis* it can be a mode of revealing death in life.[56] The magic skin, like Freud's prosthesis, exerts the power of *techne*, transforming its owner's orientation to the world so as to reveal his vulnerability to death in life, a death that deprives him of his humanity. As he is dying of prostate cancer, Anatole Broyard verifies the kind of technologization I am describing when he writes: "To die is to be no longer human, to be dehumanized."[57]

The Prosthesis as Psychic Object

Given the highly charged nature of the relationship to a prosthesis, I propose that prostheses can attain the psychic status of part-objects. Both the material prosthesis and the absent body part can take on the character of a partial object, which, as I described in the Introduction, is the part of a whole object in which sexual energy is invested. The prosthesis psychically represents a missing body part, which itself represents a lost loved object. According to this formulation, the prosthetic condition—when the body literally becomes part fleshy subject/part foreign object—materializes the fantasy part-object. I will elaborate on Kleinian thought later in this book, but for now a capsule view will be helpful, since the notion of the part-object is only implicit in Freud's work whereas it is fully "incorporated," so to speak, in Melanie Klein's. Klein proposes that part-objects are invested with persecutory or benevolent phantasies, turning them into "good" objects or "bad" objects, which are internally incorporated or projected onto others. The object, such as the mother, is split into a part-object that is hated, the "bad breast," and one that is loved, the "good breast." The destruction and reparation of part-objects is formative in the infantile stage of human development, however, Klein contends that trauma later in life can revive the mental labor they perform in mourning loss. It would not be surprising that the onset of life-threatening illness could trigger the psychic splitting that is the hallmark of the primitive part-object phase.

For Freud, the prosthesis could have been psychically split into good and bad object. As a good object, it enabled nourishment, smoking, and productive activity. At the same time, his pain would have been projected onto the obturator, turning it into a bad object that persecuted and threatened him with dissolution. As bad object, it impaired his most beloved and basic activities: eating, speaking, smoking, and to a certain extent listening, for he had lost his hearing in his right ear as a result of postoperative infections. The prosthesis becomes a "bizarre object" not unlike the psychotic projections Bion describes wherein uncanny vitality is injected into foreign matter.[58] Partial objects appear to brew in the climate of uncanniness. If the uncanny names an uncertainty as to whether a part-object might itself have an independent autonomy over and beyond the mind that presumably controls it, or further if it casts doubts upon whether something is alive or dead, prostheses carry an undeniably uncanny dimension.[59] This is not to say that prosthetic objects render their subjects defective or inhuman; rather, the uncanniness of human experience might perhaps be made more visible through prostheses.

Although she does not refer to it in these terms, Klein's paranoid-schizoid position, the earliest developmental position, which is dominated by part-objects, tends toward the uncanny. In phantasy the body is decomposed and devoured. Part-objects invade other people's bodies and phantasied organs are imagined to be cut up, roasted, and eaten. All this occurs under the pressure of the death drive, which for Klein is the agent of aggression and destruction. Just as with the prosthetic condition I have been discussing, for Klein the battle between life and death drives involves perpetual accommodation: "These two components are forever united as well as opposed, to a growing *adjustment* between them" (my emphasis).[60] Furthermore, in the early stage of human development not only is the part not differentiated from the whole nor the interior from the exterior, the animate is equivalent to the inanimate. "The child desires to destroy the organs (penis, vagina, breast) which stand for the objects. . . . This anxiety contributes to make him equate the organs in question with other things."[61]

Klein's recognition that children not only confuse but identify biological objects with inorganic things supports Searles's contention that the nonhuman environment is a necessary component of subject formation: "This crucial phase of differentiation involves the infant's becoming aware of himself as differentiated not only from his human environment *but also from his nonhuman environment*" (emphasis in original).[62] Before this moment of differentiation, Searles opines, the human experiences herself not only as coextensive with the mother but also with the nonhuman. Searles confirms the view that Winnicott had earlier advanced, that the child's capacity to distinguish between self and non-self, or in Winnicott's terms "me" and "not-me," takes shape through a "not-me possession," a nonhuman material object such as a toy or blanket.[63] Searles argues that our infantile experience consists of sensing a chaotic nonhuman environment over which we have no control, but additionally, he presumes that we harbor unconscious memory traces of "losing a nonhuman environment which had been sensed, heretofore, as a harmonious extension of our world-embracing self."[64] Searles's comment makes the lost loved object a prosthetic extension of our selves, that is to say, in our infantile or even neonatal state our world felt like a seamless extension of ourselves, and consequently that prosthetic ideal was lost and retained as the memory of a lost love object.

As mentioned earlier, Freud does not dwell upon the psychodynamics of part-objects, although most psychoanalysts locate the origins of the concept in his condensation of maternal love and nurturing in the object of the breast.[65] Understood prosthetically, the breast as part-object functions as a psychic supplement; it extends the psyche. In one of his last notes, Freud enigmatically scribbled on a sheet of paper: "Space may be the projection of the extension of the psychical apparatus. . . . Psyche is extended; knows nothing about it."[66] His note suggests that the psyche is a spatial projection, a kind of prosthetic extension. Searles calls it a "harmonious extension," although it can also be experienced as dangerous and discomforting. Under pressure from illness the spatial character of the psyche can be diminished to what Freud described as "an island of pain."[67] This description conveys a sense of disconnectedness and isolation from others, from what Paul Schilder calls the community of body images that make up our own.[68] Freud appears to have internalized what Schilder locates as a "zone of indifference" between bodies when he bemoans that his pain is "floating on an ocean of indifference."[69]

Physical decomposition dispossesses the psyche. One could represent this condition as not being *at home* in one's body. Jean-Luc Nancy, whose cancer was a by-product of the immunosuppression required for his heart transplant, wrestled with this dislocating strangeness of self-identity, or as he put it, with the distance between "me" and "me" (as opposed to Winnicott's "me" and "not-me"), a distance felt as at once alienating and intrusive.[70] This estrangement from the familiarity of one's embodiment is experienced as a loss, as Freud dolefully remarks to Arnold Zweig: "At one time a big bone chip had already been expelled and we are waiting for the repetition of this process to put an end to this episode. . . . Now one is at a loss, does not know whether this is basically a harmless delay or the progress of the *uncanny process* which we have been fighting for 16 years" (my emphasis).[71] Cancerous deterioration unhouses Freud and turns his bodily inhabitance into a disruptive intermingling of living and dying. Freud names this process as uncanny, the uncanniness of being both oneself and not oneself, the uncanniness of foreign intrusion, of rendering the body foreign to itself. Cancer's special uncanniness brings to light what ought to be hidden, and it continually recurs or threatens to return.

A Narcoanalysis of Freud's Illness

In describing the infant sucking at the mother's breast, Freud offers a term to draw out the distinction and codependence between the self-preservative and sexual instincts which are both aimed at the part-object: *Anlehnung*, which James Strachey translates with the Greek-derived term *anaclisis*.[72] I cannot help but note the *prosthetic* connotation of this word. In a footnote Strachey explains that he chose *anaclitic* "by analogy with the grammatical term 'enclitic,' used of particles which cannot be the first word in a sentence, but must be appended to, or must lean up against, a more important one.'"[73] *Prosthesis*, too, has a rhetorical meaning. David Wills notes that its Greek origins mean "the addition of a syllable to the beginning of a word."[74] Anaclisis and narcissism form the basis of two types of object-choices, according to Freud's schema. Anaclisis is "used to refer to the fact of the subject's basing himself on the object of the self-preservative instincts in his choice of a love-object."[75] One might characterize Freud's prostheses as anaclitic love-objects, which served the self-preservative function.

Paradoxically, one might also argue that cigars were an anaclitic love-object for Freud, in that he leaned upon them to sustain his creativity. Cigars were necessary to Freud's intellectual productivity. To maintain his concentration and creative output, typically Freud smoked up to twenty cigars a day.[76] A cigar can be seen as a "relic" of the infantile oral phase carried into adulthood, in the manner that thumb sucking is such a "relic."[77] Freud's addiction and consequently his cancer were centered on the earliest erotogenic zone, the mouth, which he identified as the first organ "to make libidinal demands on the mind."[78] If libido is defined as hunger, as it is in *Three Essays*, addiction, as a form of hunger, would rightly be characterized as libidinal.[79] Freud confirms in a letter to Wilhelm Fliess that smoking has a sexual dimension connected to the earliest libidinal needs and is a replacement for sexual stimulation: "It has dawned on me that masturbation is the . . . the 'primal addiction' and that it is only as a substitute and replacement for it that the other addictions—for alcohol, morphine, tobacco, etc.—come into existence."[80]

Performing a "narcoanalysis," to borrow from Avital Ronell, of Freud's addiction to nicotine is both necessary and impossible—necessary because his entire corpus was dependent upon the stimulation of cigar smoke, and impossible because, as Ronell asserts, drugs are "non-theorizable."[81] By this I take her to mean that one cannot design a consistent and rational theory in regard to the irrational incoherences of drug addiction, and that drugs not only resist theorization but actively work against it. Indeed Freud admitted his resistance to theorizing drugs, claiming his "passion for smoking" was his own "private affair" and demanding of Jones that they be left out of analysis.[82] Despite his refusal to analyze his addiction, Freud's illness and prosthetic condition are necessarily bound up with it. Much as he wanted to relegate smoking "outside of the critical economy of psycho-analysis," I argue, in line with Scott Wilson, that it remains "essential and inessential to psychoanalysis."[83] Freud cautioned Stefan Zweig, his would-be biographer, that his own internal contradictions would no doubt confound the person who tried to resolve them, namely, as he writes: "that I ascribe to the cigar the greatest share of my self-control and tenac-ity in work."[84] Of his three great passions, psychoanalysis, collecting antiq-uities, and smoking, the last is the most primal and arguably causes the most harm, and therefore makes the least sense. Warned countless times by his doctors of the ill effects for his heart, not to mention his cancer, he was perhaps unable, but certainly unwilling to part with this dependency. Both a threat to life and a salvation, the cigar, as Freud's "chemical pros-thesis," was an indispensable instrument for sustaining the paradox of what I will call "not-death."[85]

The accommodations that needed to be made for Freud to continue his smoking habit are repeatedly cited in his medical record. Pichler notes on December 2, 1926: "Some surplus backwards of prosthesis 4 reduced; reduction at palate-edge to improve occlusion for smoking."[86] And five days later: "Prosthesis 4 worn for several hours, better but still troublesome for speech and smoking."[87] Prostheses are gauged by Freud's ability to smoke with them, a criterion that is challenging to meet. The next year a new prosthesis has not improved the situation: "Has not used prosthesis 5 since

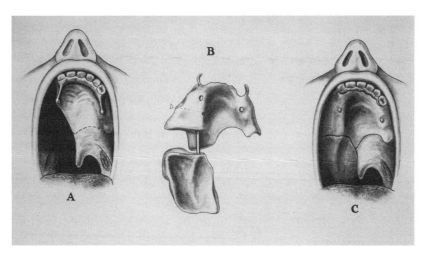

Figure 2. Diagram of V. H. Kazanjian's prosthesis for Freud, 1931. Container OV 15, Sigmund Freud Papers, Manuscript Division, Library of Congress, Washington, D.C. Photograph by Lin + Lam.

he cannot smoke with it."[88] A well-known American plastic surgeon, Varaztad Kazanjian, is finally recruited to produce three more prostheses.

The record reads: "Patient speaks much better with soft-rubber prosthesis but cannot smoke with it at all and bites his tongue."[89] Kazanjian recollects: "He was a passionate cigar smoker and wouldn't give them up. . . . I tried on one appliance that would make him able to smoke well but would not let him talk well; with another appliance he could talk well but could not smoke comfortably."[90] Kazanjian saw Freud every day while he was in Vienna working on the prostheses, sometimes two or three times a day for three to four hours. He worked in Pichler's lab for approximately six weeks.[91] Kazanjian recounts how difficult it was for the prosthesis to restore Freud's comfort and pleasures in daily activities, primarily smoking: "Normally, in order to smoke comfortably, the soft palate completely separates the mouth from the nasal cavity. The slightest escape of air reduces the pleasure of smoking, and no matter how well an appliance is made it cannot replace the normal action of the pharyngeal muscles."[92] Again we see how technological substitutes for human features always fall short. Smoking is a technical challenge more complex than speech. Pichler designates the Kazanjian prostheses with Roman numerals to keep them straight, but little does it matter how they are coded; they, like the others, eventually prove unsatisfactory. "Prosthesis I worse after alteration. Speech as bad as before, smoking also worse. . . . Guttapercha added also to prosthesis III to improve smoking."[93] To facilitate his smoking it was even "required that his jaws be propped open with a clothes peg."[94]

The prosthetic condition compounds itself with the prosthesis proper propping up what remained of the tissues of his mouth, a clothes peg propping open his mouth, and cigars propping up his capacity to work. Freud wrote to Bonaparte on September 18, 1931: "Pichler is working every day on my three prostheses, and has improved them to the point where I can smoke with all of them and speak with two of them. None of them is entirely satisfactory yet. With them it is like with the pursuit of happiness-you think you already have it in your grasp and it is always gone again."[95] This echoes Ronell's description of addiction as an incomplete and destructive *jouissance*.[96] Though obviously Freud does not speak the language of Lacan, his complaint goes to Lacan's definition of *jouissance* as the beyond of the pleasure principle, linking his addictive prosthetic condition with the painful enjoyment and compulsive suffering that ceaselessly drives toward death.

Freud's medical record reveals that his need to smoke equaled or even surpassed his need to eat and speak. This leads one to consider what psychoanalysis, the talking cure, is made of. Is the stuff of psychoanalysis smoke or speech? Within the historical context of psychoanalysis, does smoke conjure speech? If we take the ritual meetings of the Wednesday Society members, the circle of Freudian supporters who convened at his house to discuss "scientific matters" as an indication, we could presume that for psychoanalysis smoke precedes speech, and is the occasion for speech. In an anaclitic relationship smoke is the primary object upon which speech leans. In preparation for the Wednesday meetings Freud's wife, Martha, would busy herself placing ashtrays from Freud's prized collection so they would be ready at hand for the immense accumulation of ash.[97] One can imagine that the thick haze of smoke that settled on the curtains and rugs would waft into the other rooms of Berggasse 19, more easily discernable than the serious discussions held behind closed doors.

The predilection for cigars was not confined to those smoke-filled quarters. His father had passed it on to Freud, and in turn psychoanalysts of future generations modeled their habits upon the father of psychoanalysis.[98] This is consistent with psychoanalysis itself as a body of knowledge passed on through "paternal inheritance."[99] The law of the father is evident in the Oedipal myth that serves as the foundation of psychoanalytic doctrine. In psychoanalytic training an analysis is measured by its proximity to the psychoanalytic father. This patrilineal lineage of cigar smoking analysts has been documented in at least two films. The 11th Congress of the International Psychoanalytic Association, held in Oxford, England, was filmed in July 1929, and its narrator, psychoanalyst Sandor Lorand, identifies analyst after analyst lighting up. Finally he points out himself: "Here I come into the picture with my usual cigar."[100] And from 1928 to 1929, Philip Lehrman, Freud's analysand, shot footage of the psychoanalytic community that was screened for the American Psychoanalytic Association in 1950 and 1954. The screening event was recorded, and Lehrman is heard remarking that the projectionist has instructed the crowd that "the pictures will be enjoyed more and will be clearer if fewer people smoked."[101] If psychoanalysts take their pleasure in smoking, do they do so at the expense of clear pictures? That is, does pleasure inhibit insight? And if smoking is the essence of pleasure and smoking is essential to psychoanalysis whose aim is to gain clarity about the mind—how can smoking, its pleasures and dangers, be reconciled to psychoanalysis?

Freud confirms in no uncertain terms that his relationship to smoking is libidinal, and of an intensity that deprivation instigates the work of mourning. To his Wednesday Society members, "the master" is quoted as saying: "I was not allowed to smoke for two years. It was horrible. It felt like a good friend had died and I had to mourn him from morning to evening. Now I even have the same feelings for my pipe. She is a good friend of mine, my counsellor, my comfort, my guide, who smooths my way."[102] Freud had apparently cathected his cigar and then his pipe, further evidence of the central but neglected importance of nonhuman objects to psychoanalysis. In response to a questionnaire distributed to "outstanding contemporary figures regarding their smoking habits," Freud wrote: "I began smoking at the age of 24, first cigarettes but soon exclusively cigars, and am still smoking now (at 72½), and very reluctant to restrict myself in this pleasure."[103] Here Freud sets the example and foreshadows the analytic community's reluctance to master its pleasures, the very lesson that orthodox psychoanalysis is supposed to teach. So does all that talk about taming the instincts and coming to terms with the reality principle go up in smoke? Freud admits: "I have been faithful to my habit or vice, and believe that I owe to the cigar a great intensification of my capacity to work."[104] The cigar is a good friend, the pipe a counselor and guide, the smoking much like a sexual partner, a wifely habit or mistress of vice, if one puts a moral spin on it. Further situating smoking within the realm of sexual dynamics, Freud writes to his fiancée, Martha Bernays, with whom he was reluctantly parted while studying in France: "Smoking is indispensable if one has nothing to kiss."[105] The manifest meaning of this message rationalizes, since I can't have you, I must smoke. The latent meaning reveals that smoking might even take the place of his betrothed in her absence.

Smoking functions for Freud as a libidinal satisfaction that combines eroticism with the drive to produce. Following Wilson's interpretation, which links addiction to capitalist consumption, Freud's smoking can be read as a parable of how the capitalist work ethic drives the individual toward her/his own death. But if smoking is the means of his destruction, it is also the means of his production. Freud attributes to tobacco, an inert thing, the power of animation, of investing life into another thing or things, that is, creative works/texts. Nicotine, the substance directly responsible for Freud's illness and death, was simultaneously the agent that propelled his immortal legacy. Smoking, although destructive, was paradoxically reparative for Freud. A fifty-nine-year affair with the cigar, the relic of his oral phase and anaclitic love object, Freud's addiction was a paradoxical pact to survive following the illogical logic of his death drive, which is a drive toward death in life. Using the tool of his destruction for his own creative reproduction, he insisted on dying in his own fashion.[106] Freud's smoking demonstrates the problematic of the pleasure principle and its *beyond*.

Cancer as Not-Death

I now want to put Freud's medical condition into the context of his theory of the death drives, although his conception of the death drive predates his cancer diagnosis. This is because I do not claim a causal connection between the two. Rather, I seek to contemplate how the ramifications of the concept intersect with Freud's experience of morbidity and encounter with mortality. Freud's concept of the death drive uncovers ambivalences regarding self-preservation and survival that, according to his own formulations, take place specifically between the life and death impulses. The confrontation with mortality that one experiences through life-threatening illness puts the sufferer in touch with the death drive. Importantly and ironically, the death drive, as Freud conceives of it in *Beyond the Pleasure Principle*, is not simply a drive toward death. Freud is at pains to account for the struggle to survive. The death drives make up a plural concept that speaks to this embattled struggle.[107] Laplanche and Pontalis explain that Freud introduced it to answer to a need, a "structural necessity" that was becoming recognizable in his work at its turning point of the 1920s.[108] Freud proposed the death drive as a speculative hypothesis to help explain why people repeat painful experiences. The phenomenon of what we now call posttraumatic stress disorder (PTSD), which was then known as traumatic neurosis, and ambivalent complexes such as sadism and masochism, presented him with problems that seemed to refute the pleasure principle upon which he founded his science of psychoanalysis. To make sense of these puzzles, Freud put forth what he himself concedes is a "strange assumption" that was roundly dismissed as biologically inaccurate or simply off base.[109] Yet the concept has also fascinated scholars and analysts, leading to substantial studies on the topic.[110]

Freud's concept does not seek to define death in and of itself as it has traditionally been defined. The death drive is directed toward the *wish* to die—and wishes, as Freud asserted from 1895 onward, should never be ignored. Freud hypothesizes that organisms, humans among them, feel an instinctual pressure to return to their origins toward the aim of attaining an absolute repose. He postulates that *"an instinct is an urge inherent in organic life to restore an earlier state of things . . . that is, it is a kind of organic elasticity, or, to put it another way, the expression of the inertia inherent in organic life"* (emphasis in original).[111] With this bold claim, Freud concludes that all instincts are by nature conservative, and that the original instinct that arose in a living organism was to return to its inanimate state.[112] But even as he makes this assertion it gives him pause, for he must acknowledge that the sexual instincts strive toward a reproduction of life. This apparent opposition to his thesis requires him to assess whether a natural death is a biological rule of life.

To support his speculations that the drive toward death is a tendency and not a biological given, Freud draws upon August Weismann's division of the body into the mortal and immortal. Weismann divided living substance into the mortal body, the "soma," which was subject to death, and the potentially immortal germ cells, which were bound up with reproduction and survival of the species.[113] In this schema we can begin to see how death and life are entangled. In a sense, each force sustains the other. Freud describes the behavior of these germ cells as narcissistic, meaning that they retain their libido, which in this context might best be described as life-preserving energy, for their own egos rather than for distribution to external objects.[114] He turns to cancer for further evidence of narcissistic behavior on the cellular level. The death drive takes cancer as its avatar: "The cells of the malignant neoplasms which destroy the organism should also perhaps be described as narcissistic in this same sense."[115] Though the comparison to cancer may initially be surprising, it is not so far-fetched when one recalls that Freud had already made the connection between narcissism and illness. In *On Narcissism*, he characterizes the person suffering from organic illness as narcissistic in that his libidinal cathexis is turned upon his own ego rather than his love objects. At that time he foreshadowed his future plight when he quotes Wilhelm Busch on the self-absorption precipitated by a toothache: "Concentrated is his soul . . . in his molar's narrow hole."[116]

Freud's turn to narcissism will eventually find its way into the overarching dualism that he will defend throughout his later writings, that of love or Eros, a manifestation of the life instincts, and discord or strife, which is brought about by the death instincts. Narcissism, then, is crucial to an understanding of the development of the death drive. To characterize cancer cells as narcissistic is paradoxically to link the destructive forces of malignancy with love of self, as seen through the need and desire to survive. Cancer epitomizes the workings of the death drive in its aim of returning the organism to a state of inertia, and yet it also, perhaps counterintuitively, encompasses the strivings of the life instincts toward immortality. After all, cancer cells have been shown to achieve a practical immortality in cell culture.[117] Cancer cells refuse to comply with the "internal necessity of dying."[118] They proliferate profusely, and can therefore be seen as carriers of the life instincts. This is why I want to think together the two forces of life and death and to term this metaphysical condition "not-death." Not-death would be composed of the uncertainty and perpetual conflict between the life and death drives; it is signified by their contingency upon one another, that each is the condition of the other. Cancer is emblematic of not-death as the entanglement of the life and death instincts.

If we each have within us the wish and potential for immortality that the drive toward not-death suggests, this renders our own death unrepresentable to ourselves. In *Obituaries,* his last book before he died of prostate cancer, William Saroyan wrote: "Everybody has got to die, but I have always believed an exception would be made in my case."[119] This sentiment captures the disavowal at the heart of Western attitudes toward death, and reflects Freud's claim that the idea of death, specifically knowledge of one's own death, escapes us. Freud argues in *Thoughts for The Times on War and Death* that "it is indeed impossible to imagine our own death . . . in the unconscious every one of us is convinced of his own immortality."[120] Twenty-two years later Freud affirmed that protective instincts underlie the fantasy of mortal exceptionalism: "What has once come to life clings tenaciously to its existence."[121] The clinging to life, the denial of death, our ambivalence toward our own mortality, these are all reasons why death is unknown and unrepresentable to ourselves. Death itself defies representation. This is what makes the concept of the death drive both necessary and confounding.

Freud approaches the dilemma of death's resistance to representation by proposing that lived experience consists primarily in a fusion of the death and life instincts. Havi Carel identifies this as "death in life."[122] Schur speaks of "life-in-death" and Derrida "life death."[123] I put forward "not-death" because it indicates the dominance of the principles that tend toward destruction over those that sustain life, and it takes the form of negation, which Freud will come to associate with the destructive instincts. Negation is a process of denial closely allied with disavowal whereby the unconscious disowns what the ego may consciously know. The way Freud outlines it, negation appears to be imperative for higher processes of thinking. Because what is known is suppressed, "negation is a way of taking cognizance of what is repressed."[124] As such, it may be the only means by which we can accept our own mortality. If we cannot affirm our own death because that would be to unite with it, we can only grasp not-death through a process of negation.

Freud describes a biological cycle in which the survival of a species requires union between individuals for the purposes of reproduction. But because the organism desires constancy, according to Freud, a trend toward stasis counters the tensions that arise in union. Freud calls this energic pressure the Nirvana principle, which he associates with pleasure. The Nirvana principle taken to its ultimate ends would mean the death of the organism. This is how the pleasure principle can paradoxically be said to serve the death drive. Operating by the Nirvana principle, the death drive must go through the process of life to reach its end. Death is thus inextricably bound to life. The instinct for self-preservation drives the organism to reproduce, to love. Love produces difference, "fresh 'vital differences'" which Freud says must be "lived off," emphasizing the life process even as the organism moves toward its own demise.[125] This brings Freud to an impasse. He is caught in an undecidable bind between life and death or in my formulation the problem of not-death. Life moves both toward its own extinction *and* toward revitalization in a compulsive cycle. The organism seeks union *and* dissolution. Not-death consists of the perpetual oscillation between forces of integration and creation, and disintegration and destruction. Freud staunchly upheld this conceptual antagonism not so much to consolidate and defend either side (life or death as the final winner), but to describe survival as made up of this contest. When he returns to these questions in *Civilization and Its Discontents*, he articulates his morose tale of "prosthetic gods" as such: "[The evolution of civilization] must present the struggle between Eros and Death, between the instinct of life and the instinct of destruction, as it works itself out in the human species. This struggle is what a life essentially consists of."[126]

   In his deconstruction of *Beyond*, Derrida claims that Freud is speculating upon himself in the essay's structure. Noting that death pervades the works of the second period of Freud's life (1920 and beyond), Derrida quotes from Freud's autobiographical study (1925): "it seemed as though my life would soon be brought to an end by the recurrence of a malignant disease."[127] He characterizes psychoanalysis as autothanatography because Freud's own family drama and the question of death take center stage. As Derrida deconstructs it, psychoanalysis is a movement passed on through inheritance. Its genealogy begins with the death of Freud's father, which instigated the self-analysis that resulted in the foundational psychoanalytic text, *The Interpretation of Dreams*. Additionally, Freud draws on observations of his grandson, Ernst, for the *fort/da* game that illustrates repetition compulsion and signals the workings of the death drive. Ernst was notably the son of Freud's favorite daughter, Sophie, who died the year *Beyond* was published and, according to Derrida's reading, casts her shadow across the text.[128] Derrida finds *Beyond* plagued with discursive recurrence and diagnoses a metastasis of the pleasure principle.[129]

Although the autothanatography of psychoanalysis is founded upon the discourse of cancer, theorists have scarcely noted cancer's uninvited intrusion upon psychoanalysis.[130] As discussed in the Introduction, I contend that cancer has a psychoanalytic meaning, and this is not only due to its founder's protracted malady. Cancer reflects the paradoxical double meanings of the not-death drive. It names a persistent dread, anxiety, and fear of inner disintegration that is encountered by many psychoanalysts and may be innate to human beings. It is also identified with unceasing proliferation, *jouissance*, and the drive toward immortality.[131] Eerily prophetic, as early as 1899, Freud wrote to Fliess comparing his work ethic to a kind of cancer. I quote his letter at length because it so uncannily foreshadows his eventual demise:

> [It] has a hold on every stirring thought, and eventually sucks up all faculties and susceptibilities, a kind of neoplastic tissue which infiltrates into the human one and finally replaces it. . . . I have turned completely into a cancer. The neoplasm likes to drink wine in its latest stages of development. Today I am supposed to go to the theatre, but this is ridiculous—like trying to graft on top of the cancer. Nothing can adhere to it, and so from now on the duration of my life is that of the neoplasm.[132]

It is worth pointing out that Freud's major examples in *Beyond* involve significant participation of nonhuman elements, indicating that the nonhuman environment necessarily and actively facilitates the negotiation of loss, mourning, and libidinal working through of the death drive. The *fort/da* scenario hinges upon a toy that his grandson Ernst tosses into his crib so that it disappears (gone/*fort*) and then reels back out, magically bringing about its materialization (there/*da*). The spool demonstrates how the child negotiates separation anxiety and compensates for loss. The child's activities may be interpreted as an effort to come to terms with his mother's absence by mastering her disappearance and return. But in the mind of an infant the mother's absence is equivalent to death, so the game may also be understood as a means of mastering death. In play and consequently fantasy, the child overcomes death.

Read in the context of Freud's prosthetic drama, Freud continually tosses out his unsatisfactory prostheses, only to be forced to retrieve them again. They disappear and return to him in a cruel game that may have supplied if not an omnipotent mastery of death, a compulsive means of negotiating its persistent returns. Following the *fort/da* structure of disappearance and reappearance, Freud's procession of prostheses compels him to compulsively make a home for the foreign object, or to evict it. Freud's travails precisely beg the question as to who/what has the power to claim his body as home. Freud's unhomeliness at the expense of his prostheses brings to light the uncanny link between the uncanny and the death drive.[133]

Following the celebrated *fort/da* scene, which has attained the status of myth, Freud turns to literary mythology, as he is wont to do. A supernatural tree in the romantic epic poem *Gerusalemme Liberata* illustrates the compulsion to repeat. The poem's hero, Tancred, mistakenly murders his beloved, Clorinda, not once but twice, mortally wounding her in battle and later slaying the tree in which her spirit was imprisoned.[134] These two examples not only stress the centrality of death in psychoanalytic discourse, but also how it is manifested through the human relation to nonhuman objects. In the first, death is denied through mastery over a toy that can perpetually be brought home to its owner. But in the second scenario this fantasy of control is undone. Self-knowledge appears impossible, and destruction seems to be carried on without sense. Just as the problem of repetition compulsion remains a mystery to Freud, so too does the problem of death remain insoluble, or rather undecidable, as Derrida would have it.[135] The significance of the nonhuman to Freud's formulation of the death or not-death drive is not lost on Steven Miller. He analyzes not only the tree but also Clorinda's armor, which as an "inanimate shell" serves a protective function but is not invulnerable to violence.[136] Miller likens Clorinda's shell, which is "situated at the most vulnerable edge of the body," to Derrida's trace.[137] This comparison allows Miller to argue that the object of the death drive is "the nonliving trace or shell of life," another variant on not-death.[138]

When Freud turns to his nonhuman objects, he constructs a representation of the enigma of not-death. As Liran Razinsky maintains in his exhaustive account of psychoanalysis and death, "Representation is already a form of understanding. It makes of what it represents a thing, an object."[139] Freud's incomplete and contradictory representation of the death drives used nonhuman things for what may have been reparative purposes, granting himself a partial understanding (a partial object) of how his survival entailed a self-preservative drive to his own death.

His Living Prostheses

I have proposed that Freud's death drive can be understood as ironically driving toward not-death, a condition that involves a copresence of destruction and creation. I have identified how this not-death is at work in the technological predicament imposed by Freud's mechanical and chemical prostheses. Finally, I want to suggest that Anna Freud served as his living prosthesis. Contemplating Freud, his cancer, his prosthesis, and his death is inseparable from thinking about Anna. From his diagnosis to his death, "ever-present" Anna was so intimate with her father that Jones describes their relation in a letter to Schur as an "unconscious incest."[140] Anna Freud's biographer, Elizabeth Young-Bruehl, asserts: "He was, in a sense, addicted to her staying at home, to her presence, as he was to his cigars."[141] In the despair of his illness Freud confessed to Lou Andreas Salome in a letter of May 16, 1935: "I am more and more dependent on Anna's care of me, just as Mephistopheles once remarked: 'At the end we depend on the creatures we made.'"[142] With Anna as his primary caregiver, Freud submits to an almost complete dependence upon his own biological and intellectual creation. Freud associated Anna with the creation of psychoanalysis, not only because he was aware she would carry on his work after his death, but also because the birth of psychoanalysis coincided with hers. He is reported to have said that Anna and psychoanalysis were the same age, but she gave him less trouble.[143] As I have recounted, the death drive, though it tends toward a canceling or leveling out of life, as Miller parses the German, unexpectedly strives toward immortality through the act of creation.[144] Freud alludes to this through his reference to malignant cells, cells that proliferate indefinitely and can thus be said to attain immortality. I have also indicated how his addiction to smoking invites both death and immortality, through the creation of immortal works. We can therefore see how creativity and immortality are linked. Anna, as Freud's creation, was responsible for his intellectual legacy. She founded a museum dedicated to her father's memory in an effort to secure immortality for psychoanalysis. Her father's imminent destruction was the occasion for her assuming the function of a living prosthesis during his lifetime, his "mouthpiece" afterward.[145]

As is well known, Anna exerted a strong grip upon how her father was represented, which had direct bearing upon how she felt he would be remembered after his death. She objected to the public distribution of Lehrman's film, referred to previously, because it showed Freud's scar.[146] Even through a smoke-filled room the projection of these pictures would have been so clear that Freud's wound would be exposed, and consequently his disease might be negatively attributed to his addiction. Lynne Lehrman Weiner, Lehrman's daughter, who requested Anna's help in identifying the analysts in the film but was refused, recalled that Anna did not want her father to be shown in pain.[147] If Anna was loath to reveal the excruciating details of her father's demise to the public, she was utterly attentive to them in private. The Anna Freud Papers at the Library of Congress houses a stack of 203 loose leaf sheets beneath a green cover labeled "SF illness record by AF," handwritten in blue and black ink on pink, green, and yellow paper. This copy of the English translation of Pichler's notes exudes an emotionalism absent from the sterile typed document that Pichler's secretary transcribed from the surgeon's unique shorthand. Although the content is the same as the 142-page typed English translation that Schur kept, the colored papers imprinted with a daughter's schoolgirl cursive chronicling her father's eventually fatal illness cannot but invite interpretation. For this is the girl who entertained beating fantasies at the hands of her father, whose masochism is later inverted to a sadism, if involuntary, expended on manipulating her father's prosthesis.[148] These fantasies of a child being beaten Freud analyzed as meaning "Father loves only me."[149] And this prophecy is borne out in his daughter's record of devotion. Schur confirms it: "In his last years—it was only Anna."[150]

But it was not entirely only Anna. If devotion has a body many would argue that it most readily takes the shape of a dog. However, one could also argue that Anna was mediated through the Freud family dogs, for amongst Freud's devotees there was often confusion in distinguishing between children, patients, and dogs. Michael Molnar comments on Freud's infamous analysis of his own daughter-cum-analysand-cum-domesticated companion: "Through her own analysis with her father she was finally to become 'good,' that is trained."[151] Whatever she censored in her not so free association might have been mediated through the dogs, that is, especially in those last years, her fears of her father dying, abandonment, and possibly her own mortality. As several have convincingly argued, the innocent, perennial presence of dogs in the Freud household served to tame unruly feelings about mortality and death.[152] Every year from Freud's seventieth birthday the "master" of the house received a poem from one of his dogs. Via Anna, the dogs record their evolution from "emotional prosthesis" to "genuine prosthesis," as Molnar interprets it: "Their persevering jaws—will tirelessly do your chores—of chewing, and their fangs won't shirk—taking on your mealtime work. / They offer themselves up—as your prosthesis and your prop."[153] As anaclitic love objects, they chewed the food that Freud could not eat because of his surgeries, radium treatments, and difficulties with his prostheses, and thus "transformed his pain into their, and his, pleasure."[154] Above all, Freud valued dogs for their lack of ambivalence, and perhaps for this reason his own attachment to his canine prostheses, unlike his mechanical ones, was not marred by this persistent human trait. The extant films documenting Freud's daily life, including his home movies and the reels shot by Lehrman, prominently feature dogs. They are as unavoidable to the viewer as they were to Lehrman when he attempted to include himself in the frame with the Professor but was forced to continually run back to protect his tripod from the bounding creatures. And where cameras could not follow, analysands' recollections tell us that Freud's chow was a perennial presence in the consulting room.[155]

Beyond his attachment to his own dogs, how could Freud have resisted identifying with Topsy, Bonaparte's chow, who suffered, like he, from a tumor in her right oral cavity? Both were undergoing the same treatment: surgery, radium, and Roentgen ray, and the Princess even brought them to the same radiation specialist.[156] Freud and Anna together translated Bonaparte's homage to her faithful companion, *Topsy: The Story of a Golden-Haired Chow*, while they awaited clearance to escape Austria. On the eve of the traumatic disruption of exile, compounded with the accumulating debilities of cancer, Freud relied upon his living prostheses to help him mediate his ever-growing losses. Canine prostheses, Ann Pellegrini observes, can function as creative accomplices and helpmates: "Dogs offer themselves—and are offered—as a site of narrative surrogation through which to bear and tell the story of traumatic loss," the loss of home, nation, and

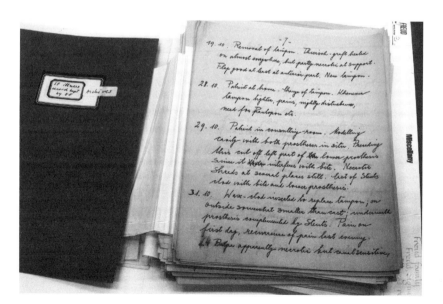

Figure 3. Sigmund Freud's illness record transcribed by Anna Freud. Container 159, Folder 2, Anna Freud Papers, Manuscript Division, Library of Congress, Washington, D.C. Photograph by Lin + Lam.

for Freud, of life itself.[157] Through the creative work of translating Topsy's story in partnership with his daughter, Freud not only could relieve his anxieties about exile and impending death, he might also fantasize an impossible recovery. Of course, Freud's mechanical, chemical, and emotional prostheses finally fail to stave off the unremitting progress of his cancer. This was corroborated by his chow's aversion to Freud when his skin and bones began to rot. The stench repelled the animal, which sadly cowered in the corner, refusing to approach his master.

In translating *Topsy* and rushing to finish *Moses and Monotheism*, among other works he left incomplete, Freud was engaged in a creative reparative process with a ferocity that frequently grips those nearing death. But in the end, it was Anna who fulfilled the demands of a reparative object. For Freud, she was his own creation who served to redress the wounds of his death and dying. As the embodiment of psychoanalysis, she becomes Freud's lasting answer to his own destruction and his mechanism for survival. Perhaps the illness record in which her devoted care is dutifully registered became Anna's reparative object to appease the pain of her father's passing.

CHAPTER 2

Keen for the First Object

A Kleinian Reading of Audre Lorde's Life Writing

.

> I found my mother
> Seboulisa
> standing with outstretched palms hip high
> one breast eaten away by worms of sorrow . . .
>
> —Audre Lorde

Within a psychoanalytic theory of human development, the first object of love, hate, nourishment, and deprivation is the breast. There are profound psychic effects to losing this first object through cancer, a loss that recapitulates the original loss all humans experience through the natural course of life. Cancer reawakens the infantile terror, frustration, anxiety, and anger of this early trauma and the destabilizations it engenders. The paradoxical and ambivalent combination of violent destruction and mournful creation that I have associated with cancer is also characteristic of the infantile oral stage. Perhaps no psychoanalytic theorist is better suited to describing this pivotal stage of psychic life than Melanie Klein, a proponent of what has come to be known as the British school of object relations, whose theories can illuminate the work of black lesbian feminist poet Audre Lorde. Why bring together two bodies of writing by women who could hardly be more different from one another? For its very incompatibilities, a Kleinian reading of Lorde's life and work is revealing. Trying to fit a square peg into a circular hole (sexual innuendo intended) may reflect some of the violences that are central to both women's projects.

In 1977, when she was forty-three, Lorde had a biopsy of a tumor in her right breast, which was determined to be benign. Nevertheless, Lorde confessed to "fantasies of chopping her right breast off, like a she-wolf chewing off a paw caught in a trap . . . She began to think of her right breast as no longer a part of her. It had betrayed her, harbored an evil that could now destroy her."[1] Lorde's fantasy is startlingly resonant with Klein's descriptions of the infantile anxieties that plague her child patients. According to Klein's ruthless drama, the baby directs its rage against its mother's breast and body, "scooping it out, devouring the contents, destroying it by every means which sadism can suggest."[2] For Klein, psychic life emerges through a savage cannibalism, what amounts to a destructive self-preservation that surfaces with regularity in Lorde's work. Furthermore, the radicality of Lorde's politics tallies with the radicality of Klein's theories. For instance, the fierce debates in the feminist movement of the late 1970s and 1980s that Lorde instigated by accusing white feminists of racism can be seen as a mirror to the controversial discussions of the 1940s between the Freudian and Kleinian schools in which orthodox Freudians were prepared to oust rebel Kleinians from the institution of psychoanalysis.[3]

Putting these two frequently contradictory but always powerful minds into conversation elucidates both women's work. Both corpuses provoke visceral reactions that can lead to a reduction of the complexities and puzzling aspects of their thought. Lorde has been accused of an essentialism that idealizes the black woman. Klein has been criticized for being obsessed with sadism, aggression, and death. Reading Lorde's oeuvre by way of Klein reveals layers of psychological complexity that are latent in its meanings. Conversely, Lorde's life writing not only usefully illustrates Klein's theories, but also highlights the narrowness of Klein's vision when it comes to the sociopolitical and cultural factors that impact an infant's survival. Lorde also politicizes Klein's normative vision of the mother/child relation by suggesting that people who have been systematically denied the status of whole persons can learn to mother themselves.[4] Lorde's notion of mothering involves claiming the parts of oneself that society would throw away, a project that enlists community support. Both women, however, portray mothers and their offspring as beset by lifelong struggle that initiates its course through the vital physical and psychic interaction at the maternal breast.

The Breast as Psychic Object

A year after her initial cancer scare, Lorde discovered a "huge lump" in her right breast. This time the tumor was malignant, and Lorde underwent a mastectomy. Alexis De Veaux, Lorde's biographer, notes that in Lorde's journals of 1979 and 1980, she "likened the physical and psychic pain of separating from her breast as 'at least as sharp as the pain of separating from the mother.'"[5] If to be separated from the breast is to be separated from mother, who would know this better than Lorde's own daughter? Lorde writes in *The Cancer Journals* that her daughter cried when Lorde told her she was going to have a mastectomy because "she was sentimentally attached to my breasts."[6] In comparing the pain of breast removal to the pain of weaning or the pain of leaving home, which can be understood to recapitulate the earlier separation from the feeding breast, Lorde implicitly presumes a psychic process by which the maternal breast becomes an object (or, more accurately, two objects, as Klein will propose) in the mind of the baby. The formation of this psychic object sets the stage for no less than human survival, a survival that is much more challenged if conditions are not favorable to its security.

Let us begin with Freud, for whom, as we all know, the penis reigns in his Oedipal logic, but who also concedes that for the child the first object is the breast. Freud locates the origins of sexuality and indeed love at the site of the breast: "A child's first erotic object is the mother's breast that nourishes it; love has its origin in attachment to the satisfied need for nourishment."[7] The breast becomes the first object toward which the sexual instinct is aimed, in conjunction with, perhaps even as a result of, activities of self-preservation. On a psychic level, the breast assumes the twin roles of sexual satisfaction and self-preservation. For Freud, our feelings of well-being take on a shape, and that shape is the maternal breast: "The sexual instinct has a sexual object outside the infant's own body in the shape of his mother's breast."[8] The shape of the mother's breast persists in a mental image we carry with us which makes possible our sense of security, our abilities to take and give pleasure, and our desire to relate to others.

Though most psychoanalysts agree upon the unparalleled position of the breast in psychosexual development, not all of their views would harmonize with Freud's. Although Freud understands love relations, of which nursing at the breast is the prototype, as inherently ambivalent, his depiction of the breast is clearly less fraught than Klein's. For Klein, the primal feelings of love and hate congeal at the breast, which will impose a greater influence upon the rest of life than any other factor. The Kleinian breast surpasses the immediate function of nourishment and sensual comfort, crucially defining the subject and her ability to recognize herself and others. It is through the process of cathecting, that is, investing psychical energy into the breast or its substitute, that the mother is "turned into a loved object."[9] This part of mother that stands in for the whole becomes the "part-object" in the infant's unconscious phantasy, which as Meira Likierman succinctly explicates it, can be "understood as 'ingested' parts of the world, or 'ingested' aspects of the mother."[10] As its first act of self-preservation, the infant splits the first object into two partial objects, the "good breast" and "bad breast," after which emotional life proceeds something like a high stakes game of psychic catch, "characterized by a sense of losing and regaining the good object."[11] The infant, according to Klein's developmental trajectory, fluctuates between experiencing the transitory gratification of its internalized "good" objects and the ruthless persecution of its internalized "bad" objects, "for both of which its mother's breast is the prototype."[12] The absence of the breast elicits annihilation anxiety, hatred, and rage, which are rejected by the baby and projected into an external object—originally the mother. One might speculate from this that when Lorde fantasizes chopping off her breast, the traumatic prospect of breast cancer prompted a regression in which she psychically detached her breast as a part-object from her body, turning her anxieties and aggressions upon that "bad" part-object.

W. R. Bion adapts and extends Klein's internal good and bad breasts to theorize thinking as the product of the absence of the good breast, what he terms "no-breast." The infant meets the breast with frustration because inevitably the baby's needs are never completely satisfied. Thus, Bion proposes that when a preconception encounters frustrated realization, it is "experienced as a no-breast, or 'absent' breast inside."[13] The "no-breast" becomes a thought if the infant has the capacity to tolerate frustration. If the baby cannot withstand frustration, rather than becoming a thought, the "no-breast" will become a bad object that must be evacuated. For Bion, dire consequences result if the bad objects the baby projects are not returned in a tolerable form. These include a failure of thinking, and with it the ability to recognize the crucial distinctions between self and other. Bion's formulation implies that an incapacity to transform the "no-breast" into cognition correlates with an inability to tolerate difference. The "no-breast" remains an object that cannot be used and must be rejected as a threatening, foreign body. Lorde's autoethnographic writing likewise shows how the inability to tolerate difference has catastrophic consequences. The "no-breasted" postmastectomy woman, the person of color, the gender nonconforming, the disabled, the poor, and the old, each of these subjects are ejected as foreign objects from a society that can only perceive of difference as endangering.

The Breast as Political Object

Klein used the terms "breast" and "mother" interchangeably and conventionally, largely bracketing the politics of motherhood. Reading Lorde through Klein puts some of the normative presumptions around the culturally sanctioned understanding of breasts and mothers into question. If the breast is a psychic object, for Lorde it is also always a political object. In the documentary about her life, *Litany for Survival*, Lorde affirms the affinity between battling cancer and battling racism or sexism: "I visualize it in very political terms. I sometimes image the cancer cells as white South African policemen."[14] De Veaux reiterates: "Lorde genuinely believed that her survival was a political issue."[15] It is fitting, then, that this "very political organ," as physician and cancer researcher Deborah Rhodes calls the breast, would be the catalyst for some of Lorde's best known and most politically outspoken writing.[16] Following her mastectomy, Lorde issued a scathing critique of breast prostheses as masking the violence exacted upon women through the collusion of the cancer, medical, and "health/beauty" industries, which turned life-threatening environmental hazards into a cosmetic problem, and rendered postmastectomy women invisible to each other. She lambasted the recommendation that prostheses could solve employment discrimination, comparing this to fighting racial prejudice by asking black people to pretend to be white.[17]

For Lorde the offenses of sexism and racism converge in their demand to cover over differences that are apprehended as transgressive. In Kleinian terms, Lorde experienced cancer, racism, sexism, and homophobia as the bad breast. She was to associate the life-threatening conditions of cancer, racism, and sexism from the time a tumor was first discovered in her breast until her cancer had metastasized to her liver. The need for self-preservation must answer to all these ills at once. To Lorde they are inseparable, and she insisted that maintaining this amalgamation of identities was necessary to her continued survival. In her refusal to dissociate the varied and messy experiences of identity, she formulated a theory of interlocking oppressions that attends to how she inhabited being not merely a black woman, but a black feminist lesbian warrior poet. Before Kimberlé Crenshaw's coinage of the term "intersectionality,"[18] she recognized that the convergence of multiple registers of identity constructed her and her sisters of color as especially vulnerable to violences of all sorts, including but certainly not limited to ill health, poverty, sexual assault, and discrimination.[19]

Lorde is, of course, not alone in her experience and understanding of oppression as a physical calamity. Frantz Fanon confirms the visceral violation of racial injury in relating an anecdote about a white boy who hails him with "Look, a Negro!" forcing him into a racialized, objectified interpellation. Fanon responds: "What else could it be for me but an amputation, an excision, a hemorrhage that spattered my whole body with black blood?"[20] Akin to the melancholic who identifies with the loved and hated object she has internalized, Lorde internalized and identified with the racial hatred and sexism that were projected onto, and in keeping with Kleinian logic, *into* her. She bemoans the "self-destructiveness implanted inside of [her] by racism and sexism."[21] This implantation was felt as a projection of racial hatred and misogyny, which she was compelled to introject. In an essay directed expressly to her black sisters, Lorde would return to the metaphor of the she-wolf who devours herself in order to save herself, questioning why black women turn against each other in their mutual oppression: "If I have learned to eat my own flesh in the forest—starving, keening, learning the lesson of the she-wolf who chews off her own paw to leave the trap behind—if I must drink my own blood, thirsting, why should I stop at yours until your dear dead arms hang like withered garlands upon my breast . . . "[22] The she-wolf that is black woman attacks itself for survival.

One could say that the poisonous projections of hatred, which Lorde experienced as a black lesbian, produced what Klein called schizoid defense mechanisms in which parts of the self are annihilated. Dismembered partobjects—paw, arms, breast—are sacrificed for the sake of the whole. Klein's theories on aggression, though not explicitly addressed to social violence, describe it in terms of injury and a threat to survival. But for both Lorde and Klein, aggression can also be self-protective, as Lorde illustrates through her metaphoric resort to self-inflicted violence in response to a greater external violence. Importantly Lorde's masochism responds to a sadism that unlike Klein's phantasied aggression extends from the reality of a hostile world.

One might protest that the literality of death sticks to cancer in a different way than it does to racism and sexism. But for Lorde, the literality of death, through cancer or social oppression, is experienced and expressed figuratively, and the figurative has the power to effect literal change. Poetry "makes you happen. It makes your living happen."[23] "Poetry is not a luxury" for it illuminates the path to survival.[24] Akin to life, poetry can overcome the threat of extinction. This is where Klein's concept of unconscious phantasy remarkably agrees with Lorde's position. Phantasies psychically express the instincts, which for Freud reside on the frontier between the physiological and the mental. Likierman explains that phantasies provide "an operative link between instinctual urges and the earliest defences of the psyche."[25] This is to say that Kleinian phantasy bridges the literal, physical stuff of the world and their internal mental representations, and it produces actual change in the form of defenses. Phantasies take root in the mire of visceral sensation. Beyond mere imagination and abstraction, they are representations that have all the force of instinctual impulses. Phantasy does the kind of work for Klein that poetry does for Lorde, which is to make thought, hence life, possible.

Lorde teaches us that the black lesbian is constituted in her differences. She is not produced in the encounter with difference. She houses difference in herself.[26] From the outset, she inhabits the position of Sister Outsider. Such a woman comes into being as alterity within herself. As such, a foreign intrusion would seem to be intolerable. Lorde loathes the idea that her body would become alien to herself. While Freud was able to take in the foreign body of his prostheses, which caused suffering but did not annihilate his sense of being, one has the sense that intrusion whether physical or psychic was devastating to Lorde, that it threatened to disassemble her self. The assault of objectification, wherein the subject is made into an object, damages the psychic differentiation between subject and object and makes maintaining them as separate entities treacherous. As Lorde narrates it, the black person, and especially the socially maligned black lesbian, precariously houses her difference at the always vulnerable divide between subject and object. She understands her oppressions to stem from a history of slavery and colonialism in which black and colored people were treated as property, things to be traded, bought, and sold. Given this charged history of objectification, the black woman is constantly in danger of having to fend off the collapse between subject and object, that distinction that psychoanalysis locates as emerging at the breast.

In the encounter with the white boy previously noted, Fanon makes *himself* into an object. Objectification is turned upon the self and accomplished by the self. Lorde's experience of cancer is similarly not only objectifying, turning herself against herself, but is also intensified by the oppression that predates her diagnosis. As a black lesbian, she was already vulnerable to attack. She did not benefit from the privilege of having her identity and identifications align with mainstream society, and was denied the ego-strengthening affirmation of always already being legible as a subject.

Objectification and Object Relations

Lorde's narrative of physical and social trauma raises a larger question: Where does objectification fit in within psychoanalytic object relations? I propose thinking very broadly about the object-ness of object relations, the object not only as a human being, but also the object as thing, and finally the human *made into* a thingly object, that is, the objectified human. While Klein hints at the depersonalizing aspects of objectification in her description of her patients' experiences of dissolution as fractured internal objects litter their psyches "in bits," her theories on how the subject contends with its constitutive decomposition fail to fully take into account the socioeconomic and cultural environment.[27] It appears that Klein conceived of the social environment primarily in terms of the mother's caretaking role. Race is not granted specific attention in terms of its formative effects upon the psyche. Klein's racial blindness can be inferred primarily through omission, but it becomes apparent on a couple of occasions when the racial and cultural "other" is expressly noted in her writing but left unanalyzed.[28] According to Kleinians, if all goes well, the child will accomplish the task of integration (from the original splitting) such that she will gain at least the illusion of wholeness, both of herself and her environment. But Klein asserts that if the world is experienced as excessively discontinuous, destabilizing, and hence dangerous, the subject has a more difficult time of stabilizing her sense of self. What integration she achieves may therefore be more fragile. Like her cells, which proved to be more susceptible to cancer, Lorde's object relations were susceptible to an environment and history of social, political, psychological, and physical abuses. While Klein's descriptions of sadistic phantasies that are projected, introjected, and identified with can be helpful in understanding the experience of such fragmented subjectivity, Lorde's writing complicates the problems that Klein's studies raise. Through Lorde's work we are prodded to ask: What becomes of the task of integration if the environment does not reflect back an image of wholeness? And what of the receiving end of projectiles of hatred and antagonism?

Lorde's poem "The Brown Menace or Poem to the Survival of Roaches" gives voice to the most despised creature on earth, showing how the processes of objectification move the object closer to the nonhuman. The reader or listener cannot help but make the equation that the black and brown races are the roaches of society, the most detested vermin, and yet the most persevering and indestructible. Lorde's identification with the roach, and the reader's identification of the poet *as* roach, involves nuanced interdependent object relations in which the speaker and spoken to are woven together. The poem's first lines are: "Call me/your deepest urge/toward survival."[29] In the process of identifying itself, the roach hails the other whose identity is known only by way of its difference from the agent of the poem. Identification is predicated on the other, for it is "you" who calls "me," who identifies me, and I who am identified in "your deepest urge," "your itch to destroy," "your most secret places," and "your poisonous refusal."[30] The poem repeatedly insists that the defiled figure reflects the hated and feared parts of the addressee:

> friend of your own image
> within me
> I am you
> your most deeply cherished nightmare[31]

In this poem, the subject that speaks does so as the object of the other. Lorde's identification with the abhorrent object of a horrified gaze, can be traced back to a childhood scene in which a woman on an A train is repelled by young Audre, as if the child were a roach.[32] Little Audre sits in confused silence as she recognizes herself as the object of the woman's hatred. Lorde will learn to speak from the position of the object of the hostile gaze, and it is the reader of "The Brown Menace" who must learn to imitate the roach's determined survival.

When her breast—the psychic home of good and bad objects and the origins of subject formation—is tainted with cancer, the fears and anxieties of Lorde's personal history are ignited, rendering her a thingly object. She laments: "I have ceased being a person who is myself and become a thing upon a Guerney [*sic*] cart."[33] Chronic illness, as in Freud's case, can transform a subject into a nonhuman object. Recalling how his carcinoma and gruesome treatments turned Freud into an island of pain, Lorde describes her cancerous body as "the island within which I had to struggle alone."[34] Indeed, she may have had cause to liken herself to an island, for she had lived on islands for most of her life, on Manhattan, Staten Island, and St. Croix. In 1989, Hurricane Hugo devastated the last island, Lorde's adopted home from 1986 until her death in 1992. Her essay recounting the destruction of the island and exhausting recovery efforts delineates the ways in which precarity is constructed through a confluence of sociopolitical and economic factors. Lorde identified with the vulnerability of the island, which was made more susceptible to the forces of nature through a history of U.S. occupation, racism, and economic disparities. And, not unlike her identification with the roach, she marveled at its tenacious commitment to survival. St. Croix after Hurricane Hugo suffered as she did from "tumors that fester and grow loathsome."[35] In using this metaphor she links her own affliction to the abuses inflicted upon the natural environment, the ugliest of which she notes are man-made.

In the aftermath of the storm the island is forced to run on generators, which "are the only sources of power, both real and symbolic."[36] If their reliance upon the generators almost seems to transform the local inhabitants into machines, the generators acquire human characteristics that likewise blur the boundaries between human subjects and mechanized objects. Lorde describes the constant drone of the motors as coughing and spitting, and they weaken as would animate beings: "Since they were never meant to be run constantly, the overworked generators soon begin to fail."[37] The plight of the generators echoes one of Lorde's most quoted phrases which concludes her poem "A Litany for Survival": "we were never meant to survive."[38] She repeats this sentiment in *The Cancer Journals*, adding and underlining her association with the nonhuman: "We were never meant to survive. Not as human beings."[39]

Orality: Creation and Destruction, Parts and Wholes

In the context of her initial cancer scare Lorde gave a lecture, "The Transformation of Silence into Language and Action," in which she associated the fears and dangers of racial and other forms of social injury with physical distress. The speech was published in *The Cancer Journals*, in which she confesses that after losing her breast through mastectomy she paradoxically began to feel "more whole."[40] Her loss unexpectedly initiates reparation. Being forced to confront her mortality leads Lorde to reflect upon what wholeness means to her. She defines a whole person as a person who makes use of her whole self, which significantly has to do with speaking out and taking action. Silence is equated with passivity, fear, betrayal, immobilization, and for Lorde this puts it on the side of the death wish. Silence leaves you incomplete, fragmented, destroyed, a condition that cancer would instigate had Lorde not summoned the power to resist its disintegrating effects through speech. Speech fosters the object relation, a relation that for Lorde is the glue that holds her bits and pieces together. She invokes her own daughter's words on the matter: "'Tell them about how you're never really a whole person if you remain silent, because there's always that one little piece inside of you that wants to be spoken out . . . and if you don't speak it out one day it will just up and punch you in the mouth.'"[41] Lorde's daughter speaks in the grammar of orality and part-objects. Silence breeds vengeful part-objects that will take out aggression on your mouth, the organ that unites with the breast for nourishment and the original maternal reverie. The transition from hostile, unintegrated part-objects to whole objects appears to occur through the medium of speech.

Lorde speaks through the language of orality, a language first acquired at the breast. The oral phase is the first psychosexual stage "in which the object that we long for and prize is assimilated by eating and is in that way annihilated as such."[42] Here Freud tells us that from their origins at the breast, creation and destruction are inextricably entwined. The destruction of the other enables the creation of the self. It is through the very process of creating oneself that the other is destroyed. Freud links these most primitive instincts with higher level processes, such as judgment: "Expressed in the language of the oldest—the oral—instinctual impulses, the judgment is: 'I should like to eat this', or 'I should like to spit it out'; and, put more generally: 'I should like to take this into myself and to keep that out.' That is to say: 'It shall be inside me' or 'it shall be outside me.'"[43] Becoming a subject and distinguishing oneself from objects extends from the foundation, and Freud might say mastery, of the oral instincts. Klein's theoretical interest is concentrated upon the oral phase, which is dominated by archaic feelings bound up with part-objects, those parts of wholes that are other to ourselves yet still feel as if they are part of ourselves. The process of introjection and projection Klein describes is fundamentally oral, following an incorporative logic that has to do with what one takes in and expels. Klein's assessment of how subjectivity comes into being through this oral process and becomes accessible for more psychologically sophisticated uses allows us to understand what survival entails for Lorde.

Lorde depicts the mouth as the organ of both comfort and threat, sustenance and aggression. After her daughter's advice to beware of the silence that threatens to congeal into a part-object that will take revenge on her mouth, she instructs her fellow unintended survivors on how to "survive in the mouth of this dragon we call america."[44] Oppression occurs on the oral level—being deprived of good objects, force-fed bad objects, and being consumed *as* a bad object. Liberation will mean taking charge of what enters and is emitted from the mouth. As a teacher at John Jay College of Criminal Justice, Lorde was faced with heightened racial tensions follow-

ing the institution of open admissions at the City University of New York.
With the influx of black and Latino students, her police officer students
attended class armed with guns.[45] Her poem "Blackstudies" addresses the
traumas of black education in the fraught urban setting of the 1970s and is
rife with oral anxieties. Lorde describes herself "nursing old gods," her
"flesh . . . covered by mouths."[46] She is terrified of being kerneled out like
a walnut, like the Kleinian children who scoop out their mother's insides.

I am afraid
that the mouths I feed will turn against me
will refuse to swallow in the silence
I am warning them to avoid[47]

As in *The Cancer Journals*, she resides "in the mouth of the enemy," but
the questions her poem raises complicate who is eating whom, for it is one's
kin one must fear and cannibalize.[48] Before the "demon father" could

devour my children
I learned his language
I ate him
and left his bones mute in the noon sun[49]

In this context, defensive gorging is not unwarranted because what she
doesn't eat comes back to strangle her. The poem concludes with a query
about what defenses and nourishment are required for survival. Lorde
wonders of her students, who have in their hands both the power to make
death or life, "what shall they carve for weapons / what shall they grow for
food."[50] These are the concerns of the Kleinian infant who is consumed by
oral anxieties about how to defend its life and fend off death.

For Lorde the dehumanization of racism, sexism, and physical illness is
taken in orally, generating the annihilating anxiety of the infantile oral stage,
which can be equated with mortal injury. Remorsefully, she poses the rhetorical question: "What are the tyrannies you swallow day by day . . . ?"[51]
In her writing she works through the many ambivalences attendant with
oral impulses: the fear of being eaten and destroyed, the urge to incorporate others, the need to devour oneself for self-preservation (the dilemma
of the she-wolf), and even the desire to be consumed. In *Zami: A New
Spelling of My Name*, Lorde recalls how she was forced to ingest the humil-
iation and injustice of discrimination instead of swallowing ice cream when
her family was refused service at a soda fountain.[52] Lorde encounters this
racist treatment on a family trip to the nation's capital, and is nauseated.
The hypocrisy of a government that blatantly fails to live up to its procla-

mations about freedom and equality for all triggers an urge to expel the toxicity she has been forced to consume.[53] In Klein's lexicon, the child Audre might have projected—spit out—the badness she had been compelled to introject. If we follow Bion's logic, had her parents acknowledged her projected bad objects, the objectifying effect of racism might have been returned to her in a tolerable state. But while her parents and sisters escaped into a submissive silence that infuriated her, she was stuck with the toxicity of her internalized foreign objects. She could not cling to her childhood fantasy that the nation recognize her intelligence and reward her. She must grapple with how to metabolize both her own and others' aggressions. In order to sustain her good objects, she needs to put her anger to use.

In different idioms, both Lorde and Klein consider hate a destructive oral instinct, one that is incorporating and annihilating. Lorde deemed hatred, a "societal deathwish,"[54] which is akin to the death instinct: "Hatred is the fury of those who do not share our goals, and its object is death and destruction."[55] Klein's infant incorporates hatred due to frustrations at the breast that awaken persecutory fears and rage. Lorde ingests the hatred that sticks to her when she is spat upon on the street. She recounts: "To grow up metabolizing hatred like daily bread means that eventually every human interaction becomes tainted with the negative passion and intensity of its by-products."[56] Put in Kleinian terms, racist brutality could revive the infantile anxiety that Lorde had experienced at the breast, necessitating a projection of the death instinct into the bad object. As with racism and sexism, cancer was an objective danger situation for Lorde that would likely have induced death anxiety. For fourteen years she fought the fear of annihilation aroused by this persecutory agency. According to Klein, an infant's defensive schizoid reaction to death anxiety might be to kill off feared and hated parts of the self. At the infantile stage the baby and breast are one, making an attack on the breast equal to self-mutilation. Lorde's fantasy of the she-wolf illustrates this psychic performance of violent self-preservation.

If we believe in Klein's "religion of the Breast," it is here that Lorde first learned how to make use of her anger to strengthen her ego.[57] Stress upon the value of using feelings pervades Lorde's writings. Hate and guilt cannot be used by life; they can only be used for death. They are therefore wasted suffering. However, anger and pain are feelings that can be used. They are used for survival, which requires suffering. According to Klein, it is only through aggression that the infant can achieve and negotiate a new ego position, the "depressive" position, which will lead, if all goes well, to a balancing of hatred and love, and will enable the subject to determine self from other, internal from external reality, and ultimately to make lasting bonds with other human beings. In an unfinished 1940 paper on death, Klein contemplates reactions to the war.[58] She speculates that the inability to dissociate love from hate in the form of a separation between good and bad objects produces a paralyzing effect. She suggests that the only way to overcome political paralysis is to turn hatred outward to the actual enemy. This mode of action aligns with Lorde's strategy. For Lorde, speech and anger, which serve action, harness the power of love and self-protection.

Klein's depressive position performs the task of integrating the pieces of oneself that have been torn to bits in the sadistic paranoid-schizoid position. The compensatory reparative efforts that characterize the depressive position allow for, according to Klein, the stabilization of an internalized good object, which in turn enables a person to overcome adversity. *Zami* can be read as a recollection of how Lorde came to secure an internal good object. As a child, Audre relished crawling into bed under the covers next to her mother, a move that Klein might interpret as wanting to get inside of mother. She would wriggle inside the womb-like cocoon of bedding, "feeling the smooth deep firmness of her breasts," indicating her continued devotion to her first object.[59] Lorde's mother's West Indian mortar was a good external object that comforted her child. Lorde remembers, "The heavy sturdiness of this useful wooden object always made me feel secure and somehow full."[60] Its potential for oral gratification, its substantiality and use in the preparation of her favorite food link it to her first love object, the nourishing, erotic, self-validating breast. Lorde's attachment to this charged material object reflects her internalized good mother, which Klein describes as something felt unconsciously "having the nature of kindness and wisdom."[61]

After acquiring her first pair of eyeglasses, Lorde reports that they were "rapidly becoming a part of me."[62] As my account of Freud's case dramatically depicts, a prosthesis is never something simply to exalt or to abase. The eyeglasses that became a part of Lorde, who was legally blind, show how a good prosthesis is more than a prosthesis; it can in some sense become an internalized good object. As an adult, Lorde makes the connection between her prosthetic dependence upon inanimate and animate objects. Of her lover Muriel, she recalls: "Re-seeing the world through her unique scrutinies was like re-seeing the world through my first pair of glasses."[63] Like her glasses, Muriel functions as her prosthetic good object. But Lorde's relation to Muriel also suggests that even in adulthood her internalized good object was still vulnerable to fragmentation. She identifies Muriel as an external part-object that stands in place of and outside of herself: "I could cherish and protect this piece because it was outside of me."[64] It is only when the good object is externalized that she can value it. This puts her in a precarious position according to Klein's formulations because to attain stability of the self, the good object must be reborn inside of oneself. The maturational achievement of the depressive position can only be attained through an integration of good and bad internal objects. If the good object cannot be protected or repaired, the subject may remain caught in or regress to psychic fragmentation.

Continually beset by external aggressions that destabilized her good objects, Lorde might have felt herself to be conscripted to the oral phase of part-object dominance. She complains: "I am constantly being encouraged to pluck out some one aspect of myself and present this as the meaningful whole, eclipsing or denying the other parts of self."[65] The internalized tendency to divide herself into parts persisted throughout Lorde's life, not least because of a social system that demands that those who do not fit neatly into dominant categories disown parts of themselves. Lorde describes a paranoid schizoid world that infantilizes certain populations who are relegated to the status of perpetual part-objects. This is why she so fervently defended her right to defiantly and inclusively name the pieces of herself as black, feminist, lesbian, poet, mother, warrior. She denounced the hierarchies of oppression that sought to rank pieces of people as better or worse than others. When she was terminally ill, she prayed to the Black Mother goddess to protect her "from throwing any part of myself away."[66] Translated into Kleinian terms, Lorde continually strived to defend her good objects, so as not to resort to the schizoid mechanism of expelling hated and feared parts of herself. With her own body a betraying agent, she consciously and resolutely determined to care for and make use of her good objects to combat her death anxiety. Her project was to lay claim to all of her part-objects so that she herself could determine her own wholeness.

The Breast as Fetish Object

To the extent that she had secured an internalized good object, Lorde was able to mount a powerful and, even by today's standards, radical critique of breast prostheses as "bad" prosthetic objects. Lorde's good objects empowered her to campaign against breast prostheses, which to her mind supported only pretense. She vehemently opposed the prosthesis that mimes normativity, for to her the normative constrained her own "extraordinary body," which had always been regarded by dominant society as aberrant.[67] Lorde's criticism of breast prostheses reveals the ways in which sexual objectification mirrors racial objectification and exposes the degree to which the cancer complex in this culture perpetuates and is itself produced through the normative construction of gender and sexuality. Lorde's rejection of breast prostheses extended from her belief that gender non-normativity could be a form of power. In the prologue of *Zami* she announces a desire for gender variance: "I have always wanted to be both man and woman."[68] In her self-created genre of biomythography, Lorde constructs her own myth, repudiating the expectations she feels are imposed on her by external sources. With the exception of this confession, however, Lorde's discourse tends toward the woman-centric, *Zami* taking its title from the women loving women of Carriacou.[69]

By contrast, Klein's writings presume a heteronormative subject. The desire for a "third designation"[70] is unaccounted for in Klein's writings, although she does relate her boy patient's terrors of a hermaphroditic phallic mother, "a combination of father and mother in one person" who houses the penis inside her body.[71] Klein, like Freud, holds to an essential bisexual nature, though this is only to the extent that each individual possesses a masculine and feminine side. For her, sexual identity is restricted to males and females who, if psychologically "normal," are driven by heterosexual desire. Klein's theories can be read against the grain, but they reach some limits when faced with the radical difference of alternative gender identity.[72] Breast cancer troubles conventional and fixed notions of gender and necessitates a more complex view of the first object than either Klein or Lorde fully discussed.

When Eve Kosofsky Sedgwick was diagnosed with breast cancer, her immediate response was: "Shit, now I guess I must be a woman."[73] But who, in fact, possesses the breast? Women are defined as having breasts. Men are defined against that norm. As a gender theorist, Sedgwick intended her remark as an ironic commentary on breast cancer ideologies that equate women with presumably female organs. The fact that men have breasts and are also susceptible to breast cancer is rendered moot by this equation. Sedgwick goes on to say, "The formal and folk ideologies around breast cancer not only construct it as a secret, but construct it as the secret whose sharing defines women as such. All of this as if the most obvious thing in the world were the defining centrality of her breasts to any woman's sense of her gender identity and integrity!"[74] The "truth" about breast cancer must remain a secret, hidden behind prostheses and breast reconstruction, because in a society that defines only women as having breasts, the breast's vulnerability to disease and amputation threatens the very definition of "woman," and by opposition, of "man." When the sexual characteristics that dominant Western culture takes as defining gender categories are not visible or are transgressed, gender categories are in danger of collapse. In her discussion of sex reassignment surgery for transgender people, Gayle Salamon tells the story of a transwoman whose surgeons rejected the breasts she had grown and insisted that she have breast implants:

> According to the surgeons, what they could craft out of silicone were "real breasts," but the appendages that her own body grew, though they might have looked exactly like breasts, were merely gynecomastia, the abnormal development of the mammary tissue in a male. The breasts that her body grew were duly removed, and replaced by "real" surgically crafted breasts.[75]

For the doctors to recognize the trans woman as a woman she must not only display the shape of breasts but also those breasts must not originate from biologically male tissues. As these surgeons would have it, the breasts fabricated for a trans woman, like a postmastectomy woman's reconstructed breasts, are meant to hold apart a clear distinction between "man" and "woman." A woman's absent breast is seen to signify a deficiency or deformity, a punishment, a reminder of disease and apprehension around its recurrence. The absence must be filled or remedied by a prosthesis or reconstruction. As Lorde remarks, "the idea that a woman can be beautiful and one-breasted [or to invoke Bion, no-breasted] is considered depraved, or at best, bizarre, a threat to 'morale.'"[76] The gender ambiguity that arises as a result of gender realignment and breast removal surgery exposes anxieties around gender that this culture seeks to disavow.

Lorde describes the "prosthetic pretense" that is recruited to assimilate postmastectomy women to their pre-mastectomy state as regressive:

> After a mastectomy, for many women including myself, there is a feeling of wanting to go back. . . . It is this feeling, this nostalgia, which is encouraged by most of the post-surgical counseling for women with breast cancer. This regressive tie to the past is emphasized by the concentration upon breast cancer as a cosmetic problem.[77]

She suggests that the traumatic removal of the breast recalls the loss of the first object in infancy and can awaken infantile anxieties. Referring to Freud's late words on identification illuminates how this regression takes place. He writes of how the breast exemplifies the ways in which object relations evolve from identifying oneself as an object to differentiating oneself from one's objects: "Children like expressing an object-relation by an identification: 'I am the object.' 'Having' is the later of the two; after loss of the object it relapses into 'being'. Example: the breast. 'The breast is a part of me, I am the breast.' Only later: 'I have it'—that is, 'I am not it'. . ."[78] On a psychic level a woman who loses her breast to cancer may regress to the earlier state of identifying herself as the lost object, which may underlie the urgency with which a restoration of the breast/self is sought. The woman who has acquired a surgically reconstructed breast may look at the mirror and echo her infantile past: "I am the breast." In this light, breast reconstruction after the loss of the first object works against the mode of "having" and encourages the postmastectomy woman to retreat to the domain of "being" wherein the lost object can only be grieved through identification, by becoming it. Rather than being experienced as an object a woman has, the breast becomes the object that allows the woman to feel herself to be a woman. Identification with the breast may enable the postmastectomy woman who seeks reconstruction to feel complete as a woman.

Freud describes the fetish as a substitute for something treasured that the fetishist refuses to give up.[79] According to this definition, breast reconstruction is a form of fetishism. A fetish is a thing that substitutes for that which is felt to be missing, the absence of which threatens the fetishist's very sense of being. Klein's study of early symbolization reveals that fetishism is a structure of belief to which humans may all tend, or it may be more accurate to say regress, as traumatic events revive infantile fantasies. Speaking of the stage when identification and symbolization are taking shape and external objects are in the process of being drawn into the interior phantasy life, Klein discloses that persons and things are felt to be equivalent.[80] This is to say that the equation of a reconstructed breast with its biological predecessor may descend from the infantile equation of things with persons.

To the fetishist, the fetish conceals its own phantasmatic nature, but it does not necessarily exert its magical power on others. This is apparent when a Reach for Recovery volunteer asked Lorde if she could tell her (the volunteer's) unaffected from her artificial breast. Lorde's response was to think, "both breasts looked equally unreal to me."[81] Lorde's reaction exposes the illusory aspects of our biologically given organs. What fake breasts may effectively reveal is the artificiality and fetishism that underwrites the symbolic function of all body parts. As Anne Anlin Cheng observes, "Fetishism as a defensive structure unleashes the very sexual uncertainty that it labors to cure."[82] Contemporary breast reconstruction can be seen as a fetishistic mode of hiding these uncertainties. If breast cancer puts its sufferers in the depressive position, breast reconstruction supplies for some a means of reparation, of compensating for the losses of disease and disfigurement. Breast reconstruction promises a refigurement, the return of the first object that provided both a sense of completion and individuation. The definitions of breast reconstruction reveal some of the contradiction and confusion that signal its fetishistic character.

> Breast reconstruction is surgery to rebuild a breast's shape after a mastectomy. It cannot give a woman back her breast—a reconstructed breast does not have natural sensations. However, the surgery offers a result that looks like a breast.

> Breast reconstruction is a surgical procedure that restores shape to your breast after mastectomy—surgery that removes your breast to treat or prevent breast cancer.

> Breast reconstruction is surgery to recreate a missing breast.

The first definition of breast reconstruction, offered by the U.S. National Library of Medicine, clearly states that a reconstructed breast is the result of a surgical intervention that approximates a breast's shape. This fundamental recognition of the actual results of breast reconstruction practices is frequently muddied by internal contradictions, demonstrated by the second definition, offered by the Mayo Clinic. If, by its own definition, a mastectomy removes a breast, then how is it that breast reconstruction restores shape to a breast that is no longer there, as the third definition, that of Susan G. Komen, makes plain? The fetishistic logic of a misrecognition that disguises itself as recognition is everywhere apparent in the discourse surrounding breast reconstruction. In making his case for breast reconstruction following mastectomy, my breast surgeon told me an anecdote. He had performed a double mastectomy on a patient who recovered well and was now happily a new mother. The doctor congratulated her and inquired if she was breastfeeding. "Why of course not, doctor," the woman replied, "don't you remember you removed my breasts?" If the breast surgeon is capable of both knowing and not knowing that the breasts he removed are no longer present, and further that their replacements are so convincing that they can be imagined to perform their original function of nourishment, then the reconstructed breast can truly be said to have attained the status of a fetish, an overvalued, trauma-induced object that conceals an underlying gender confusion.

The expectation that women without breasts undergo breast reconstruction today is not unlike the "prosthetic pretense" that Lorde identified in the 1980s.[83] Lorde labeled the use of a breast prosthesis a pretense to normalcy, a kind of false advertisement that the body in question had not undergone any change and that the postmastectomy woman should still be regarded as the same woman she had been prior to surgery because she displayed the visual signifier of a woman with the shape of her symmetrical breasts. Contemporary breast reconstruction continues to focus on breast cancer as a cosmetic problem for which a solution can be found in the highly sophisticated surgical advancements and medical technologies that deploy a woman's own tissues to produce a breast mound. The technological success of contemporary breast reconstruction only reinforces Lorde's observation that the time, research, and money spent upon breast reconstruction surgery was time, research, and money not spent on how to prevent cancer but how to pretend that our breasts were not gone.[84]

The topic of breast reconstruction made a highly publicized appearance in May 2013 with Angelina Jolie's prophylactic double mastectomy as a result of her BRCA+ status.[85] Reactions to this news have tended toward consternation over the perceived extremism of preventative mastectomy or commendations for her bravery.[86] Media responses in the news, blogs, and social networks pivot around whether or not Jolie should have had her breasts removed, rarely around whether or not she should have had them replaced. Breast reconstruction is considered a given. It is taken for granted as a norm that does not merit inquiry, at least not within mainstream medical practice and media. Jolie's decision has been reported as having "redefined beauty" by *Time* magazine and *USA Today*, but in what sense has beauty been redefined?[87] The sex symbol's appearance on the red carpet looking buxom and regal just a few months after her mastectomy affirms how much breasts continue to connote beauty, femininity, and womanhood.

Within the breast reconstruction industry, emphasis upon shape and silhouette falls under the tyranny of symmetry. Federal law specifies that if insurance covers a mastectomy, then breast reconstruction must also be covered, including reconstruction of the other breast to restore symmetry. Every state law concurs with this with some deviation in terms of the time lapse between surgery and reconstruction.[88] The aspiration toward breast symmetry is symptomatic of an ideology that seeks to erase difference for the purposes of maintaining a fixed notion of what constitutes a woman. This idea of "woman" is visually equated with symmetrical breasts. For this reason, not only is reconstruction urged upon a postmastectomy woman as a solution to the "problem" of her absent breast, but her healthy breast is often viewed as faulty, requiring adjustment to maintain the proper symmetry of acceptable female breasts.

As Judith Butler might put it, breast symmetry is a regulatory norm through which sex is materialized. The woman without a breast in Butler's terminology is considered "abject," living under the sign of the "unlivable."[89] As Lorde experienced, in order to obtain cultural intelligibility as a woman, the one-breasted or no-breasted woman must elect breast reconstruction or wear a prosthesis. Over thirty years after Lorde summoned a one-breasted army of women to descend upon Congress to demand that research investigate how to prevent cancer rather than direct funds toward improving the cosmetic appearance of artificial breasts, women who appear flat-chested or asymmetrical still face the painful failure of cultural intelligibility.[90] Photographer/model Matuschka conspicuously rejected the abjection of the one-breasted woman with her postmastectomy self-portrait, which shocked readers of the August 15, 1993, issue of the *New York Times Magazine*. However, at the age of fifty-nine, twenty-two years after her boldly revealing cover photo featuring nothing but a scar where her right breast had been, Matuschka underwent reconstruction on her right side. The reason she gave was: "The world is never going to really embrace a one-breasted fashionable chick."[91] The CBS news reporter who conducted the 2013 interview characterizes Matuschka's decision as "moving on." How it is that living without a breast registers not as an acceptance of present conditions but as a refusal to move on? Matuschka's experience suggests that the one-breasted woman becomes the melancholic object for a sexist culture that can only move on if she reembodies the fantasy of symmetrical breasts.[92]

Within my proposition of the reconstructed breast as fetish, the breast that has gone missing is not the actual breast in reality so much as it is the breast in fantasy, a symbolic breast, the image of which is conjured in the infant sucking her first object. Indeed breast reconstruction nourishes fantasies of imagined plenitude. The reconstructed breast is erected as a memorial to the lost loved object, both commemorating and warding off feelings of loss, fear of ill health, and aging. But the immediate reparative gesture of breast reconstruction can also be seen to paradoxically prolong suffering because it obstructs recognition of the real. A regressive impulse in breast reconstruction is embedded in the term itself. By virtue of its name, the procedure is not viewed as a "construction," the creation of a new form, but recalls the past, as if the breast could be restored.

In addition to unsettling gender determinants, the fetish has a racial dimension, its anthropologic iteration emerging from a history of colonialism. Homi Bhabha argues that colonial fantasy operates through the tropes of fetishism as a denial of the play of differences, between races, genders, discourses, and knowledges, resulting in a fixation upon stereotypes.[93] Freud's well-known reference to woman as the "dark continent" reiterates the imbrication of race and sex, making "woman" a racialized fetish and tying together two vexed terrains for psychoanalysis.[94] And why not conflate woman as sexual fetish with the racial fetish, for as Bhabha notes, both pose the same questions: "In Freud's terms: 'All men have penises'; in ours: 'All men have the same skin/race/culture'—and the anxiety associated with lack and difference—again, for Freud 'Some do not have penises'; for us 'Some do not have the same skin/race/culture.'"[95] Freud's fetishized phallic mother excites a phobic reaction that is not so dissimilar from what Fanon termed "Negro-phobogenesis" in which the myth and the fantasy of the Negro triggers castrating anxiety among whites.[96] Dovetailing on Bhabha and Fanon, Mary Ann Doane observes that in so far as the white woman and the black man both function as phobogenic objects, they arouse anxiety and occupy comparable positions within psychoanalytic discourse: "To the extent that [the black man] poses the possibility of another body, his position would appear analogous to that of the woman in psychoanalysis, who embodies the threat of castration."[97] Using the language of oral gratification, Fanon relates how blacks nourish the white claim upon humanity: "The presence of the Negroes beside the whites is in a way an insurance policy on humanness. When the whites feel that they have become too mechanized, they turn to the men of color and ask them for a little human sustenance."[98] Racism, sexism, and fetishism are linked as psychic defenses mounted against the dread of difference. If fetishization means becoming a substitute for something imagined to be lacking, the black woman is doubly positioned to be fetishized. Lorde resists allowing any part of herself to become a fetish. She discounts anything that masks difference as pretense. Rather than fetishize the lost breast, Lorde would use her pain to recognize loss. In this regard, she undertakes a Kleinian process of mourning.

Mourning the Lost Object

The fetishistic drama that ensues in the aftermath of breast cancer diagnosis and surgery discourages women from interacting with themselves, as Lorde writes, "as physically and emotionally real," that is, as subjects of loss.[99] The self-protective triumph of the fetish defends against mourning and may therefore run parallel with melancholia, or an inability to mourn. According to Darian Leader, "Mourning involves . . . a recognition of absence and loss. We accept that a presence is no longer there. Melancholia, on the other hand, involves the affirmation of a negative term. The lost loved one becomes a hole, an ever-present void which the melancholic cannot give up his attachment to."[100] Leader underscores the difference between the experience of loss and its registration. The work of mourning requires psychic processing and representation in order for a loss to be registered as real. Leader proposes that the work of mourning may be enacted by creating a "frame for absence."[101] The production of a frame is a creative process, not a work of substitution or restoration, but a creation that recognizes and frames absence, enabling the work of mourning.

Klein's discourse is rooted in mourning. By her account, mourning is the creative process that enables survival. For Klein, the establishment of a relationship to reality involves a process of mourning, in which the subject comes to terms with loss: "The object which is being mourned is the mother's breast and all that the breast and the milk have come to stand for in the infant's mind: namely, love, goodness and security."[102] The pivotal movement from partial objects to whole objects "forms the foundation of that situation called the loss of the loved object."[103] Love and loss are inextricably bound together in Klein's conception. Loss cannot be completely felt unless one has gained the full capacity to love. "Not until the object is loved as a whole can its loss be felt as a whole."[104] Yet, as Klein understands it, one cannot truly love unless and until one has lost the loved object and secured it inside oneself. Loss is a necessary precondition for progress to be made. The process by which the love object is installed in the ego involves a repetitive destruction and creation. Having passed through the sadistic phase of cannibalizing partial objects, the infant gradually incorporates whole love objects and mourns the devastating effects of its cruel history during which it had psychically killed and maimed its good objects. The depressive position is achieved through the mourning of loss, which is bound up with the attempt to make reparations. Creativity coincides with the desire to repair the damaged objects and make good the injuries inflicted. Mourning and love are creative acts of reparation meant to attend to the fallout of unbridled aggression initially aimed at the breast. Grief in later life, as Lorde's life writing has shown, revives this early mourning.

Unsurprisingly, Klein regarded the breast as the first creation, as an object that is the original source of creativity as well as a psychic creation in the mind of the baby: "The 'good' breast that feeds and initiates the love relation to the mother is . . . felt as the first manifestation of creativeness. In this fundamental relation the infant receives not only the gratification he [*sic*] desires but feels that he is being kept alive."[105] The Kleinian baby conjures a feeding breast that unites creativity with survival. Love and life itself are sustained through the very processes of mourning and creativity. Winnicott drew from Klein's association between the breast and creativity: "The breast is created by the infant over and over again out of the infant's capacity to love."[106] For Freud, the sexual aim is initially directed outward toward the breast before it is turned upon the self, indicating, if not even inaugurating, an ability to love oneself.[107] Love of self arises out of the love and loss of the other. According to all these psychoanalytic accounts, in the absence of the breast, we discovered our potential for love by turning to ourselves, to self-love. It is this message that Lorde hopes to express when she contends that prostheses offered "the empty comfort of 'Nobody will know the difference,'" for it was that very difference that she wanted to affirm as a mode of self-love.[108] After the loss of her first object, she turned to herself, to mothering herself in the company of her sisters. Her prescription for her fellow women of color is to learn to "mother ourselves."[109]

By now we should not expect a comforting portrayal of mothering from either of these two fierce mothers, Klein or Lorde. Although Lorde found some fleeting moments of succor with her own mother, these lines capture their intense oral struggles:

> My mother had two faces and a frying pot
> where she cooked up her daughters
> into girls
> before she fixed our dinner.[110]

This biting portrayal eerily echoes Klein's description of her patient's dream of a crying kidney protesting being fried alive in an oven by his mother.[111] In the dream, the patient heard the squeaking of a live creature being burned in hot oil and tried to explain to his mother that this was torture. Klein interprets the kidney in the oven as a baby inside his mother's body who was to be killed.[112] Lorde's first published story, which told the tale of a woman who consumes her children, parallels Klein's carnivorous infanticide. Lorde was well aware that her attraction to the Medea parable stemmed from unresolved oral aggression towards her mother. With Kleinian inflection she admits: "I didn't deal at all with how strong my mother was inside of me."[113] Later she composes a poem that grieves over the death of a black child murdered in the streets by a white police officer who was acquitted by a jury of eleven white men and one black woman. The poem, entitled "Power," torments over the agony of sacrificing oneself for the sake of one's children. Its first lines read:

The difference between poetry and rhetoric
is being
ready to kill
yourself
instead of your children[114]

Poetry can resuscitate life against the deadening rhetoric of mainstream media and public opinion. Lorde puts herself on the side of poetry as a reparative salve. She identifies with the lone black woman on the jury who collapsed under the weight of the jury's power inequities and betrayed her spiritual son, but she wants to assume the power of preserving life, even if that means extinguishing her own. Self-inflicted annihilation, the specter of the she-wolf, is the trade-off for survival of the species. What can mothering mean in the context of such rage and sorrow? Motherhood, tragically derailed, disintegrates into oral objects strewn across the crime scene: "my mouth splits," "my stomach churns."[115] Mothering as a creative force must be redeemed. Mothering, which also means mourning, must be made to perform the work that poetry does. Lorde will situate this mothering project within the context of community engagement.

Lorde takes ownership of her outsider status and turns it into a strength, a weapon and mode of survival. She "figures herself as inassimilable, so unique in body, birth, history, and behavior that distinction becomes the principle of her identity and her power."[116] In the introduction to *The Cancer Journals* she writes: "The outsider, both strength and weakness. Yet without community there is certainly no liberation, no future, only the most vulnerable and temporary armistice between me and my oppression."[117] Without community, Lorde has only herself and her oppression, which is to say that she would be at the mercy of cancer, racism, sexism, and homophobia, whose disruptive impacts threaten to dismember her into discontinuous part-objects. Lorde famously declared that "the master's tools will never dismantle the master's house."[118] If the female breast, through its history within patriarchal objectification of the female body, has become the master's tool, Lorde warns against its use, or fetishistic substitutes for it, to dismantle patriarchal structures. However, one can use a different kind of body as a tool to build one's own house of difference.

Lorde offers herself to her black sisters as she would medicine to the ill or a tool for useful production: "I am who I am, doing what I came to do, acting upon you like a drug or a chisel to remind you of your me-ness, as I discover you in myself."[119] She makes herself into a veritable transitional object, which Winnicott defines as the first possession that aids the baby to discover "me" and "not-me."[120] In that transitional space where subjects and objects are blurred, where she finds Kleinian introjects inside herself, Lorde celebrates and makes demands on her community of black women allies. True to the contradictions that manifest within her life and work, Lorde learns to use herself fetishistically and is used fetishistically by queers of color today.[121] Although she advises them not to mythologize her after her death, the lesbian/poet/mother/warrior encourages her community to use her as a tool, as a fetish.[122] Michel Leiris identifies fetishism as "a love . . . projected from inside to outside . . . which we can use in that strange, vast room called space."[123] Thus conceived, fetishism involves a movement not unlike Kleinian projection from an intensely personal interior to the external world. Lorde's self-love is projected outward into the strange space of difference, modeling how mothers might cannily reclaim themselves as the uncanny original site of home.[124] Through projective identification, others who were "never meant to survive" might introject this projection and identify with her, constructing novel houses of difference that honor and productively fetishize her legacy.

Before I was diagnosed with breast cancer, I dreamed that I had gained a new internal organ. It was called a "keen," which afterward I thought might be a hybrid of my kidney and spleen. I didn't know if it was intended to purify me of toxins, the task my kidney performs, or to serve some essential but unknown purpose as my spleen does, or merely to occupy a space,

Figure 4. Original box containing draft of *The Cancer Journals*, preserved in the condition of receipt at the Lesbian Herstory Archives, Brooklyn, New York. Photograph by Lin + Lam.

which would then be sensed as an absence should it be removed. I didn't know what this organ "keen" was supposed to mean to me, how it was supposed to serve me. Was it a kind of anticipatory recompense for a loss I was yet intended to suffer? I knew only that I looked the word up in the dictionary and found that it is the word for the wail of grief for the dead, sung at Irish funerals. I also discovered that Lorde wrote a poem, "Holographs," a critique of South African apartheid, the second stanza of which begins: "60,000 Pondo women keening/on the mountain . . . "[125] Each of its three stanzas ends with a question and a plaint on death and dying. The first on malnourished babies dying prematurely, the second on fathers going off to fight to their deaths, and the last on the imbrication of death and life. In the aftermath of my mastectomy, I asked myself how an artwork might respond to questions of bodily uncertainty, how art might react to bodily crisis. As an artist this was a predictable question for me to ask. Through her writing, Lorde thinks creatively and critically about the meaning of bodily absence, corporeal suffering, and defamiliarization. Her answer to my questions is to make creation of destruction. In a sense, she mobilizes the oscillation between destruction and creation, between death and life, putting death to use such that survival amounts to an insistence upon "not-death." She does not try to imagine a world without pain and hardship. She tries to imagine a world that can make use of it. She tasked herself to create something new, something that did not seek to restore the past or fill the absences that remained in the wake of devastation. She used words to speak back to her losses. As a psychoanalyst, Klein was also especially attuned to words. She proposed a word for the emotions bound up with losing the loved object. To represent the sorrow, concern, fear, and longing for the lost object Klein selects the word "pining."[126] We pine for the object we have lost and we mourn its loss through keening.

Lorde's longtime friend Adrienne Rich wrote a poem about a childhood friend of hers who had died of breast cancer, "A Woman Dead in Her Forties": "we never spoke at your deathbed of your death/but from here on/I want more crazy mourning, more howl, more keening."[127] Rich's verse bemoans the silence of death and calls for the reparative gestures of speech and mourning. It echoes the lament that Lorde hears from the South African mountaintop and the cry that she utters in miming the keening she-wolf. I give myself language in naming an imaginary part of myself "keen." My keen, like Lorde's and Rich's poetry, might be regarded as a creation that can be used for mourning absence, that symbolizes but does not substitute for the lost object.

CHAPTER 3

Object-Love in the Later Writings
of Eve Kosofsky Sedgwick

In her primer on living with advanced breast cancer, literary critic and queer theorist Eve Kosofsky Sedgwick tells a perplexing joke that she has brooded over increasingly as she gets deeper into her own cancer experience. Someone asks a farmer about his pig's wooden leg. The farmer goes into a long story with many examples of how the pig saved his son's life, his daughter's and her boyfriend's, and his own with progressively extraordinary feats of ingenuity that far exceed anything a pig would be capable of. But despite reciting the details of the pig's heroism, the farmer never explains why it has a wooden leg. Finally, the inquiring man beseeches the farmer to speak more directly, and the farmer says he thinks it should be obvious: You don't eat a pig like that all at once.[1] This odd tale can be seen as an analogy for living with cancer as a process of attrition in which corporeal wholeness is gradually eroded.

The allegory of the pig whose life and bodily integrity are subject to both danger and conservation encapsulates the major themes of this chapter. It supplies an open-ended instruction on survival, it ruminates upon death through gallows humor, it involves prosthetic part-objects, it grimly delights in the disassembling of the body into fragments, and unexpectedly it has to do with love. Who loves whom and how that love is shown is put into question.

Sedgwick was diagnosed with breast cancer in 1991. She lived with cancer for eighteen years before succumbing to it in 2009. As in the case of Audre Lorde, her cancer supplied the occasion to reflect upon what is entailed in continued survival in the face of loss. Sedgwick's later writing mediates her relation to loss and mortality, and demonstrates how she learns to come to terms with enduring an illness without cure. In addressing her attitudes toward "living on" as a slow process of dying, she formulates a pedagogy of love in such writings as her contributions to *MAMM*, a magazine for "women, cancer, and community," and *A Dialogue on Love*, a memoir of her therapy. These two bodies of writing deal explicitly with illness and are arguably the least studied of her oeuvre—at least this is the case for the *MAMM* articles.[2] Sedgwick's "cancer journalism" and *Dialogue* represent a public discourse on love, which is intended to be used as "good pedagogy" to counteract the "bad pedagogy" of received knowledges from which threatened groups (queer, disabled, racially othered, poor, diversely shaped, to name a few) do not profit.[3] In her later writings, Sedgwick learns how to grasp what sustains her by paradoxically letting go. One can view this as letting go of a desire for wholeness by embracing her own dissolution. By disseminating pieces of herself in her published works Sedgwick strives to serve as an instrument for good pedagogy. Detaching herself from the need to be the sole author of her experience, she mobilizes the destruction of cancer and its treatment into a process of collective reparative work—with her therapist and with her readers. These reparative labors are acts of impersonal and anonymous love. Through a generalized care for the world, Sedgwick learns to care for herself as an object of love.

A Public Discourse of Love

MAMM was conceived by Sean Strub, founder of *POZ*, a publication targeted to an HIV-positive or AIDS demographic. The first consumer magazine geared to people affected by breast and gynecologic cancers hit newsstands in October 1997 and was discontinued in 2009. Survival was an issue for *MAMM* since its inception. Initially its subtitle was "Courage, Respect and Survival" before it was changed to "Women, Cancer and Community." Cynthia Ryan titles her ethnographic study of editorial practices at *MAMM* "Struggling to Survive," foregrounding the rhetoric of survival that perennially attends cancer discourse and placing it within the financial constraints of a periodical that seeks to uphold high standards of medical

Figure 5. *MAMM*, September 2000. Courtesy of Hal Sedgwick.

journalism, while retaining advertising loyalty. *MAMM*'s predicted viability was initially favorable, given the one in eight women in this country to which it would presumably appeal, but its advertising base quickly and steadily declined soon after its initial publication.[4] Despite the fact that both magazines jointly won the *Village Voice* best health/lifestyle award in 2002,

POZ, initiated four years earlier than *MAMM*, has outlived its sister publication and continues to this day.[5]

In its June/July 1998 issue, *MAMM* published Sandy Fernandez's history of the pink ribbon that has now become synonymous with breast cancer culture.[6] Fernandez traces the pink ribbon initially to the yellow ribbons that signaled hope for the safe return of Iranian hostages, then to the iconic red AIDS ribbons, and last to a confluence of Susan G. Komen Breast Cancer Foundation's distribution of pink ribbons at its 1991 New York City Race for the Cure and a collaboration between *Self* magazine and Estée Lauder that resulted in 1.5 million pink ribbons being distributed at cosmetic counters across the country. This was the beginning of a mass mediatization of breast cancer culture in North America where malls and websites flood potential consumers with sneakers (Lace Up for the Cure), food processors (Cook for the Cure), and even toilet paper graced with pink ribbons to benefit the irreproachable cause of "breast cancer awareness." As Gayle Sulik succinctly puts it in *Pink Ribbon Blues*, "breast cancer is an illness that now functions as a concept brand."[7] In an influential 2001 *Harpers* article, Barbara Ehrenreich lambasts what she calls the "cult of pink kitsch." She underscores the infantilization of women who are offered pink teddy bears upon diagnosis with her often quoted, pithy retort: "Certainly men diagnosed with prostate cancer do not receive gifts of Matchbox cars."[8] In league with Ehrenreich, Marita Sturken identifies the teddy bear as the poster child of "comfort culture."[9] Situated at the intersection of trauma and consumerism, the teddy bear has a depoliticizing function meant to reinforce the idea that hardships need only be endured—rather than actively interrogated as an impetus for change—with the help of a product that will make them "bearable."

Not long after Ehrenreich's critique of what she would later label the ideology of positive thinking, Breast Cancer Action (BCA), an activist organization based in San Francisco, launched its "Think Before You Pink" campaign. BCA coined the term "pinkwashing" to refer to the hypocrisy of corporations that prey upon consumer's charitable feelings to market products whose manufacture either cause cancer or are linked to the disease.[10] Pink buckets of Kentucky Fried Chicken and Estée Lauder's pink ribbon cosmetics are two of the worst culprits. Sulik woefully summarizes the depleted discourse that circulates in contemporary breast cancer culture: "Courage. Strength. Goodness. Hope. Fight. Survive. Win. . . . The war on breast cancer when united with pink femininity leaves few other words from which to choose, and we speak with the words we have."[11]

Although Ehrenreich cites *MAMM* as complicit in the compulsory optimism of breast cancer culture, Ryan argues that *MAMM*'s staff explicitly

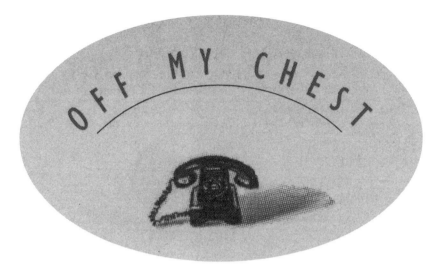

Figure 6. *MAMM*, April/May 1998, 36. Courtesy of Hal Sedgwick.

attempts to counter the "traditional restitution narrative."[12] Instead, their mission is one that Sedgwick would share as a contributing editor, to produce a manual for surviving with cancer, one that does not portray the cancer "survivor" as necessarily restored to an ideal of wholeness but as struggling with the disruptions of living with a chronic disease. The original editor, Regan Solmo, announced in its first issue that *MAMM* was a "guide to life. For anyone living with or affected by cancer."[13] This is an apt description of Sedgwick's goals in "Off My Chest," which performs love as a public discourse within a scene of identification and instruction.

In a review for the *Lesbian and Gay Studies Newsletter*, Sedgwick recounts how the medical editor of a local daily newspaper in Durham County, North Carolina, phoned her because he wanted a human angle on his piece and had heard that she was public about her diagnosis. Her conversation with the reporter suggests some of her motivations for undertaking her own cancer journalism. They spar for a bit:

REPORTER: So tell me, I know it isn't lucky to have cancer, but do you feel you're lucky that your cancer was detected early?

EKS: It wasn't detected early. And even "early" isn't early. According to current understandings of breast cancer, by the time it's detectable on a mammogram or by touch, it's already systemic.

REPORTER: But they got it all?

EKS: What part of the word "systemic" don't you understand?

The reporter then asks if Sedgwick has any advice for other women.[14] Sedgwick replies that she has lots of advice for women diagnosed with cancer. But the reporter corrects her, saying he was looking for advice for the "average woman." Sedgwick responds that she hasn't any except to avoid growing up five blocks from a major toxic incinerator.

Though this journalist did not seek her advice, Sedgwick was eager to offer it to the people whom she thought she could help, those who suffered from cancer. Her advice column, "Off My Chest," appeared in *MAMM* from February 1998 until January 2003. The recurrent illustration that accompanied her column was the image of a telephone, as if Sedgwick were waiting for a call from someone unlike the aforementioned journalist for whom she could be of use. Much like the psychoanalyst whom Freud compared to a telephone receiver, positioned to hear the patient's messages, Sedgwick might have symbolically embodied the telephone.[15] On the other hand, she may very well have used the column as a forum in which to work through her own confusions and fears regarding her cancer which had metastasized by the time she began contributing to the magazine. In an interview that took place in January 2000, she confessed to making up all the letters because, much as she wished for correspondents, no one wrote in for advice.[16] Composed in a populist, highly accessible and humorous style that skillfully reproduces the advice column genre, "Off My Chest" lands somewhere between talking to herself and talking to another. It has its ambiguity of voices in common with *Dialogue*, which I will elaborate upon later in this chapter. In her *MAMM* articles, Sedgwick gets to play both roles at once, the distraught, complaining, or bewildered questioner and the more settled, stable, sage advisor. Interestingly this multiplicity of selves materializes in her advice column moniker, eves@mamm.com, which reads as many Eves inviting you to "get it off your chest."

Advice is by definition proffered at the onset of a problem. Sedgwick-as-Eve positions herself (or the team of Eves position themselves) as problem solver(s). The problem is how to survive a grave illness. Cynthia Franklin argues that *Dialogue* "extends to readers a form of impersonal intimacy, one that allows for forms of identification that make useful the narcissistic impulse of the therapy and one that provides provocative crossings between the private and the public, the personal and the political, the intimate and the public."[17]

Sedgwick's contributions to *MAMM* function similarly, albeit through a distinctly different style and format. By virtue of the shared narcissistic injury of cancer diagnosis she prompts identifications that move across the private and public, the personal and the political, stimulating their interpenetrations. When she first publicly disclosed her diagnosis, she maintained that her purpose was to be available for identification. "It's as though there were transformative political work to be done just by being available to be identified with in the very grain of one's illness."[18] Additionally, Sedgwick regarded it her task to make people smarter, as she describes it in *Dialogue*.[19]

These two persistent goals—identification and instruction—are entwined and come under the rubric of "love." Identification, a necessary step toward the capacity for object-love, is a mode of learning. Freud connects love as identification to education, which helps us to both differentiate ourselves from and bind ourselves to sociality. He makes this connection through the figure of the poet, a figure to which Sedgwick had a life-long devotion. The poet, for Freud, submits himself as the first ego ideal, much like Sedgwick aspired to in setting herself up as a model for identification.[20] Through his invention of heroic myth, the poet hands out imaginative advice on the nature of living and loving. Through her invention of "Eves," an alter ego ideal who alternately takes the position of heroic leader and supplicant, Sedgwick doles out instructions on how to care for ourselves by identifying with her, which is to say, by loving her.

To understand identification as a form of love, it is useful to examine how Freud came to view identification as foundational to the formation of the ego. In his most extensive rumination on identification, which tellingly appears in his commentary on group psychology, Freud states more than once that identification is "the earliest expression of an emotional tie with another person," or "the original form of emotional tie with an object."[21] Referring to his thesis that in cases of melancholia the attachment to a lost loved object takes an inward turn toward the self and is replaced by an identification, he asserts: "To the ego . . . living means the same as being loved."[22] By this account, life consists of the love of others who have been taken into the self. And this does not only apply to those suffering melancholia. In *The Ego and the Id*, Freud realizes that replacing a lost object with an identification is, in fact, typical, and furthermore, that it may be the very means by which the ego is built, providing, as Deborah Britzman says, the "raw material for character."[23] The process by which a love object that is lost or abandoned becomes a part of the ego resembles something of a love story itself. As Freud narrates it, "When the ego assumes the features of the object [that is, when it undergoes a process of identification] it is forcing itself . . . upon the id as a love-object and is trying to make good the id's loss by saying: 'Look, you can love me too—I am so like the object.'"[24] Not only is this a transcript of love, but it is also one of reparation. In this case, reparative efforts are directed toward the id as compensation for losing its love object. Sedgwick latched onto identification as a political project for its reparative potential. According to both Freud and Sedgwick, identification engenders transformation. It alters the ego and is the basis for change. Sedgwick invites her readers to transform their egos through their identification with her. For instance, her cancer comrades might identify, as Sedgwick did, with the absurdity of the peg legged pig's deferred yet inevitable demise. Or, Sedgwick might assume the role of the prosthetic wooden leg for her readers, propping them up anaclitically. This desire to become an object of transformative identification (and, as we shall see, a transgressively identifying subject) becomes increasingly pronounced as she feels her own mortality more acutely.

"A Scar Is Just A Scar: Approaching that First Postmastectomy Tryst" is the first article in "Off My Chest" to include the name of an advice seeker, "Alice."[25] Perhaps Sedgwick refers to the famous Alice who tumbles into a bewildering world in which her size and scale mutate, who endures the alienation of finding her body foreign to herself. But this same Alice encounters a fantastic realm of possibility where she literally undergoes a transformative experience. When Sedgwick leads her readers down the rabbit hole of cancer-related confusions, she conveys it as a hall of mirrors, never casting simply a single reflection, but rather a multiplicity that must be maneuvered. In the last of the series, B.F. asks whether their thirty-seven-year-old girlfriend should get a mammogram.[26] Though published in 2003, this article is eerily relevant to today's ongoing debate on a well-worn and fraught subject. Sedgwick's reply situates the mammography debate at the tip of an iceberg: "As patients, we are likely to find ourselves making decisions with less and less certainty rather than more and more. Under these stresses, it's hard—though exciting—to remember that the iceberg's name is progress."[27] She swiftly places cancer research within a Benjaminian drama of medical uncertainties, misdiagnosis, missed diagnosis, overtreatment, and ineffective treatments piling up as a wreckage of catastrophes. Yet Sedgwick is not nearly as pessimistic as Walter Benjamin, for she appreciates the excitement of medical developments just as years earlier she recognized that she found her illness "full of stimulation and interest."[28]

The painful quandary of living with cancer provocatively poses a stimulant to thought for Sedgwick. "Off My Chest" indicates her desire to translate both her fear and enthusiasm to a public domain. Though her need to love and be loved manifests itself covertly in *MAMM* through the gift of advice, the giving and receiving of advice—even when none is solicited—

shows her to be capable of loving and being loved. *MAMM* disperses Sedgwick's objects of love to a public sphere of anonymous readers and allied patients.

Love as Comic Instruction

Sedgwick expresses her love through comic instruction. Humor is the medium through which she teaches her readers how to cope with the failed heroics of cancer treatment and survival. How might one read the pig story that lingered with Sedgwick throughout her treatment as a comic tale of love? The pig demonstrates its love through heroic sacrifice. The farmer shows his love for the pig by postponing its death. Although this strange anecdote may fall into the bewilderment/illumination structure that Freud found characterized some jokes, it makes greater sense to consider it in terms of gallows humor.[29] Freud associates gallows humor with the parental superego that caretakes the child ego, offering a mechanism for relief and defiance of suffering.[30] Through her advice column, Sedgwick's superego takes care of her own child ego just as it gives care to her readership.

It is impossible not to relate the pig's story to cancer treatment, since that is the context in which it has been raised, and Sedgwick points to how the story sticks with her the further she descends into her cancer ordeal. The unexpected outcome of the pig's dark comedy is the opposite of what one feels the pig deserves. One would assume that the farmer would preserve the creature that saved his life, and yet he consumes it and considers his slow process of consumption a means of honoring the pig, and, in fact, prolonging its life. The farmer thinks it is obvious that his treatment of his prized possession has been charitable. Cancer treatment is similarly offered as a means of extending life and maintaining survival, but the question this joke forces one to ponder if one takes the story as an analogy for how to survive cancer is whether it benefits the pig to part with itself bit by bit, or whether its piecemeal destruction is really only beneficial to the farmer or those who have a vested interest in the pig's prolonged life/slow death. The pig's death-defying acts of heroism win the survival of others, but is it ultimately a sacrificial victim? The pig is meant to be eaten. Despite its heroics, it is still destined to die. Its heroism only buys time, a kind of prognostic time of slow death.

S. Lochlann Jain describes "living in prognosis" within the cancer complex as being both "prognostic subject and cancer object."[31] By this she means that cancer sufferers gain a statistically manufactured subjectivity from their all important prognosis that renders them cancer's object—the object of risk assessment, cancer trials, all the mechanisms by which the cancer industry dictates the balance of their life in death or death in life. Unsurprisingly, in Sedgwick's cancer primer, her ABCs of living with cancer, in addition to "Pig," "P" stands for Prognosis No. 1 and 2. She compares two prognoses from different oncologists, two years apart. Although Sedgwick's cancer had "barely progressed" in that time, the prognoses are exactly the same since the second oncologist relied solely upon statistics.[32] Jasbir Puar follows on Jain to discuss "prognosis time" as a queer temporality that puts pressure on presumed able-bodiedness.[33] Within Jain and Puar's frameworks it becomes bleakly amusing to consider what the prognosis time is for Sedgwick's incrementally consumed pig. The pig's prognosis time consists of chronic debility management that will occur until its predicted demise. Its situation can be likened to what Lauren Berlant calls "slow death," referring to the disenfranchised, specifically the poor, the obese, the racially oppressed and the depressed: "In the scene of slow death, a condition of being worn out by the activity of reproducing life, agency can be an activity of maintenance, not making."[34] Those afflicted with metastatic cancer no doubt experience the maintenance of life at some point as a condition of slow death. Berlant turns to the "unheroizable case" of so-called obesity to show how capital articulates this inexorable attrition of the subject as survival.[35] She critiques the "crisis" rhetoric that is appropriated to distort the duration and scale of what is a "defining fact of life for a given population."[36] Designating a persistent, environmental phenomenon a "crisis event" misrepresents the ongoingness of everyday structurally enforced suffering. Crisis anxiety and the call for heroism are related. Locked into an attrition for which it has been marked, the pig performs Sisyphean deeds that constitute a failed heroism analogous to the "unheroizable" phenomena of obesity and cancer.

The impossibility of heroism, but nonetheless the call for and desire for heroism, is a latent theme throughout Sedgwick's cancer journalism. Many of her *MAMM* articles deal with the specific ways that cancer boggles the mind in addition to messing with the body, demanding an unattainable and therefore ineffectual heroism. Sedgwick's first contribution to her advice column testifies to the dilemmas that cancer so effectively produces, that of an ambivalence between two uncertainties, or a kind of lose/lose scenario. Her first post concisely illustrates this with the problem of being too fat or too thin. Two questioners are represented, one who is mistaken for losing weight on a successful diet rather than through the rigors of advanced cancer, and another who is gaining weight as a side effect from chemo and her current medication, which people who know she is ill presume means she is improving and people who don't know think she is "letting herself go." Sedgwick launches into her response with the exclamation: "Holy double bind, Batgrrls!"[37] It is as if cancer patients need to transform into superheroes in order to tackle the hazards not only of life-threatening disease but also of draconian treatments and demoralizing social interactions. Sedgwick fabulates the breast cancer Batgrrls and the peg-legged pig to upend the pervasive optimism that is promoted by the cancer industry and taken up by "survivors" who are trapped between false hope and despair.

The species of optimism that Sedgwick refuses and mocks resembles what Berlant will later deem "cruel." Cruel optimism is the affective sensibility that drives "people [to] maintain their binding to modes of life that threaten their well-being."[38] Within Berlant's argument, it takes shape around a "cluster of promises."[39] What kind of promises might a potentially fatal disease pose? While Sedgwick was not caught up in the fantasy of the good life or even of a cancer-free life at all, she nonetheless maintained a degree of attachment to and certainly ambivalence in regard to her cancer. Cruel optimism's further criterion is "the condition of maintaining an attachment to a significantly problematic object."[40] Metastatic cancer is nothing if not "significantly problematic." For Sedgwick the diagnosis of a serious illness was a stimulant to thought, a provocation for transformation and creativity. Despite the terror and pain it arouses, the continuities of malignancy can, like cruel optimism, extend "something of the continuity of the subject's sense of what it means to keep on living on."[41] Is it cruelly optimistic to remain bound to a life-threatening object from which it is impossible to detach? Sedgwick both supports and overturns her own brand of cruel optimism with a wicked wit that does not service the compulsory positive attitude that cancer patients are often shamed into upholding, but acknowledges, for instance, the ironies of being dependent upon a medical industry whose corporate practices (collaboration with companies producing environmental toxins) and treatment modalities (radiation and pharmaceuticals that cause cancer) aid and abet the very affliction it means to fight. Sedgwick's humor exposes how the pig's failed heroism cruelly secures its piecemeal survival, making it only a spectacle of an "extraordinary body" until it is no body at all.[42]

The most striking feature about Sedgwick's contributions to *MAMM*, if it has not already become obvious, is how funny they are. She directly addresses people who have cancer with inside jokes appealing to those in the know about cancer culture. For example, in her ABCs of cancer, "E" is for ER (+ or –) which she says is sometimes used to describe your tumor's hormonal status but mostly describes your television viewing habits.[43] The

MAMM articles seek to perform a curative function, suggesting that the therapeutic form can be understood as a comic genre. But if laughter is the best medicine, it is not so much because of its medicinal properties as its powers to instruct. "Living with Advanced Breast Cancer: The ABCs" provides direct schooling, explicitly giving lessons on living with cancer. The tutorial begins with "A" for "Advanced: Welcome to the upside-down world of metastatic cancer. Advancing and progressing are bad!"[44] In this inverted world the superhero "Metastatic Cancer" does not dive in to restore stable order to our lives, but just the opposite: "Metastatic cancer goes to the root of our desires for control, security and knowledge—and takes them away."[45] Although one might anticipate that an advice column, especially one oriented to those who have a serious illness, would nurture, Sedgwick does not coddle her readers, sometimes taking people to task. The disjunction between her sharp, teacherly voice and the supportive, maternal tone one might expect from its vehicle of expression adds to the column's charge. In "The Guy Factor in BC Support Groups," she jokingly admonishes S.W. for complaining about why a man would want to join the breast cancer support group she is coordinating. Rather than punish the questioner for wrongheaded thinking, she turns it into an opportunity to teach. In this case, she is able to publicize the lesser-known fact that men can develop breast cancer as well as underscore the false sense of common ground women presume to share with other women.[46] She frankly enumerates the many ways in which people are different from one another that can have much more impact upon whether they can sustain supportive group cohesion than what chromosomes they have. With good humor, she finds ways to slip in a gender critique while also playing into the gender conventions she imagines her readers may uphold: "You're probably cringing at the thought of exposing this poor guy to a lot of girl talk. . . . Maybe he's on tamoxifen. Ask yourself: is he supposed to go to his bowling buddies for the lowdown on hot flashes?"[47]

When R.G. complains that cancer pundits wrongly blame the victim even though they did everything right in terms of taking care of themself, Sedgwick points out how poorly R.G. would feel if they actually smoked, was fat, hated veggies, and didn't exercise. She shows how the advice seeker is guilty of internalizing a grandiose sense of their own control over their own health. While she is correct that this hypothetical questioner is flirting with omnipotence, who is the one displaying grandiosity in this fictional drama? Ann Pellegrini points out how in *The Interpretation of Dreams* Freud casts hysterical identification as a one-woman play.[48] Sedgwick's insistence upon playing all the parts in her advice serial makes her a candidate for hysterical identification. Hysterics, according to Freud, "suffer on behalf of a whole crowd of people."[49] Indeed Sedgwick humorously drama-tizes her own suffering on behalf of her readers to garner their love, encouraging a mass mediated hysterical identification. One might suspect that she aims to incite what Freud labels a "psychical infection" in which her symptoms are empathically shared and assimilated by her actual and invented fellow patients.[50]

Sedgwick's Forms of Love

"Off My Chest" not only depicts Sedgwick's comic flair, it also reveals a deep-seated interest in psychotherapy, as she plays therapist to her reader-ship and imagined questioners. It is therefore not surprising that Sedgwick's cancer diagnosis was her "presenting problem," her trigger for entering psychotherapy herself. *A Dialogue on Love*, Sedgwick's memoir, chronicles approximately four and a half years of work with her therapist, Shannon. In it she defines love as "suddenly, globally, 'knowing' that another person represents your only access to some/vitally/transmissible truth."[51] Love, in Sedgwick's world, exposes itself in the dependent relations between patient and therapist or doctor, or between student and teacher. As Frank-lin formulates it, "*Dialogue* charts how Sedgwick comes . . . to understand dependency as a form of love."[52] Opening *Dialogue* with the line, "Appar-ently it's as a patient that I want to emerge," Sedgwick confesses to an invest-ment in her status as "patient," a role that one could argue is nothing if not dependent.[53] Franklin contends that by turning her therapy into her own publication, "Sedgwick not only subverts and invests the role of 'patient' with agency . . . [but also] through the process of narrative, gives the love she experiences from Shannon a form of permanence."[54] Continually trou-bled by the impermanence of objects, which was connected to her fear of losing them, Sedgwick's publication of her experiences as patient preserves the seemingly impermanent co-creation of therapy. Making permanent the relations of love in *Dialogue* is a "performance of love," most explicitly between a patient and therapist, but also between a writer and her readers.[55]

Dialogue is self-consciously produced in multiple voices, forecasting the ambiguity of voices in Sedgwick's *MAMM* pieces. Employing the seventeenth-century Japanese poetic form, *haibun*, Sedgwick splits the voices in *Dialogue* into diaristic prose and elliptical haiku. Additionally, in an unusual move, Shannon gave Sedgwick his therapy notes, which are incorporated into the text in "all caps." Even with upper and lowercase letters designating each voice there is considerable blurring since Shannon frequently writes his notes from his patient's perspective, confusing whether "I" means Shannon or Eve. As if to confirm her interest in displacing the solitary, authoritative authorial voice, Sedgwick admits: "There are times when even I can't tell whose first person it is."[56] As she has argued elsewhere, "I" is a heuristic, which Sedgwick clearly means to exploit in the formal strategy of *Dialogue*.[57] On other occasions Shannon's notes omit the subject altogether, further contributing to the uncertainty around voice. *Dialogue*'s ambiguity, ellipses, and fragmentation, its embrace of the empty spaces of the page, instruct the reader on how to stay with irresolution and unknowing, and to learn by reading on. One can analogize that one can learn to live by living on, in the face of unpredictability, the unknown, and emptiness. Michael Moon observes that the way in which *Dialogue*'s prose and haiku switch between each other suggests something of Sedgwick's "sense of the relations of form and its effects to illness and pain."[58]

In *Dialogue*, the form of love is constructed through a relation of voices. Producing a weave of voices that disperses the first person, *Dialogue* materializes Sedgwick's attachment to the plurality of voice: "a texture book wouldn't need to have a first person at all, any more than weaving itself does."[59] Sedgwick's delighted realization indicates that the *form* of her multivoiced illness memoir is itself therapeutic. Together Shannon and Sedgwick craft a therapeutic space, braided together with poetry and prose, as a form of psychic holding. Sedgwick moreover emphasizes that it is important that Shannon holds her "*impersonally*" (emphasis in original).[60] *Dialogue* provides Sedgwick a means of disseminating a love that is impersonal in the sense that it is ambiguously authored and potentially received by an audience that would remain anonymous to her.

Therapy evokes for Sedgwick "a voice that never otherwise comes into being," a "voice that speaks in a quiet double way, the being alone but not being alone."[61] Therapy is a form of relating that affords a speaking and hearing unique to its strangely distant yet profoundly intimate artificial space. This formal attitude even begins to escape the confines of the consulting room and session for Sedgwick: "The strange form of address is taking shape in my head again, the unmistakable one that's somewhere between talking to myself and talking to another person."[62] The plurality of being simultaneously internal and external answers Sedgwick's need for autonomy and ego support. She revels in her "favorite pronoun: the dear/ first person plural," *we*:

Promiscuous we!
Me, plus anybody else.
Permeable we![63]

She attaches to a plural, "permeable we" as her labile, queer object-choice, which is not a singular identifiable "other" towards whom erotic love is aimed, but an "us" made up of multiple, potentially unknown identities woven together. It is the space of these distant yet intimate relations that constitutes love for Sedgwick.

—Not in love with a
person—but with the place the
person inhabits
and with the space of
my friendly distance from him.[64]

I detail the formal characteristics of *Dialogue* because its form is inextricable from what it means to do. *Dialogue* is intentionally performative. It *does* what it says. It enacts Sedgwick's growing dependency upon and trust in Shannon not only by telling us what transpired between them, but simply by including more and more of Shannon's voice in the text. *Dialogue* performs Sedgwick's love for Shannon as well as for herself, and extends this love toward an anonymous audience of friends and readers. This is precisely the mode of writing that one might expect would evolve out of Sedgwick's attraction to the performative. Drawing on J. L. Austin and Judith Butler's discussions of performatives as citational speech acts that enact their meaning rather than merely index it, Sedgwick strived to exploit and expand upon the potential of her experimental writing not only to enact her agency but also to activate the desires of her readers.[65] Attending to the performative dimension of Sedgwick's writing, Philomena Tsoukala emphasizes how Sedgwick's text produces feelings in her, how it does things with and to her.[66] Tsoukala tries to pinpoint exactly what it is that "Eve" has done to her in Sedgwick's "A Poem Is Being Written," which interrogates the relation between spanking and lyric poetry. Tsoukala comes to the conclusion that "Eve was right there (hence the singular of familiarity) engaging in a sadomasochistic erotic relationship with me through the text . . . spanking me and then consoling me through the obligatory resignification of her violence as love. . . . To wit, I finished reading the text and it felt like I had just had sex with Eve Kosofsky Sedgwick."[67] Tsoukala encapsulates the feelings that many critics express of an intensely transferential reading in regard to Sedgwick's work, that is, in her writing "Eve" *makes love* to the reader.[68] As much as she makes love to the reader, Sedgwick is equally invested in a desire to *show herself to be loved*.[69] When she feels herself to be understood by another, like Shannon, she experiences this as love and could thus be seen as *lovable*. In her homage to psychologist and affect theorist Silvan Tompkins, which was compiled during her therapy, Sedgwick expressed her commitment to publication as a mode of loving.[70] For Sedgwick to discover writers, such as Tompkins and Proust, who captured so well her own sensibilities, was to feel loved by them. Her identification with their subjectivities, which mirrored her own, was a demonstration of her capacity to love and be loved. The give and take of the therapeutic exchange, not unlike the giving and taking of advice staged in "Off My Chest," affirmed her ability to love and worthiness of love.

Object-Use, Object-Love

Sedgwick's public discourse of love, which she deployed to mediate her relationship to illness and mortality, can be further understood by examining the transference dynamics involved. No doubt transference, which Britzman identifies as "built from the analysand's inchoate demand for love," permeated Sedgwick's therapy.[71] When she reveals that "the space of Shannon is both myself and not," Sedgwick's blurring of self and other takes place in the transference where one cannot clearly discern one's own voice from one's parental figures, one's lovers, and one's therapists.[72] The dual voices Sedgwick hears, talking to someone who is not quite herself and not quite other, signal the transference of her ingrained and inherited feelings onto Shannon. Freud came to see transference as itself a neurosis and called the transference neurosis an "artificial illness."[73] This transference neurosis induced by psychoanalysis has in common with slow moving or indolent cancers the characteristics of an incurable but not necessarily debilitating illness. Sedgwick suffers from both types of affliction, and *Dialogue* is her effort to reflect upon the forms of love that these illnesses teach her.

Transferential relationships turn upon identification. If identification is a mode of love, then when Sedgwick and Adam Frank ask what it means to fall in love with a writer in the preface to their Silvan Tompkins reader, they are hinting at what it means to identify with a writer. They admit to having written a "literary-critical lover's discourse" to a man who existed at a different time, at another theoretical moment than they.[74] When I say I love Eve Kosofsky Sedgwick in the manner that Sedgwick and Frank love

Silvan Tompkins, it is also to say that she, in part, defines who I am or how I currently recognize myself. Or, that I recognize myself in how I recognize or misrecognize who she is/was. In this, I am describing a form of transference love. Tsoukala, who I described earlier as feeling like she had sex with "Eve," enjoys the performative effects of her transference to Sedgwick. One reason for our susceptibility to Sedgwick's charms is that above all "Eve" wished to make herself available for identification and use. Identificatory love is related to transference love. Diana Fuss tells us that "to be open to an identification is to be open to a death encounter, open to the very possibility of communing with the dead."[75] Transference is a communion with the dead who populate one's inner world, the voices of those figures with whom one has identified and sometimes against whom one has disidentified.

When I was diagnosed with breast cancer, I looked to Eve Sedgwick on a hunch that she might have something to say that would refute the "normalizing feminine aesthetic," to use Sulik's phrase, that pervades breast cancer literature.[76] Having read very little of her work, I was aware of her as a public intellectual who had struggled with breast cancer. When I read that her initial response to her diagnosis, as I mentioned in the previous chapter, was that it dawned on her, "Shit, now I guess I really must be a woman," I had the same reaction Sedgwick had upon reading Silvan Tompkins.[77] I nearly fell out of my chair. As a woman who has never comfortably identified as a woman per se (or as a man, for that matter), I was both shocked and pleasantly surprised that someone else would have shared my lack of female identification. If this was the start of an identificatory love with Sedgwick, it was only enhanced when I discovered from her husband, Hal, that she and I shared the same oncologist. What could lend itself more to a transferential reading of her work than knowing that we had undergone some of the most intimate, invasive, and terrifying procedures at the behest of the same doctor? It was like finding out we had slept with the same person, or that we had the same mother.

In "White Glasses," written in honor of her beloved friend Michael Lynch, who died of AIDS, Sedgwick comes out publicly as having cancer. She announces her intention of making herself available for identification as a political responsibility. The death and dying made aggressively palpable through AIDS and cancer give identification a special urgency. Sedgwick locates her identifications across gender, across sexuality, across "perversions," and "across the ontological crack between the living and the dead."[78] This dispersion and flexibility confirms that identifications and the identities that accumulate them are far from stable. Fuss argues that the recognitions and misrecognitions that produce identity at once call that identity into question. If, according to Fuss, "identification is the detour through the other that defines a self," it can potentially derail or be derailed.[79] Later in "White Glasses," Sedgwick relates her eviscerating experience at a performance, an "evening of wit, wisdom, and storytelling for lesbians," when the comedian makes a comment about the lack of funding for "our" disease in comparison to AIDS research. Sedgwick is so incensed by the inaccuracy of this claim, the mistaken exclusion of women from the AIDS crisis, as well as the presumed solidarity of women around "that-disease-that-is-not-AIDS," she feels compelled to disown her identification as a woman.[80] She rejects the association between breast cancer and breasts as essentially female, and she points out the ways in which cancer treatment challenges familiar gender conventions and identifications. "Just getting dressed in the morning means deciding how many breasts I will be able to recognize myself [*sic*] if I am wearing (a voice in me keeps whispering, *three*)."[81] This scene is reminiscent of the one in which Audre Lorde was faced with a Reach for Recovery volunteer who requested that Lorde identify which of her (the volunteer's) breasts were fake, and Lorde thinks to herself that they both looked unreal.[82] Cancer treatment highlights the construction of gender and exposes the shaming of those who can no longer or refuse to maintain its illusion; however, it also affords an opportunity to mock and maybe even overturn those normative conventions. Sedgwick's slyly defiant suggestion that she sport three breasts invites us to imagine identification with the boundless expressivity of science fiction characters or super heroines and works toward resignifying the norms on this planet. Elaborating on the disempowerment and empowerment that comes with the revised state of her health, she underscores how the vulnerability of identities is precisely what allows them to be creatively transformed: "Every aspect of the self comes up for grabs under the pressure of modern medicine. . . . I have never felt less stability in my gender, age, and racial identities, nor, anxious and full of the shreds of dread, shame, and mourning as this process is, have I ever felt more of a mind to explore and exploit every possibility."[83]

Even before her diagnosis and treatment, Sedgwick was attuned to the ways in which people identify and disidentify with, against, across, or around expected identifications. In "A Poem," she had already pronounced that her strongest identification as a woman was *as* a gay man.[84] In culling together writings for a posthumous anthology of her former student, gay African American poet Gary Fisher, Sedgwick dreamed "not of Gary, but *as* him."[85] Sedgwick's identification with Fisher is not unproblematic but it is illuminating. Her own racial and class status as a highly educated white woman are likely what enable her to cross identify along both gender and race, while such "transgressions" are foreclosed to others. If identification is the detour through the other, there are clearly some who are afforded more access to travel its course. The insight Sedgwick gained from such privilege is that identifications are not necessarily formed from likeness but rather may be forged through difference.[86]

She builds her identifications with men who differ from her in race, age, size, and sex, to say the least, upon the limits of her knowledge.[87] What she does not know, and can never know, about them and their experience is, for her, what makes them available for love and identification. "The opacity of knowledge, figured in the cross-mirroring faces and forces of available identification, is the kind of disorientating refraction that Sedgwick sees as constitutive of a self, *her* self."[88] Irreducible distance—the distance between self and other, but also the distance between parts of oneself—is paradoxically the condition of intimacy and the very condition for love and self-acceptance. That Sedgwick regarded distance as a precondition for love may explain why she implies that therapy as well as Buddhist prayer present opportunities for impersonal love. Additionally, the distance of impersonal love applies to her relationship with her readers.

I turn to D. W. Winnicott to unpack the complicated trajectory by which an object-love built upon distance, and paradoxically destruction, may be secured. Winnicott developed the concept of object usage through working with patients who were incapable of benefitting from their analysts as real people who existed in the external world. He distinguishes object-relating from object-usage, which entails an acknowledgment of real objects in the external world, and thus extends beyond the subject's projections and internalizations of objects. According to Winnicott, the overlooked psychic mechanism that enables a subject to use an object and not just relate to it is destruction. Winnicott transcribes his patient interaction, his own dialogue on love, as, "Hullo object, I destroyed you. I love you."[89] First comes "subject relates to object," then comes "subject destroys object," and then may come "object survives destruction by the subject." But survival is not guaranteed.[90] If the object indeed survives, it acquires value to the subject because of its survival, and becomes available for use. In this sense, the object's destruction and survival contribute to the subject's construction of reality. Winnicott concludes: "This destruction becomes the unconscious backcloth for love of a real object."[91] Sedgwick continually "destroys" Shannon by insulting him, doubting his intelligence, and idealizing him, and yet he survives her fantasied projections of him. Shannon becomes an autonomous object who has survived her destruction, and can go on to contribute to her faith in the well-being of the world. Sedgwick enters therapy with a deep dread of the destruction of her love objects, a loss that she fears would disable her ability to love the world around her. Shannon's survival allows her to maintain her love of the world and interest in surviving herself.

Winnicott contends that the subject can only come to terms with reality and make use of objects in the world if she can learn to tolerate the essential paradox of needing to both create and destroy the objects of her love. Living with a life-threatening disease seems to intensify this paradox. Presenting itself as a classic double bind, the cancerous object destroys and yet in Winnicottian fashion may enable a different construction of reality. As cancer treatment disseminates her body into a collection of part-objects, Sedgwick grapples with destruction and creation on the level of reality and fantasy:

> As my body got weirder with the treatment, I kept feeling that I had to choose, and couldn't. Either the girl in the fantasy would have one breast, or she would have two. Either she would have hair, or she would be bald. . . . If she was me, a bald woman with one breast, that ruined the fantasy—and if she . . . wasn't marked in those ways, then that ruined the fantasy, too.[92]

Cancer strips her of the power to construct a vision of herself as stable. Shannon's session notes evidence the peculiar incarnation of her dilemma:

> "OH HERE'S A COMFORTING THOUGHT; I MIGHT HAVE AN INCURABLE ILLNESS" BUT THEN IT'S NOT A COMFORTING THOUGHT, BUT I STILL ORGANIZE SO MUCH OF MY ENERGY, THINKING, ETC., AROUND THAT. HABITUALLY, IT OFTEN IS ODDLY COMFORTING, LIKE GRABBING ONTO YOUR CROTCH FOR REASSURANCE.[93]

How can cancer be comforting? Is it because, for those once diagnosed, it is a constant companion in one's thoughts if not in one's cells? There may be something poignant (in the sense of piercing) about how determined cancer cells are to make a home in one's body and how tenaciously they wish to stay. Sedgwick makes an analogy to grabbing your crotch, which true to her identification, is a gesture conventionally attributed to a man. What is Sedgwick grabbing? Winnicott might say that to regulate her anxieties she creates an object there in her mind, an object to be destroyed. Although consciously bewildered by the reversals her interior life has been subjected to, her comment suggests that she may have unwittingly accommodated to a cycle of unconscious creation and destruction that is, after all, life sustaining.

Has Sedgwick managed to make of her cancer a kind of "transformational object," as psychoanalyst Christopher Bollas defines it? Bollas introduces the concept of the "transformational object" as a medium for transformation, "the object as enviro-somatic transformer of the subject."[94] These objects can be persons, ideologies, or things, and have the tenor of being sacred.[95] Ahab's whale is Bollas's prototypical transformational object. Can we conceive of Sedgwick's cancer as her whale, the object that plagues and destroys her, yet also galvanizes her? Berlant usefully parses how *Dialogue* reveals and maintains the dynamic of creation and destruction that underlies survival:

> The very shifting of the subject in response to its own threat to its self-attachment can be the source of an affective creativity that is not just a fantasmatic toupee, but also the possibility of a recalibrated sensorium, as when a comic orientation toward aggression and pleasure produces new capacities for bearing, and not repairing, ambivalence. Eve's work is a training in being in the room with that ambivalence, which she also called unbearable, in its revelation that having and losing are indistinguishable.[96]

The self-provocations that cancer produces in Sedgwick generate not only the reassurance of a fantasmatic phallus (grabbing the crotch) but also provide the impetus for creativity. In fact, Sedgwick was so overtaken by an obsession with arts and crafts just as her cancer metastasized that she and Shannon joked that she must have had a tumor pressing on the Sculpey node in her brain.[97] The intimate levity with which they explain Sedgwick's creative impulse in connection to her illness exemplifies the role of the comic in bearing the unbearable. Berlant's account highlights the degree to which the comic is a mode of creativity that is instructive of how to suffer ambivalence, and indicates that this is key to Sedgwick's particular pedagogy. In contrast to her advice column, on its surface *Dialogue* does not read as humorous except in isolated instances, but Sedgwick regarded it as essentially comic in tone. She thought of it as a "comedy of underdetermination, of sudden relaxation."[98] The underdetermined comedy of *Dialogue* is a counterpart to the overdetermined comedy of her *MAMM* articles where she channels the destructiveness of cancer to construct a pedagogic performance of love designed to comfort her own anxious mind as well as readers who identify with her and her fantasmatic questioners.

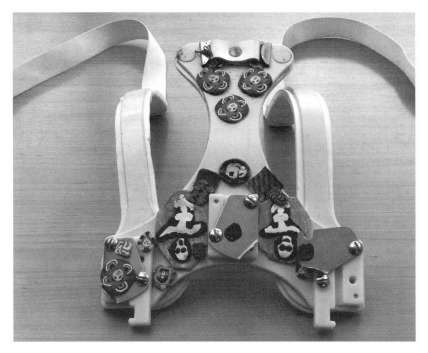

Figure 7. Eve Kosofsky Sedgwick's neck brace. Photograph by H. Lan Thao Lam.

Bad Pedagogy/Good Pedagogy

In calling Sedgwick's work "a training," Berlant affirms that reading Sedgwick's writing is a pedagogic experience. As mentioned earlier, Sedgwick was invested in the idea that she makes people smarter.[99] In regard to *Dialogue*, she stated: "I think it's clear that a pedagogical desire underlies this narrative—desire both to inhabit but equally to offer this radically, ever newly unpreempted space."[100] *Dialogue* and "Off My Chest" are intended as instructional offerings that open up a therapeutic space from the intimate dyad to the "permeable we" of a broader, anonymous public. Rather than relegated to merely its institutional iteration, pedagogy is, for Sedgwick, above all "a mode of relationality."[101] Sedgwick's humor teaches her *MAMM* pupils how to destroy themselves as subjected objects and to produce a more compassionate, one could say permeable subject that can better tolerate the unsettling predicament of incurable illness. As Berlant puts it, "a Sedgwickian teaching hits one like this: it requires becoming undone

in proximity to one's object and yet in that undoing one is no longer subjected to one's ego or one's world, and thus both may become more possible (less impossible)."[102] Berlant's appraisal of Sedgwick's pedagogy
resonates with Winnicott's claim that an object must first be destroyed in
order for it to become useful for the subject, or in Sedgwick's lingo, in order
for the subject to be "made smarter," which in this case, is to learn how to
live with a grave disease. Following Berlant's formulation, Sedgwickian
instruction may be deployed to detach the prognostic subject from the
cancer object, in some sense undoing its composite character. Sedgwick
points out that the insights that illness can give on the processes of living
and dying have long functioned as master teachings: "The sickbed or deathbed is continually produced as a privileged scene of teaching."[103] What she
calls the "pedagogy of illness and dying" can short circuit temporal expectations of vitality and destabilize customary relations between teachers and
students.[104] For instance, the young student dying of AIDS can advise the
older professor who has been diagnosed with cancer.

A pedagogic language and attitude pervades cancer treatment, subject-
ing the patient to the rigors of assessment but without facilitating the
enlightenment one comes to expect from good pedagogy. The questioner
of "I Got it Good . . . and That Ain't Bad" inquires why she sometimes feels
bad when she gets good test results. An illustration of a hunched over
woman with a morose expression receiving a grade of A+ for her checkup
accompanies the article. Here the physician is teacher and the clinical situation a scene of evaluation but not one that is edifying. As advice columnist
and lay analyst, Sedgwick empathizes with the distraught "high performing" patient: "Oh, dear—will you feel even worse if I pronounce your
psyche perfectly healthy?" She confirms that the language of test results is
"emotionally ass backwards."[105] "Cancer free" in the "upside-down world
of metastatic cancer" is designated "unremarkable."[106] She complains that
when her brain scan was deemed "unremarkable" she wanted to hit her
doctor.[107] The same logic (or lack thereof) dictates that when cancer is not
spreading, the physician teacher reports its behavior as "indolent," like a
delinquent student who makes "no progression." For compliant subjects,
as so many have been trained to be, especially within the disciplining institution of modern medicine, the rhetoric of oncological assessment is difficult to swallow. "Ac-cen-tu-ate the negative, e-lim-i-nate the positive:
That's the disorienting ditty that swirls through our heads when we're
waiting for test results."[108] On the one hand, when the news is good, the
negative appraisal encourages the patient to feel disappointed. On the other
hand, when the news is bad, the blame is placed upon the poorly perform-

ing patient. Hal Sedgwick recalls someone standing up at an annual San Antonio Breast Cancer Symposium and threatening to scream if the presenting oncologist, using the field's conventional terminology, referred one more time to patients who "failed" the treatment.[109]

"Advanced Degree: School Yourself in Resilience to Beat Depression" continues with Sedgwick's comic pedagogy, further elaborating on how language constructs patients in ways that many are uncomfortable with. Heather H. asks about the term "survivors" for advanced cancer patients. She doesn't expect to survive the disease and doesn't want to be required to be upbeat. Sedgwick responds that it gets on her nerves as well. One of the pleasures of reading "Off My Chest" with the insider's knowledge that Sedgwick devised the questions herself is imagining her coming up with criticisms and then agreeing with herself. She surely must have used the column to affirm and work through her own feelings, while also reaching out to others. For Heather H., Sedgwick proposes an alternative arsenal of terms that are more suited to the patient's experience, at least to hers. Since calling herself "sick" is kind of "blah," she suggests the acronyms: PWC (Person With Cancer), PBGO (Person Barely Getting Over), BBP (Bald Barfing Person), WAPHMO (Woman About to Go Postal at HMO), PSHIFTY (Person Still Hanging In Fine Thank You), QIBIFA (Quite Ill But, Inexplicably, Fat Anyway), and WOBT (Women On Borrowed Time). PSHIFTY is my personal favorite, though "ontologically abbreviated" is classic Sedgwick. She herself ends up voting for "undead," and is planning on "differently extant" for when "undead" no longer applies.[110]

While on the surface it calls to mind zombies and vampires (another kind of failed superhero), "the undead" is more likely drawn, albeit obliquely, from Sedgwick's long investment in Buddhist study. "Differently extant" would seem even more related to the ultimate Buddhist aspiration toward a non-self. Buddhism is allied with illness on the terrain of pedagogy, which is one reason why Sedgwick was attracted to it. For Buddhists, life and death are subsumed in the project of reincarnation, a "very complex learning project" in which one lifetime resembles a year of school.[111] Sedgwick contributed an entry on "Pedagogy" in *Critical Terms for the Study of Buddhism*.[112] This essay was anthologized in *Touching Feeling* under the title "Pedagogy of Buddhism." In it she writes of her appreciation for *The Tibetan Book of Living and Dying*, which advertises itself as a "manual for life and death," situating itself immediately within the realm of instruction.[113] She describes *The Tibetan Book* as involving readers in "a series of complex, affectively steeped pedagogical relations."[114] Demonstrating what Sedgwick calls the "mobility of teacher-student positions," Sogyal Rinpoche introduces the book as an infant and concludes it as a teacher. While he maintains his dependence on his "master," Sogyal Rinpoche has been recognized as an incarnation of his master's own teacher.[115] Given this fluid set of relations, Sedgwick asks how readers are to identify who is teaching them. For Sedgwick, Sogyal's book interpellates the reader "into a rich yet dissolvent relationality of pedagogy itself."[116]

Is it possible to conceive of *Dialogue* and "Off My Chest" as likewise manuals for life and death that turn on and overturn the "master"/student relation? Each work features a different form of ambiguous authorship. Who is teaching whom? Is it I or Sedgwick who is learning from Eve or Shannon or Heather H. or a pig with a wooden leg? And who am I, for that matter? Am I a Batgrrl, PSHIFTY, or "differently extant"? The ambiguity that Sedgwick fosters in her writing reflects the ambiguities of living and dying with cancer, and sits well with the Buddhist principle that pedagogy entails learning what one already knows.[117] In her later writings Sedgwick attempts to model this learning as a coming to terms with what one knows about oneself. She aims to substitute "good pedagogy" for the kind of "bad pedagogy" that the medical industry dispenses. And we can extrapolate from her work in general that she means to counteract the debilitating effects of heterosexist, homophobic training. But contrary to her earlier work, which advocated direct political action, her later work invokes what I have related to Winnicott as a self-destruction that creates a non-self. Steeped in Buddhist philosophy, Sedgwick's later teachings demonstrate the value of letting go of one's tight grasp upon oneself. (Perhaps not needing so readily to grab hold of one's crotch.)

In her ABCs of living with advanced breast cancer, Sedgwick refers to poet Elizabeth Bishop's "One Art," with its repeated refrain: "The art of losing isn't hard to master." Against the "art of losing" in which people schooled in advanced cancer have often obtained an advanced degree, Sedgwick proposes an "art of *loosing*," by which she means "letting life and loves sit freely, for awhile, on the palm of my open hand."[118] In the introduction to *Touching Feeling*, Sedgwick puts forward a virtually identical sentiment to describe her book's goals: "Ideally life, loves, and ideas might then sit freely, for a while, on the palm of the open hand."[119] Preceding both these compositions, *Dialogue* sketches an "art of loosing" through the expansive holding environment that Shannon and Sedgwick craft together. She tells Shannon that she always feared losing the people she loves, and supplies an open ended list of names, "concluding" with "and, and, and the big spreading field of intimacy where love just grows wild."[120] This embracing attitude toward a public sphere of love recalls her mantra in "White

Glasses" to "include, include" as many people as possible in a community of witnesses who oppose state violences.[121] Sedgwick's capacious community is the source of both affirmation and danger, for while the people she loves nourish and would seem to offer her a holding environment, they are vulnerable to death and can be lost to her.

It is, rather, *language* that can better serve her as a holding environment. Shannon speculates that words have an ontological importance for Sedgwick, that things do not exist until they have been spoken. She responds, "maybe it's more about loss—things *exist* without words, but without words I've no safeguard against losing them the next minute."[122] Sedgwick's fear of loss shows its pathological character in her dreams and fantasies, and arrives in the guise of forgetting. After the last of three finches, gifts from a friend, dies, she tells Shannon her dream: "HER OLD DREAMS, E.G., OF HAVING A CHILD AND FORGETTING TO FEED IT AND BEING REMINDED OF THAT BY FINDING IT DEAD. RELATED TO THE LONG HELD SENSE THAT IF I LOOK AWAY FROM SOMEONE I AM AFRAID TO LOOK BACK BECAUSE THEY MIGHT BE DEAD, NOT CONTINUOUSLY ANIMATED BY MY GAZE."[123]

Death is the consequence of looking away, of forgetting, of losing omnipotent control over the vulnerable objects in and around her. Incidentally, the preceding excerpt grammatically enacts its loss of control over the stability of its subject pronoun. "She" becomes "I," raising the previously posed question, who is speaking to and about whom?

Even before her mastectomy, Sedgwick's own part-objects are objects of loss and forgetting:

> even when
> I had the two breasts
> I kept forgetting them. They
> weren't there for me.[124]

This ever-present fear of forgetting, losing and becoming lost elicits a craving to be held, to somehow be safe and contained and (impossibly) found. When Shannon asks how he can support her, she fails to say, but wishes she had said:

> Well if you wouldn't
> mind could you please just fold me
> up in your billfold,
> carry me like that
> around in your pocket for
> a couple of weeks?[125]

The security of the womblike recesses of a pocket is echoed in the title *Gary in Your Pocket*, the anthology Sedgwick edited. The pocket reemerges as portable holding environment when Shannon writes his home phone number on his business card, giving it to her in case she needs to call him. At home she reaches into her pocket to happily feel the comfort of his card, and realizes she needs to wash her pants before leaving for a trip. "It isn't for half an hour that I picture them tumbling around the washer and realize . . ."[126] She has again forgotten a fragile item and lost Shannon's card to the sudsy water. And yet in some sense it has already served its purpose. She has already internalized it as a good object that "holds" her and appeases her psychic fragmentation. Earlier, when she is anxiously awaiting test results that will confirm malignancy, she imagines Shannon holding her hand as an acceptable form of support.[127] She then transfers the capacity to profit from being held by Shannon's hand to her own when she reaches into her pocket to feel for his card. The narrow limits of safe space, which were relegated to the holding environment of the pocket, begin to open up through her own hands. Psychic holding moves from the sheltered confines of the pocket to the open palm, facilitated by the literal and symbolic helping hand, Sedgwick reaching for but *not grasping* the card with her outstretched hand. This gesture enables her to practice the art of loosing, "letting life and loves sit freely" on the palm of her hand.

"Loss," Lee Edelman maintains, "is what, in the object-relation, it's impossible to lose."[128] Edelman believes that when an object changes, for better or worse, it leaves a space, and loss measures the distance that relation requires: "Loss, in such a context, may be a name for what survives. . . . As relationality's constant, then, loss preserves relation in the absence of its object, affirming the object's contingency . . . even if or when the object is mourned as irreplaceable."[129] According to this formulation, relationality persists despite the loss of its object, as does loss itself. Loss is always felt as that which supported relationality, even when the object is no longer present. Take, for example, the first relation. The infant experiences loss as the distance from mother that subtends its former unity with her. If the infant did not experience this loss, it could not be said to experience a relation to mother.[130] The infant bears this loss as the immaterial substance that binds it to mother. The loss survives so that both infant and mother can endure as subjects for themselves and objects for each other. This experience of loss as a means of relating carries through for the person who takes herself as object. Expanding upon Winnicott's notion of the use of an object, Bollas discusses the ability of the subject to use itself as an object as an essential form of self-management.[131] To maintain a healthy intrasubjective relation with oneself, to be able to think and act self-consciously, a person must be able to use herself as an object. For Freud, as Bollas points out, this mental work is conducted through the superego who speaks to the self as its object.[132] This is not unlike Sedgwick writing letters to herself for her advice, using herself as an object to facilitate her own survival. And the loss she has suffered provides the necessary distance to uphold a loving relationship to herself.

Edelman informs us that when an object changes its place or state, loss materializes to fill that gap. When a person suffers a life-altering event, such as a cancer diagnosis, the object of health that the person could formerly rely upon fails to provide the security it once did. Loss is felt in its place. Loss preserves the relation one has to oneself as an object who needs care. It is important to note that this occurs even as a result of a pleasurable event. An event in which you gain something may transform the ways in which you identify yourself, and thus unhinge your former relation to yourself and produce a loss. Edelman's view directs us to see that loss can hold the place of the lost self-object so that the changed self can recognize herself. A subjectivity of survival, as I have been describing it, is essentially supported by loss. Cancer's intrusions upon one's bodily and psychic well-being render such a subjectivity in chronic need of repair. This leads me to the concept to which Sedgwick was so strongly drawn, that of reparation.

"Let Another Finish the Poem . . ."

In her 1997 essay "Paranoid Reading and Reparative Reading; or, You're So Paranoid, You Probably Think This Introduction Is about You," Sedgwick famously "came out" as an advocate of Melanie Klein's concept of reparation, which she says, is another name for love.[133] Reparation, according to Klein, is associated with the depressive position. The infant assumes a depressive position when it recognizes that an "object which is loved can also be lost."[134] As discussed in Chapter 2, psychic reparation involves the infant attempting to make good on the damage done to its loved objects through its hatred and sadism. Klein's infant, in order to survive, must adopt a cruelly optimistic attitude toward a "significantly problematic object," one that frustrates and disappoints, and yet is necessary for continued life.[135] Reparative reading offers for Sedgwick a teaching project involving those of us who suspect, in Audre Lorde's words, "we were never meant to survive."[136] As Sedgwick writes, "What we can best learn from such practices are, perhaps, the many ways selves and communities succeed in extracting sustenance from the objects of a culture—even of a culture whose avowed desire has often been not to sustain them."[137]

Sedgwick closed *Dialogue* with a reparative moment that guides not only a reading of her memoir but also her later work in general. She describes arriving for therapy early one day, deciding to walk to the corner gas station, and tripping on the shrubby border between parking lots, dislodging some mulch. As she returns she spies upon Shannon gathering up the mulch she had displaced, and then patting it in place, restoring its integrity with the rest of the mulch. Sedgwick writes to her friend Tim, reflecting on how Shannon occupies "the place where I was, encountering my ghost without recognition, unmaking my mistake—me, turning back, seeing it. And I love that his care for me was not care for *me*."[138] Tim's reply places Shannon's act of generalized, anonymous love in the context of Klein's reparation. "An immediate, involuntary substitution: anonymous shrinks, doing reparative work—in their spare time."[139] Shannon's impersonal form of love works to restore Sedgwick's wounded bodily ego. She finds momentary relief from her narcissistic injuries through the reparation of the modest destruction she leaves in her wake. Within a text narrated by a continuously mobile author, the final "I" rests upon the therapist. Sedgwick cedes to Shannon the last word of her memoir: "SHE REMEMBERS TELLING ME HOW SHE WAITS FOR SOMEONE TO TELL HER SHE CAN 'STOP NOW'—E.G., DIE. . . . SHE ALSO TALKS ABOUT HAVING COME TO BE ABLE TO HEAR A VOICE LIKE MY VOICE INSIDE HERSELF . . . I CAN IMAGINE THE VOICE TELLING HER SHE CAN STOP."[140] This voice is in some sense Shannon's while it is also Eve's. She has internalized his voice as her good object, which enables her to make use of her pain and to enact self-repair paradoxically through contemplating self-destruction.

Sedgwick was aware that her move toward a depressive pedagogy of love might also be a flight from a political activism dependent upon paranoid/schizoid aggressive, destructive energies.[141] Yet the process of reparation is not free from destruction. Far from disavowing hate, love is a means by which humans come to terms with its enduring presence in our lives. Reparation is, according to Klein, "a lifelong activity of restoration" that seeks to address the sadistic destructiveness of human beings.[142] For Sedgwick, reading and writing repair the self-destruction that is the precondition for Klein's reparation. Reading and writing is a reparative performance of love. Sedgwick's *Dialogue on Love* amounts to precisely what its title suggests, a discourse directed at the seemingly elementary question of love.

In *Group Psychology*, Freud reminds us that although sexual love predominates in our definition of love, "self-love . . . love for parents and children, friendship and love for humanity in general, and also devotion to concrete objects and to abstract ideas" have "a share in the name 'love.'"[143] Freud's enumeration unexpectedly proposes that love is a word, a name, as much as it is an energy, a relation, and a set of ideas. Indeed, *Dialogue* and the *MAMM* articles exemplify the textual as well as collective character of love for Sedgwick. Her determination to serve as a model for group identification indicates that she shared with Freud the insight that "groups are held together by Eros, for the sake of love."[144] She wrote her lesson plan on living with advanced cancer, addressing it to a public whom she may have hoped were held together by their love and identification with her. Her alphabet of cancer survival strategies literally spells out the name of love. Her final entry in this primer is "zen," whereupon she quotes Chinese master Wu-Men: "Let another finish the poem . . ."[145] This passage links the idea of living and loving with textual creation and collectivity. It is suggested that life is analogous to Japanese *renga*, or collaborative poetry. According to Wu-Men's poetic instruction, authorship is unselfish and dependent on unknown others. Sedgwick gives these words to her readers to intimate that living is a creation that is not contained to the individual but is picked up and passed on by anonymous strangers, as a work of love. The phrase echoes Sedgwick's wish to cease living, doing, and striving expressed at the end of *Dialogue*. To stop doing is not to end life but to concede to its continuation by others. She has learned and teaches how to love by granting to others the collaborative project of living.

Tibetan Buddhists understand dying, meditation, sleep, and dreams as privileged instances of reality, which they call bardos, or gaps in which the possibility of realization is heightened.[146] Buddhist scholar Rick Fields specifies that "the bardo of dying begins when you are diagnosed with incurable illness [and ends only when you enter the bardo of after death]."[147] Sedgwick observes that modern medicine has enabled earlier diagnosis of grave diseases, such as AIDS and cancer, and hence has delayed mortality such that the bardo of dying can now last for many years. During this time of "living in prognosis," it is often questionable whether one is ill or well. Sedgwick mentions that at one point postdiagnosis when she was feeling rather well, her oncologist ruminated upon the philosophical question of in what sense she could be said to be sick. This reminds me that shortly after my own diagnosis, during the many interviews with different oncologists, a nurse had asked me the same battery of questions about symptoms and then said, "So, overall you are in good health?" I hesitated, unable to quite answer, wondering why I was sitting in a cancer clinic, why my life had been consumed with waiting rooms, exams, poking, prodding, needles,

X-rays, biopsies, etc. She then helped me along with, "aside from the cancer." "Oh, yes," I replied when prompted. "I'm in fine health."

Even when one's cancer is in remission one can never inhabit the cancer-free zone in which one existed prior to diagnosis. Affiliation with others in the same uncertain state of health led Sedgwick to the idea that companionship within the bardo of dying could produce a novel public sphere.[148] In an interview she states: "I think just the recognition of [the bardo of dying] as a distinct place that many people spend a fair amount of time in, out of which they can speak directly to others as well as to themselves . . . affords its own opportunities, its own tasks and also anxieties."[149] AIDS activism arose out of such conversations, and Sedgwick regards other slow-acting diseases as presenting a similar potential. The bardo of dying is a pedagogic space in which one learns from identification not only with shared disease but also with others' experience of pain and confusion. The trauma and stigma of affliction binds one to others with whom one can empathize, having in common the destabilization of one's self and world. Sedgwick, a self-described fat white woman with cancer, relates to Gary Fisher, a black man with AIDS, on the grounds of the suffering they have both endured. Sedgwick commiserates with Fisher about being entranced in a narcissistic self-absorption due to the narcissistic insult of chemotherapy-induced baldness. Fisher admits to a similar obsession with his sarcoma lesions, spending "sometimes whole days of months, paralyzed in front of his mirror, incredulous, unable . . . to constitute there a recognizable self. Impaled by the stigma."[150] Moreover, Fisher's sister later tells Sedgwick that this is how she believes Gary experienced being black.[151]

Fisher experienced his racial stigmatization in the same manner as he experienced the stigmatization of AIDS. Just as he identified with being black and being ill, he was also appalled and unable to recognize himself as either species of outcast. Fisher's predicament highlights the problem of identification for those who are compelled to identify with something that, as much as it constitutes them, poses a threat to their lives. As stated earlier, Sedgwick had the privilege of experiencing this double bind in a less constrictive manner than Fisher, or rather, she had the privilege of regarding identification as more mobile than was possible for him. Hence she forged a path out of her impasse by identifying with her own mortality, or as she says, with the very grain of her own illness: "If one isn't going to cling desperately to a self, however, another point might be to become *it*; to identify with the fabric and structure of this discohesive fate itself."[152] Advanced cancer thrusts its aggrieved into the bardo of dying, which involves a process of identification, an identification with a self undone.

Sedgwick's message suggests that one can learn from one's cancer, as one learns from Buddhism, how to accept human vulnerability and transitoriness. Contrary to the tyranny of positive thinking that converts the negative into the positive, Buddhist practice urges the acceptance of the negative. We all know we are going to die, but often we do not *realize* it until we are undeniably confronted with our mortality. The project of Buddhism is to train its adherents to realize this fact that they already know. With a particular cruelty, incurable illness can also lead toward such realization. Sedgwick remarks: "Perhaps nothing dramatizes the distance between knowledge and realization as efficiently as diagnosis with a fatal disease."[153] For Sedgwick, the irrefutable evidence of the imminent reality of her death brought on by metastasis worked to close the gap between knowledge and realization. "The proximity to death suspends life," Rosi Braidotti insists.[154] In these terms the bardo of dying may hold open the space of life, not unlike how loss preserves and supports what is lost, as Edelman proposes. The bardo can relieve one's hunger for company in this specialized space, acting as a public sphere where one teaches and learns how to die, how to live, how to live on, how to accept and appreciate mortality—one's own and others, how to grieve and come to terms with loss, and how to love. I recognize this pedagogical space in which the dying make efforts to *realize* what it is to be human as a space of love. Braidotti casts humans in an amorous or at least welcoming relation with death: "Making friends with the impersonal necessity of death is an ethical way of installing oneself in life as a transient, slightly wounded visitor."[155] If for Sedgwick, life is defined by impersonal love, following Braidotti's cue, it may be an impersonal love of death, which is to say, an embracing of death as the precondition of life and of the future. This life that is constituted by death might be called "not-death," as I termed Freud's death drive.

In his remembrance of Eve Kosofsky Sedgwick, Ellis Hanson recounts how when someone close to him died, Eve comforted him with the maxim: "People are fragile."[156] With the same elegant distillation of complex ideas and feelings as her axiom, "People are different from each other," Sedgwick's seemingly commonplace observation reverberates in a world where increasingly sophisticated technologies cannot prevent and likely abet ever more ways of dying.[157] Sedgwick's work has spoken to the fragility of life in the face of loss. Words have been her means of honoring those who are especially susceptible to such losses. Words provide a holding environment that works against the threat of disintegration, a place of holding but not gripping, for words model an art of loosing through their openness to interpretation, and the flexibility of their authorship and reception. Sedgwick called for a reparative reading implicit in which was a call to reparative writing. *Dialogue* and her *MAMM* contributions answer to this demand. So, too, does *Gary In Your Pocket*, in which her rationale for compiling Fisher's writing reflects a conviction that words operate as talismans against loss: "The indignity, the promiscuity of book publication . . . answers eerily to the indignity of death; but also to the survivors' yearning for a potent, condensed, sometimes cryptic form of access to the person who would otherwise be lost."[158] Sedgwick's publications can function as such for those of us who survive her, and who, like myself, may fall in love with a writer they have never met.

It is not so strange, after all, that I have had so powerful a transferential response to reading Sedgwick, for, as Freud defines the transference phenomena, they are "new editions" or, one could say, promiscuous new publications of old stories.[159] This Eve I have never met and yet somehow know and love has distributed parts of herself in her books and through her words. Her discourse on love enters me as part-objects with which I identify. She teaches me that publications are vital, animate, collaborative objects that perform the work of mourning and love. They also register her own survival. *A Dialogue on Love* and "Off My Chest" thereby impart a reparative public discourse of love, preserving objects that survive to speak back to the irrevocable call of death.

CHAPTER 4

Reparative Objects
in the Freudian Archives

So far, I have been arguing that cancer produces a psychic rupture in the sense of embodied self, or what Christina Crosby calls "bodymind," that is fundamentally destabilizing.[1] This process of discomposure can be interpreted through a psychoanalytic theory of maturation as reverting the subject back to the infantile, oral phase in which existence is dominated by part-objects. A sense of wholeness, a presumed unity with oneself, is lost, producing a psychic state that calls for repair. The losses imposed by cancer are countered by this urge to repair, a process that is inherently creative. According to Klein, the path toward integration from the chaos of fragmented part-objects to a psychic cohesion involves mourning, which she describes as making amends for the destruction that has been inflicted upon one's internal objects. Klein calls this mental labor "reparation." For Lorde, this involved expressing her self-love through her life writing and inciting her community to mother themselves. For Sedgwick, reparation entailed disseminating a public discourse of love and mourning through publications and pedagogy.

We return now to the scene of Freud's dying amid his profuse collection of antiquities, which served a reparative purpose in mitigating his suffering from illness and exile. Keeping the body of psychoanalysis alive has been a project split between two rival museums, one in London and one in Vienna. The London Freud Museum secures its survival through its inheritance of Freud's possessions. It sustains the life of his personal collection of "death objects" by entombing them. The Vienna Freud Museum mourns the irremediable absence of both Freud and his possessions with the Jewish psychoanalyst's expulsion from Nazi-controlled Austria in 1938. The Vienna Museum enlists fetish objects to symbolically and psychically repair the ruptures of war and dispossession. Just as physical trauma can threaten the security of bodily intactness, historical catastrophe may unseat the totalizing myth of historical continuity or aesthetic completion that museums are often charged with affirming.

The question as to whether material forms can perform the work of repairing wounded psyches guides this chapter. How can the forms that we creatively construct—through writing, collecting, photography, or museum exhibition—repair traumatic fissures? Freud's conception of the psychoanalytic technique of "construction" serves as an entry into understanding how the Freud Museums grapple with the loss of their loved objects, historical rupture, and the consequent fracture of the body of psychoanalysis into a collection of part-objects. In "Constructions in Analysis," Freud declares that the job of the psychoanalyst is to construct or reconstruct forgotten material from the patient's memory traces. To sort through the meaning of constructions in psychic life, it is appropriate that Freud turns to the archaeological metaphor of which he was so fond, for the questions of recovery—whether of memory, from illness, or from wartime disaster—have substantially to do with material form. Both psychoanalysis and archaeology, he writes, "have an undisputed right to reconstruct by means of supplementing and combining the surviving remains. . . . For the archaeologist the reconstruction is the aim and end of his endeavors while for analysis the construction is only a preliminary labour."[2]

An archaeological reconstruction serves as an end in itself, whereas within psychoanalytic treatment a construction should incite recollection, initiating a process that is theoretically interminable. While the destructive effects of illness and war inspire a need to reconstruct—to redress damages and restore past forms intact, psychoanalytic construction suggests that survival is built upon creative endeavors that are oriented to the present and future. The patient relies upon the analyst to stitch together memory fragments into a "contingent whole."[3] Although he repeatedly insists that the analyst wants to *recover* the patient's forgotten memories, Freud's preference for the term "construction" for this reparative procedure implies that something is being *made*, something new for which there is no precise prior form. Freud's concept of "construction" embraces the creation of something new and points to an acceptance of its incompletion. His custom of giving a ring to members of his Committee, his most trusted psychoanalytic confidantes, illustrates how reparation can be materialized in creative forms. As factions in this intimate analytic community grew, and members departed or were dismissed, Freud discontinued this tradition.

But he made an exception for Ernst Simmel, presenting him with a gift of a ring and a note that read, "Forms may pass away, but their meaning can survive them and seek to express themselves in other forms."[4] Meanings survive in the wake of destruction, and forms are devised to keep those meanings alive. Reparative efforts, though, cannot so much restore a lost whole as construct a present and a future that mean to accommodate life's inevitable discontinuities.

The Museum as Creative Construction

Theodor Adorno reflects on the close relation between museums and death: "The German word, *'museal'* [museum-like], has unpleasant overtones. It describes objects to which the observer no longer has a vital relationship and which are in the process of dying. . . . Museum and mausoleum are connected by more than phonetic association. Museums are like the family sepulchres of works of art."[5] If all museums are places of dying, then how is it that they might also be reparative? For Klein, the reparative impulse is bred in the depressive position, on pain of death. It is to defy death and dying, as felt through the psychic annihilation of internal objects, that a reparative response is recruited. In a similar fashion, the act of collecting, which is to accumulate objects in an effort to ward off death, and the preservation of those objects, can work against the threat of destruction and disappearance. Adorno quotes Marcel Proust, who claims "it is only the death of the work of art in the museum which brings it to life."[6] Adorno pits Proust's adoration of the museum's revivifying powers against Paul Valéry's view that objects are entombed within the confinement of the museum. Such art and artifacts are held captive in a deathlike frozen moment in time, severed from the external world and from the animated social life in which they were handled and used.

Hal Foster argues that the apparent opposition between Valéry and Proust's positions, in fact, uncovers the antinomy that underlies modern art and the modern museum. For Foster, art history is constituted by repeated crises of "fragmentation and reification of tradition" which entails a commitment to "remedy through a redemptive project of reassembly and reanimation."[7] One might, then, situate the reparative projects of the Freud Museums within the larger reparative projects of museum practice that repeatedly contend with the crises of ordering disorder and reordering that which has been violently or passively deranged. Douglas Crimp, who begins his elegy to the modern museum with Adorno's reflection on the deathly connotations of museums, writes about the demise of the museum as an ordered and ordering universe that safeguards the aura of works of art.[8] He refers to Flaubert, who describes the museum as an "absolute heterogeneity" that requires something like a myth to organize its otherwise incomprehensible and unruly bits into a coherent whole.[9] In the absence of a museum's structuring fiction an incoherent heap of "bric-a-brac" recalls the fragmented realm of part-objects.

The museumification of objects can thus be seen to mimic the path of integration by which part-objects become "whole." Museums undertake a creative construction to represent their collections by way of an overarching, totalizing narrative, one that makes coherent and seemingly complete the disarray of its isolated artifacts. Not unlike many human beings, museums, in general, share a desire for totality, for completion, for a sense of wholeness that may be materialized, for instance, in the wish to obtain the complete collection of Freud's possessions. The Freud Museums might be thought to produce the kind of construction that Freud himself discovered as a psychoanalytic technique, which is a speculative, ordered narrative of the patient's past life. The Freud Museums make something new of the surviving remains of Freud's life, resuscitating forgotten memories culled from historical documents, constructing a present account of the past. But Freud's legacy remains incomplete at both sites of Freud's memorialization, and it has also been substantially distributed to the Freud Papers at the Library of Congress and even the Augustus Long Health Science Library of Columbia University, where a collection of Freud's books is held. This dispersal of the Freudian archive may point to the fantasy of ever being able to collect the entirety of a person's life. That is to say that after our deaths, all of our lives will remain in some sense incomplete.

Remedy and Reanimation at the Freud Museum, London

Freud was eighty-two when he was exiled. He had delayed his exit from Vienna, the "prison" which he both loved and hated, for as long as possible, but when the Gestapo arrested his daughter Anna, though they eventually released her, he fled to London with fourteen members of his family.[10] With the help of his world renown and powerful allies, he was able to transport to London almost all of his important possessions, including more than two thousand Greek, Egyptian, and Roman antiquities; thousands of books; and most of his furniture. Freud would live in London from June 1938 until his death in September 1939. In 1971, thirty-three years after Freud was forced to leave Berggasse 19, the Sigmund Freud House opened to the public at the site of the analyst's former home and offices in Vienna. In 1986, four years after Anna Freud's death, the Freuds' private house at 20 Maresfield Gardens, where Anna had continued to live after her father's death, was opened as the Freud Museum in London.

Maresfield Gardens is located in Hampstead on the outskirts of London, whereas Berggasse 19 is in the inner city of Vienna. Despite the architectural and geographic differences, the Freud Museum in London can be seen as a reconstruction of Freud's Viennese study and consulting room with its congregation of his ancient cult figures and library arranged into two adjoining rooms, and the placement of his chair at the head of his couch so that the reclining patient would face away from him. This orchestration of bodies and furnishings continues to serve as the model "stage set" of psychoanalytic therapy, spawning myriad reconstructions with their requisite couch, strategically positioned analyst's chair, and any number of objects set out as a feast for the patient's eyes.[11] It is reported that Anna Freud preserved her father's consulting room and study as they were at the time of his death, even leaving his eyeglasses on his desk. But the extent to which this exactitude is accurate is subject to some debate. David Newlands points out that if indeed the rooms were left precisely as they were since September 23, 1939, there would only be two globe lights in the room.[12] Nevertheless, the proliferation of objects showcased at Maresfield Gardens evidences the impulse to preserve a lost love object and to restore a lost environment. While its excess of objects appears to contrast it with the Vienna Museum, the Freud Museum in London shares with its rival the looming absence of its namesake. The former director of the London Museum confirms this interpretation in its guide: "The museum is the scene of Freud's absent presence."[13]

Visitors typically come to museums dedicated to "great men" with the hopes that the memorialized life will in some sense be recreated. They seek and are reassured by the impression of a world in which time has stood still, an illusion Anna Freud was at pains to preserve at Maresfield Gardens. Her father's portrait would forever remain poised above her own couch in her consulting room which was itself a copy of her father's. The Freud

Museum, London, delivers on visitors' expectations, maintaining the recon-struction of Freud's Viennese library and office that the Freud family and their maid, Paula Fichtl, undertook so that Freud could weather the upheaval of his exile and advancing cancer "enveloped by his reconstituted old envi-ronment."[14] Freud's couch, swathed in Persian rugs and topped with plush pillows, his wall-to-wall books and exotic artifacts produce the sort of mise-en-scène that can provide reassurance that history is continuous and ultimately progressive rather than regressive, fractured, or subject to disre-pair.[15] The London Museum strives to express a narrative of wholeness and integrity even with the absence that binds it at its core. Through the "great man" fiction the assorted objects at the Freud Museum, London—the Biedermeier furniture, Gradiva bas-relief, bronze porcupine, and oddly shaped desk chair—are assembled into a comprehensible and seductive whole that is easily translated into bite-sized social capital: "I saw the famous psychoanalytic couch!"

The Vienna Museum wishes to call to mind a time of plenitude before Freud's departure, but it is only able to succeed in preserving a sense of his absence. One would imagine that the Museum at 20 Maresfield Gardens would succeed where the Vienna Museum must fail. Indeed, the London Museum communicates much of the fullness of Freud's life, that he had been welcomed by London, was able to enjoy freedom, light, flowers, idols, and books. Yet London, too, is haunted by Freud's absence because it suggests that the only thing that is missing from this scene that recon-structs the rooms of Berggasse so well is Freud himself.

Newlands records the antagonism that existed between Vienna and London before the opening of either museum. Arnold Horwell, an inter-mediary for The B'nai B'rith Jewish organization in London, wrote to Anna Freud upon news that she had been asked to approve the Vienna Museum and to donate Freud's furniture, books, antiquities, and other artifacts: "It is only right that his possessions should share the fate of the great man himself and should find [a] final resting place here in London."[16] His comment indicates that more than a decade prior to an establishment of a Freud Museum in London, advocates of such a museum were making claims upon Freud's material possessions as a means of appropriating and securing the myth of the "great man himself." Anna Freud responded to Horwell's letter with: "I do wish the Viennese would not make so much undignified noise now. . . . I must say that I preferred the quiet and neglect that preceded it."[17] The irony of her remark is striking when one considers that the most persistent and resonant sound that echoes throughout the reverberant because largely empty and uncarpeted rooms at the Vienna

Museum is Anna Freud's own voice, narrating her family's home movies. Although these are played at Maresfield Gardens as well, the carpeting and furniture absorb a good deal of the "noise" in the London Museum. Anna Freud was able to obtain her quiet in the suburbs of London where her father's mute statues, books, prints, rugs, and couch remain as the silent witnesses to his last days.

Before its official museumification, H.D. had already compared Freud's unique office setting to a museum.[18] Both museum and mausoleum, 20 Maresfield Gardens was a place of dying. Freud lived there for just under a year. Commemorating Freud's death as much if not more than it memorializes his life, the London Museum is inextricably connected to death, not least due to the collection of antiquities that survive him, for collecting in general is known to be a ritual undertaken to fend off death. Among Walter Benjamin's collection of quotations, for example, we find: "The need to accumulate is one of the signs of approaching death (Gui Patin)."[19] More specifically, Freud's relics have been interpreted in relation to death because he initiated his collection following his father's death in 1896 and because so much of it consisted of funerary equipment withdrawn from tombs: Egyptian funeral masks, mummy bandages, and *shabti* figures that accompanied the deceased into the afterlife.[20]

Figure 8. Freud's desk, Freud Museum London, 2015. Photograph by Karolina Urbaniak.

At least a decade before acquiring his first art object, in a letter to his fiancée, Martha Bernays, Freud recounts visiting the antiquities wing at the Louvre and extols praise over the "dreamlike world" of the ancient gods.[21] This attraction to the things of the past motivated what would become a museum-like collection that influenced Freud's psychoanalytic theories and provided him lasting comfort to endure his illness, exile, and death. At least six glass cases at 20 Maresfield Gardens overflow with terracotta statues, plaster busts, and marble reliefs of Egyptian, Greek, and Roman gods and demigods, including the Sphinx, Venus, and Artemis and six or seven representations of Eros.[22] While the collection is heterogeneous and idiosyncratic—Rubén Gallo calls it multicultural in rejecting norms of antiquity collection that categorize artifacts by origin and type— there are more statues than other types of artifacts, and most originate from the Mediterranean.[23] Though he prized certain items, the act of collecting was more important to Freud than any single piece. One gains this impression because the treasures are almost all displayed in groups, and were not so much showcased for public presentation as for his own benefit. Segregated from the rest of the house, Freud kept them confined to his study and consulting room. He stuffed drawings in drawers and crammed sculptures into the inaccessible corners of cabinets. The diverse pieces of the collection—its glass bottles, jade bowls that doubled as ashtrays, mirrors, stelae, cylinder seals, urns, rings, gems, amulets, lamps, prints, and fragments of sarcophagi—seem to have only one shared characteristic: Freud's intense fascination with the origins of civilization.

The Life and Death of Objects

Because collecting organizes the experience of possession and is ultimately a reflection or even embodiment of the collector, collections "facilitate the mutual integration of object and person."[24] Collecting, on Jean Baudrillard's account, is the activity through which objectivity and subjectivity might be integrated. The collected object for Baudrillard is therefore reparative in that it facilitates an integration. Humans accumulate reparative objects, sometimes compulsively, in an attempt to overcome the irreparable losses that accompany the human condition. "It is precisely this irreversible movement from birth towards death that objects help us to cope with," Baudrillard asserts.[25] Cancer brings this irreversible movement into relief, and the figures I have discussed throughout this book deploy creative solutions, such as collecting, writing, and smoking, to psychically defend against and eventually come to terms with this unwanted knowledge. Baudrillard argues that the "game of possession," a game in which Freud was an avid player, defends against the existential crisis presented by the inevitability of death. Baudrillard likens this game to another, Freud's game of *fort/da*, in which the player counters anxiety by performing mastery, thereby warding off the fear of absence and death.[26] Through accumulating possessions, people defy death: "A person who collects is dead, but he literally survives himself through his collection, which (even while he lives) duplicates him infinitely, beyond death."[27] Baudrillard implies that there may in fact be something alive in the objects humans collect, just as there is something dead in the collector.

I earlier described how cancer brings humans closer to the status of things. Baudrillard finds that collecting likewise has a deanimating power on collectors who "invariably have something impoverished and inhuman about them."[28] However, the intimacy between collector and collection also transmits human characteristics to collected objects, a transference that Freud experienced in the close proximity to his prosthesis. Ultimately, according to Baudrillard, by integrating oneself within the "system of objects," one takes part in a grand series not unlike the collaborative project of life that Sedgwick discovered through Buddhism, the accumulated life that remains incomplete in and of itself, yet is continued by another. An individual life within the system of objects may be merely a part-object that works toward an integrated whole, which is itself never complete. Benjamin echoes Baudrillard when he refers to the collection as achieving a "peculiar category of completeness" that is accomplished through integration of parts into a historical system.[29] He proceeds to describe the compulsion of the collector as a fight against dispersion.[30] By the same logic as the museum, the impulse of collection is therefore fundamentally reparative.

Benjamin describes the relationship between collector and collected objects as one of love and reverence. An object that is acquired by a collector, a book in his case, is rescued from loss, amounting to its veritable "rebirth" or "renewal."[31] For Benjamin, collecting as a reparative activity was invested with a passion akin to religiosity. With gleeful pride he recounts his greatest moment of acquisition, when he was able to obtain an 1838 edition of Honoré Balzac's *La peau de chagrin*, the last book that Freud read before he died. Freud, like Benjamin, was a collector of books, amassing between two and three thousand, but his antiquities arguably form his more celebrated collection. Also like Benjamin, who regarded the library as a living thing, Freud understood his collection to be living as long as it was kept alive through ongoing additions.[32] When the owner no longer

added to it, he considered it dead.[33] Historian of psychoanalysis John Forrester credits Anna Freud with fostering the transformation of Freud's
"living collection" into a "dead museum."[34] He represents Freud's collection as an imbrication of death in life resembling what I have termed "not-
death": "Freud's collection of antiquities elegantly demonstrates how a
collection can symbolize the battle of life within death, of life being infil-
trated by death, of a space cleared for the expression of this battle by the
objects the collector has chosen as his personal representatives."[35] Freud's
collection embodies the paradoxical interdependency between death and
life exhibited in the death instinct.

Throughout his career, Freud turned to archaeology to understand
psychoanalysis, and specifically to explicate the ways in which both practices exhibited powers of reincarnation, of awakening the dead. Donald
Kuspit summarizes this comparison: "Each is a way of engaging and
articulating what remains alive—in effect immortal—and continues to
determine our humanness, yet seems dead and buried and lost forever."[36]
Freud emulated archaeologists who were able to reanimate the lifeless and
dismembered shards of antiquity and could thus reconstruct something of
a whole picture of the past. He saw both professions as oriented toward
repair, piecing together "mutilated relics" and restoring missing parts.[37]
The antiquities Freud collected were for him "preserved pieces of the
mind, petrified parts of the psyche" akin to distorted memory traces
retrieved from a forgotten past.[38] In describing how Freud would illustrate
therapeutic points with his "grubby gods,"[39] H.D. affirms that by analogy
they functioned as a kind of reanimating reparation for Freud's patients:

> Fragmentary ideas . . . were often found to be part of a special layer or
> stratum of thought and memory . . . these were sometimes skillfully
> pieced together like the exquisite Greek tear-jars and iridescent glass
> bowls and vases that gleamed in the dusk from the shelves of the cabi-
> net that faced me. . . . The dead were living in so far as they lived in
> memory or were recalled in dream.[40]

Freud's classical objects and figures embodied and revived memories of
the deceased. H.D. recalls Freud's escorting her to his study to physically
handle a particular object, demonstrating that the collection's therapeutic
purpose was not merely symbolic but material.[41] The psychic constructions Freud endeavored to make with his patients were reinforced by their
connections to material objects. H.D. confirms that the memories and
dreams conjured in the analytic space are "as real in their dimension of
length, breadth, thickness, as any of the bronze or marble or pottery or

clay objects that fill the cases around the walls."[42] Asserting the tangible reality of psychic objects, for H.D. at least, contributes to their healing power.

But perhaps more than for his patients, the collection seems to have been curative for Freud himself. Much attention has been given to the objects that crowd Freud's desk, acting as an assenting audience as he struggled to bring to life difficult theories.[43] For instance, Max Pollak's famous etching *Sigmund Freud at His Desk* contributes to the impression that Freud drew intellectual inspiration from the statuettes that peered back at him as he wrote.[44] Freud even took them with him to his summer-houses to ensure their continued support. As fetishes, they gave him plea-sure and afforded him the opportunity to rediscover, as Forrester describes of the collector, "his narcissism in the charm of the objects, which each reflect back to him a portion of his lost libidinal objects."[45] Freud showed his passionate attachment to his treasures in many ways, both in words and in action. His housemaid verifies that he used to lovingly fondle his Baboon of Thoth "as he did his pet chows" and that when he entered his study he greeted the Chinese Scholar who stood on his desk.[46] Judith Bernays Heller, Freud's niece, remembers the "'Eindringlichkeit' a sort of affec-tionate way of describing the thing, when he talked about the Egyptian and Roman objects in his cabinets while showing them to you. And the delicate way he had of handling them and stroking them."[47]

Freud described the effect that his antiquities had upon him as one of *Erquickung*, which Lynn Gamwell translates as a kind of revitalization or enlivening comfort.[48] Writing to Max Eitington, he describes being fitted for a new prosthesis following one of his many oral surgeries on his cancer-ous jaw and confesses to buying himself a consolation gift of a dipylon vase "to fight my ill humor."[49] Paradoxically his deathly objects gave him life, analogous to how his prosthesis enabled him to eat and speak. But in con-trast to his monstrous prosthetic jaw, they offered resuscitation and refresh-ment.[50] He would bring new acquisitions to the dinner table and commune with them; they provided a distraction during the painful production that eating had become.[51] In a sense, what the prosthesis could not restore, his antiquities did, and he relied upon them as much as he did his oral appli-ances. Freud's collection took on the positive aspects of dependency, leav-ing to the prostheses largely the negative ones.

While staying in a sanatorium in Berlin where he was having a new prosthesis made, Freud records visiting his antiquities dealer six times in two months.[52] The aging psychoanalyst seems to have had as many dealers as doctors, Philipp Lederer, Theodor Graf, Fröhlich, Glückselig, and Robert

Lustig among them. He routed his daily constitutional around the Ring-strasse to visit his favored tobacco and antique shops, seeing his antiquity suppliers as regularly as patients see their therapists—at least twice weekly.[53] But Lustig made house calls, bringing special items to Freud's office at least once a week, increasing his contact with Freud from two to three times a week, a difference in frequency that in psychoanalytic terms elevates psychotherapy to psychoanalysis.[54] Collecting, then, fulfilled the psychoanalytic task of relieving his suffering, while simultaneously, as in the case of his jaw prosthesis, it revealed his addiction. If Freud's prostheses were material evidence of his addiction to smoking, his antiquities were evidence of his compulsion to collect. Freud himself recognized the interplay between his two compulsive habits, and sought the compensatory pleasure of collecting when his health required him to abstain from smoking. This solution was, however, not always viable, as he complained when he had been forced to temporarily quit smoking due to heart problems: "I am only missing cigars, whatever measures I try against that fail, wine drinking, letter writing, eating dates are no substitute. Antiquities may have been one, but one cannot buy so many."[55]

I read "Freud's toys" as reparative objects in the sense that they appeased his anxieties about the process of dying, mitigating his fears of mortality.[56] They served the purpose of resisting death, even as they symbolized death. In his laconic diary, Freud jotted down his acquisitions, putting them on par with his surgical operations, ailments, adjustments to his prostheses, along with the deaths of friends, colleagues, and public figures, and world events such as the election of Hitler and "Finis Austriae" on March 12, 1938.[57] His favorite statue, the Athena that held center stage on his desk, preceded Freud to freedom and functioned as a watchful guard when he fled his mother country. Marie Bonaparte had managed to smuggle her out of Vienna when it was uncertain whether Freud's collection could be transported, and the Princess also supplied Freud with a small army of Greek terra-cotta figures to oversee his desk until his full battalion arrived. In his thank-you note, he wrote, "we left proud and rich under the protection of Athene."[58]

Once he was welcomed to London, friends and visitors continued to bring him gifts of gods to compensate for the combined indignity of being uprooted while he suffered from illness and old age. Freud's bed was brought down to his study so that he could look out into the garden and die where his pagan deities could help him reconcile himself to death. As Ernest Jones describes it, "his beloved objects from antiquity must have done something to console his last hours. He attached very special value to those pieces in his collection that had been perfectly preserved. They were beings that had lived for centuries, or else come back from the dead, without suffering any impairment of their integrity."[59] They, unlike he, would survive with their bodies intact. Benjamin confirms that the miscegenation of humans and objects extends the life of the owner who haunts his objects: "Ownership is the most intimate relationship that one can have to objects. Not that they come alive in him; it is he who lives in them."[60]

The perseverance of these personified, reanimated objects persists beyond Freud's death. His collection itself is a survivor of war. Not only had it escaped Austria, but it also survived the bombings in London. The pieces that Anna ultimately donated to the Vienna Museum were stored in the cellar of 20 Maresfield Gardens where, "damaged and blackened," they nonetheless eluded complete destruction.[61] Even as they suffer from erosion and disrepair, Freud's deathly objects have ultimately outlived him and signify an eternal lifelessness that exceeds death.

The London Museum expends the same loving attention as Freud did to the collection that it has inherited. It keeps two of Freud's prostheses stored in the top drawer of his desk. On the desk is a toothbrush that I was informed was kept there by the Museum, not by Freud. I imagine it is to be

Figure 9. Children viewing Freud statue, London, October–November 1970. Container XI, Folder 10, Anna Freud Papers, Manuscript Division, Library of Congress, Washington, D.C. Photograph by Lin + Lam.

used for dusting off stray particles, but it is amusing to think that even after
its owner's demise the prostheses would still require brushing, and suggests
that the abundant objects that people 20 Maresfield Gardens remain in
some sense still uncannily alive.

Questions about the potential life and death of objects are raised when
a young boy whose daily path crossed the statue of Freud that formerly
stood outside of the Swiss Cottage Library not far from 20 Maresfield
Gardens remarks, "every day he is dead."[62] Gino's definitive, yet ambiguous statement may refer to the recurrence of Freud's death, but also to
the statue's continued survival. Personifying Freud's death, the statue
uncannily persists. Filmmakers Chris Marker and Alain Resnais support
the view that artifacts hold the capacity for mortality with their 1953 film
The Statues Also Die (Les statues meurent aussi). Marker and Resnais's film
critiques the colonialist appropriation of African art and culture for exhibition in European museums.[63] Indeed, although frequently overlooked,
Freud's collection is a violent cultural appropriation. Archaeologist Peter
Ucko quotes Neal Ascherson's appraisal that Freud was a "shameless
patron of tomb-robbers," and Pål Harmat's more succinct designation of
the psychoanalyst as "art smuggler."[64] The London Museum reinforces
and at the same time renders invisible the colonialist dimension of Freud's
ardor for collecting by downplaying the antiquities as artifacts with specific historical and cultural pasts. They are presented en masse without
labels to communicate an aura of the "climate of opinion" that Freud
has become.[65] All that guides their placement is an approximation of
Freud's display preferences, which like many personal collections makes
little sense to outsiders. As mentioned, Freud imposed no classificatory
system upon his collection, no division in terms of chronology or origin.
With great precision, the London Museum reenacts that lack of coherence. In regard to its inheritance, the Museum, like Freud, is guilty of
uncritically romanticizing an exotic past and laying claim to it for its own
purposes.

This is a common trait of collectors. Benjamin also neglects his own
colonizing salvage mentality when he heroically describes endowing his
collected books with freedom, comparing his exploits to "the way the
prince bought a beautiful slave girl in *The Arabian Nights*."[66] The first
words of the voiceover of *The Statues Also Die* proclaim: "When men die,
they enter into history. When statues die, they enter art."[67] This is precisely what has transpired at 20 Maresfield Gardens. With his death, Freud
entered into history, and his ill-gotten, yet reparative statues live out their
days as fetishized art objects.

Figure 10. Freud's consulting room, 1938. Photograph by Edmund Engelman, © 1976 Thomas Engelman.

Melancholia and Reparation at the Sigmund Freud Museum, Vienna

In April 1938, Edmund Engelman, a young photographer and engineer, was asked to photograph Freud's home and office at Berggasse 19, where Freud had lived and worked for the past forty-seven years. After the annexation of Austria into the German Third Reich, the psychoanalyst August Aichorn anticipated that a record of the original site of psycho-analysis would be essential in reconstituting the past at some point in the future. Engelman, also a Jew, was charged with preserving the very image we have of psychoanalysis. Any contemporary understanding of the origins of psychoanalysis is still very much conditioned by these photographs. Almost every image in the popular imagination of the analytic couch in its bourgeois scene replete with Greek and Egyptian idols is derived from Engelman's photos.

Since its inception, the Vienna Museum has seized upon these photo-graphs that reconstruct a time prior to world historical tragedy as a means of reconciling its own relationship to its troubled past. The Museum, I believe, deploys the photos as reparative objects with the hope of healing the rupture of Freud's forced departure. The photographic framing of the Museum's lost objects reveals how substitute objects are enlisted in an effort to mitigate loss. Yet despite fetishistic desires to disavow it, absence forms the core of the Vienna Museum experience.

While the formidable bureaucratic and diplomatic procedures that would permit Freud to escape were underway, Engelman packed his camera bag with a Rolleiflex and Leica and two lenses, a 50mm and 28mm.[68] When he approached Berggasse 19, a Nazi flag was already hanging from the roof of the building, and a swastika emblazoned its entrance. In four days, Engelman shot 106 photographs, taking care not to be observed by the Gestapo agents who were stationed across the street.[69] Because of this surveillance, he worked only with available light and without a flash.

Engelman's photos resonate with a particular affect because of the long exposures required for shooting without floodlights or flash. On my viewing, they do not evidence his anxiety at taking them under duress. Rather, they appear extremely methodical and purposeful. Due to the long exposures, all the images were taken with a tripod, giving them a sense of stability. Additionally, because he did not want to disturb Freud, almost all of the interiors are unpeopled. For these reasons, the photographs exude a peculiar calm. Engelman's slow progression from public exterior to private

Figure 11. Berggasse 19, Vienna, 1938. Photograph by Edmund Engelman, © 1976 Thomas Engelman.

Figure 12. Freud's study, 1938. Photograph by Edmund Engelman, © 1976 Thomas Engelman.

interior parallels the painstaking process of detachment that Freud observed with mourning. And yet, the photos elicit a melancholic response. Rather than encouraging a withdrawal of libido from the lost object that mourning entails, they pull the viewer in more intimately toward objects that have been retrospectively lost. In the photos, the objects are *not yet* lost. Within the photographic frame there is no trauma to be seen. Contrary to the discourse of trauma that has developed post-Holocaust, these photographs do not perform the work of testimony or witnessing, at least not in the usual sense. These images document a moment that *precedes* trauma; they in fact *anticipate* it. By virtue of the abundant presence of loved objects within the photo's frames, the viewer is invited to unconsciously identify with these lost objects, even and perhaps especially in the face of their absence at the site of their display. Situated within the now emptied location in which they originated, the photos *of* Berggasse 19 are recruited *to* Berggasse 19 to ameliorate the very trauma that prompted their creation.

Paradoxically, returning the photographs to their origins serves to underscore Freud's evacuation along with the prized possessions that accompanied him into exile. In the Vienna Museum the photos undergird

Figure 13. Freud's study, Sigmund Freud Museum Vienna, 2013. Photograph by Lin + Lam.

copious quantities of documents that attempt to reconstitute Freud's life and substitute for his missing possessions. Because so few original objects are present for the task, the space as a whole is also enlisted to aid in the project of psychic reparation. The Museum seeks to compensate for its enduring losses by requesting a studious, even a demanding relationship with a cerebral as opposed to a material reconstruction of Freud's life. Could the labor of looking at the Sigmund Freud Museum, of trying to see what is actually not there to be seen, be made to fill in its visible absences?

In 1938, about 166,000 Jews lived in Vienna.[70] Most of them resided within a twenty-two-square-kilometer radius of the Second District and Ninth District, where Berggasse 19 is located.[71] About 100,000 Jews emigrated before the war, approximately 18,000 of which were later caught in other European countries.[72] Around 65,000 Austrian Jews were sent to concentration camps.[73] Trauma haunts psychoanalysis through the victims of the camps, as well as the many psychoanalysts and their families who fled but whose lives were stripped of the securities of citizenship, employment, and community.[74] Although Freud managed to escape, he died a stateless refugee, and four of his sisters were exterminated in concentration camps. Engelman's photographs archive a way of life before its disappearance, marking both the end of an era and a desire to preserve its history.[75]

But the way in which the photos are appropriated in the Sigmund Freud Museum differs from Aichorn's original intention, which suggested a hope that a museum would replicate the state of things as they once were, that is, that a museum could reconstruct the origins of psychoanalysis. To the extent that this is possible, the Freud Museum in London succeeds in just this sort of memorialization. Rather, the Vienna Museum is caught between a desire to authenticate itself as the original site of psychoanalysis, which compels it to showcase images of its "former glory," and a sense of historical accountability, which requires it to maintain the absence that resulted from massive political, social, and economic turmoil. The curious part-memorial, part-museum, part-house, part-gallery, part-library, part-archive, part-research center at Berggasse 19 is itself conflicted with regard to how to position its own presentation. It is troubled by the melancholic's ambivalence.

Whereas the Freud Museum in London suffers from an embarrassment of riches, the Sigmund Freud Museum in Vienna suffers the embarrassment of its losses. Yet, crowds flock to the Vienna Museum at more than three times the rate of the London Museum, which would seem to indicate that it is the site itself, boasting one of the most famous addresses in the world according to the Museum's audio guide, that draws visitors.[76] With a mixed attitude of regret and pride, the tour guide notes that the Museum is a special place because "there are hardly any originals; we have the floor, we have the doors, we have the windows." What is the meaning of these bare material remnants of where Freud lived and worked?

The voice on the Museum's audio guide greets the listener with, "If you came to see the famous couch, I will unfortunately have to disappoint you." The presumption is that a visit to Sigmund Freud's former abode will in any case begin with disappointment, upsetting expectations of finding oneself in the presence, and under the assurance, of the Father through symbolic objects carrying the force of the paternal imago. But Lydia Marinelli, the Museum's former research director, construes the Museum's apparent lack as one of its strengths. "As an empty place," she writes, "which has nothing but an address to mark it and serves as a permanent reminder of obliteration and banishment, the room resists the affirmative construction of meaning and remains inherent as a block in traumatic constellations."[77] Marinelli explicitly associates the Museum with trauma, an association that describes the specific interplay of visuality and temporality operating in its physical and psychical space.

As a "site stripped of its material core" by a history of war and exile, the Vienna Museum, according to Andreas Mayer, was "an institution in search of an anchor for a representation of its collective past."[78] This anchor obviously could not be found in the celebrated objects associated with the Freudian legend, but would be formed around what Marinelli identifies as a "constitutive absence."[79] Marinelli emphasizes that the typical visitor as well as the Museum workers struggle with a sense of incongruity between expectations and actuality. As she stresses, "it is precisely this function of reassurance that the Vienna Freud Museum cannot fulfill. The expectation of finding certain traces of an individual, a particular history, is frustrated."[80] How, then, can the Museum respond to the absences that constitute it? Whereas the mourner, according to Freud's schema, endures an external paucity, emptiness rather pervades the melancholic's internal world.

Because the scandal of its impoverishment simultaneously defines it, the Vienna Museum remains bound to a depressive relation to loss. I suggest that the Museum's current strategy of display can be interpreted as an attempt, in the form of idealization, at recuperating its lost objects. Psychoanalyst André Green understands idealization, which is essential to melancholia, as a dematerialization or spiritualization.[81] In this case, through the sublimation enacted by the Museum in its display, the memory of the father Freud is idealized and dematerialized, one could even say spiritualized, perhaps as an unconscious means of atoning for the violent

Figure 14. Freud's consulting room, Sigmund Freud Museum Vienna, 2013. Photograph by Lin + Lam.

history that necessitated his departure. The compensatory idealization at work in the Museum enables me to interpret the scene of psychoanalysis at Berggasse 19 as a melancholic response to loss, one that takes place through a complex negotiation of visuality, spatiality, and temporality.

If the Vienna Museum is what Griselda Pollock has described as an "empty shell," this shell could be understood as a photographic container.[82] To authenticate them as the original spaces where Freud practiced his new science, the Museum obsessively exhibits Engelman's photographs in each of the rooms outfitted for museumgoers. They are placed strategically to designate as closely as possible the location and arrangement of all the absent originals. To accurately point to items deemed especially significant, such as the missing couch, Freud's desk, chair, books, and favored statues, the images are often cropped and repeated. Photographic plenitude stands in the space of emptiness and stands *for* the lost objects of Freud's legacy. Rather than through traumatic imagery or artifacts, the way in which the aftermath of trauma is negotiated at Berggasse 19 has more to do with the intersection of two-dimensional representation and three-dimensional space. Collapsing clear-cut divisions between two-dimensional and three-dimensional space, and simultaneously conjuring the past and constructing a present, Engelman's photographs, as they function in the Vienna Museum, are made to bear the task of compensating for unbearable loss.

When the Museum first opened in 1971 as the Sigmund Freud House, Harald Leupold-Löwenthal, cofounder of the Sigmund Freud Society and assembler of the opening exhibition, conceived of the Museum experience as integrally constructed through photographs. "The basic idea of its design had already been worked out: to present the 1938 appearance of the rooms by means of enlargements of Edmund Engelman's photographs," he writes.[83] During this era, Forrester visited the Sigmund Freud House, noting that "it was dominated visually by photographs, blown up to life size, of how it once had been, photographs that stood in for all the objects that had been removed to London when the Freuds escaped from the Nazis. It had a derisible atmosphere," he continues, "perhaps one deliberately induced to remind visitors of yet one more loss that the war had visited on Vienna."[84] Although, in the Museum's current rendition, Engelman's photographs have been downsized and compete with masses of additional documentation for wall space, the visitor standing within the walls of Berggasse 19 is still struck by the redundancy of occupying a space composed largely of multiple images of itself. Ironically, photographs of the Museum interiors do not do justice to the phenomenological and perceptual strangeness of

Figure 15. View to Freud's study, Sigmund Freud Museum Vienna, 2013. Photograph by Lin + Lam.

this environment. The redundancy of the photographic and physical space can be easily overlooked when reduced to two dimensions. However, the photographic mimesis of the physical space exerts a psychic impact stemming from a temporal doubling wherein the past is displaced and forced into the present.

Stepping into Berggasse 19, one encounters layers of mediation produced through a redundant dynamic between architecture and photography. The architecture appears both inside and outside of the photographs, both containing and contained within them. The photographs physically frame the architecture, its windows and doorframes, but are also framed by them. There seems to be an excess of framing devices, which leads me to think about the place of the psychoanalytic frame within this picture. We can conceive of the psychoanalytic frame as a clinical injunction in both literal and figurative terms. The purpose of the frame is to contain the transference, those unruly feelings that spring from other people and other times that the patient projects onto the figure of the analyst in the consulting room. The apparatus of the frame consists of the appointed hour of sessions, the agreed upon fee, the fundamental rule of free association, and so on.

But Freud provides an analogy that opens up the frame to a more metaphoric reading. He instructs the analysand on free association by telling

Figure 16. Freud's study, Sigmund Freud Museum Vienna, 2013. Photograph by Lin + Lam.

her to imagine looking through a train window and describing what she sees.[85] The narration of the unconscious in this scenario takes place within the frame of the window where interior and exterior are superimposed. The superimposition of the internal self and the external world is accompanied by a similar superimposition of present and past. The patient is always in the current moment narrating her historical past. The layout of Engelman's photos at Berggasse 19 demonstrates this temporal fusion, and thus the temporal experience of the Museum can be seen as analogous to the psychoanalytic process itself. Joanne Morra points out that the "excess of archival documentation" that fortifies the "seemingly empty" Museum forces visitors to glance about the space in order to light upon something of interest.[86] This is precisely how an analysis proceeds by free association: images, events, and memories pass before the analysand's eyes like the moving landscape in the frame of a train window until the analysand captures something upon which to dwell at length.

In her description of her analysis with Freud, H.D. alludes to the unique temporality that psychoanalysis fosters. "It was not that he conjured up the past and invoked the future," she writes. "It was a present that was in the past or a past that was in the future."[87] H.D. captures the temporal disruptions that psychoanalysis imposes upon its subjects. It is this temporal discontinuity, an understanding that the time of memory can go against the grain of chronological time, which Freud introduced through concepts such as *Nachträglichkeit* and screen memory. The temporality of *Nachträglichkeit*—translated into English as "afterwardness," retrospective reaction, or deferred action—can be understood as a present-past, a present conditioned by the past in which the present has agency, for better or worse, to shape the import of the past upon the present. It is the traumatic event that occasions *Nachträglichkeit*. In her genealogy of trauma, Ruth Leys asserts that the concept of *Nachträglichkeit* "calls into question all the binary oppositions—inside versus outside, private versus public, fantasy versus reality, etc.—which largely govern contemporary understandings of trauma."[88]

Freud's concept of *Nachträglichkeit* helps to describe the specific temporality of the space of psychoanalysis as it is represented at Berggasse 19. We can consider the Museum's efforts to come to terms with, and represent, a history of loss and exile in relation to the temporal operation of *Nachträglichkeit*. The prominence of Engelman's photographs within the Museum space provides a counterpoint to the chronological presentation of the "great man's" life. It is almost as if the Museum asks the visitor to consciously follow the chronological timeline, while on an unconscious level the Engelman photographs—which line the lower third of the walls and thereby accompany the visitor at seemingly any point in time and space— belie the reassurance of this conventional notion of time. Engelman's photographs serve as a tacit reminder that the past occupies the place in which one currently stands. History's "obliteration and banishment" is permanently inscribed in the Museum's present tense through photographs that work with and against the barrenness of the space. Within this discordant context, the photographic volumes can precipitate for the viewer an experience of *Nachträglichkeit*, an encounter between the past and present in which the present could revise our understanding of the past. Rather than remain caught in the melancholic loop that the photographs and Museum appear to invite, it is possible to imagine counterintuitively that a visitor might temporally reorient herself to the potentiality of a history subject to revision.[89]

Fetishism of the Lost Object

In addition to melancholia, fetishism is another defense against loss that dominates the psychic landscape of the Vienna Museum. The psychoanalytic couch has become a metonym for, even an icon of, psychoanalysis.

The lack of material objects in Vienna's Museum, epitomized by the missing paternal symbol of the couch, can be read as a figurative castration that the museum attempts to cover over through the overdetermined usage of photographs, documentary, and archival materials. The absence of a material "seat of power" at the Vienna Museum provokes fetishistic responses that strive to defend against the horror of absence. The *Sigmund Freud House Catalogue*, published in 1975, opens with a floor plan of Apartments 5 and 6 at Berggasse 19. A grayed-out rectangle appears in the consulting room with an arrow pointing to it labeled "couch."[90] It is the only piece of furniture that is designated on the floor plan, and it singles out an object that cannot be found at Berggasse 19. Very similar floor plans are included in both the English and German editions of *Berggasse 19–Sigmund Freud's Home and Offices, Vienna 1938*, the most complete publication of Engelman's photographs. In the English edition, like in the 1975 catalogue, an arrow is directed at a box with the word "couch" next to it.[91] In the German edition, the word "couch" is inserted in the rectangular box.[92] These empty signifiers, like Engelman's photos, indicate the absence of the referent and emphasize that the metonymic function of the couch as a stand-in for the whole of psychoanalysis cannot be physically rendered at the Vienna Museum.[93] Although such representations of the couch cannot operate as proper fetishes in themselves, they carry an "as if" quality that resembles the fetishist's refusal to know its own loss. They evidence the work of disavowal characteristic of fetishism: the knowledge of the desired object's absence and yet the simultaneous refusal of that knowledge.

The Museum is not alone in grappling with the disavowal that accompanies fetishism. Thirty-three years after Freud's forced emigration from Vienna, his offices were opened to a public that appeared to share the Museum's pathological disposition. Marinelli reports that visitors frequently and adamantly recall seeing the couch at Berggasse 19 on a previous trip to the Museum.[94] When visitors insist that they remember seeing the couch in Vienna, they reveal their fetishistic attachment to a pretraumatic moment. According to artist and writer Victor Burgin, fetishism fills the gap between knowledge and belief: "The photograph as fetish object" he writes, "provides a representation that can bridge two-dimensional surface and three-dimensional space, that is, it moves the viewer between knowledge and belief."[95] Drawing on Burgin, I contend that the movement away from the actual space at Berggasse 19 to the photographic reproduction is one of fetishism. Fetishism moves the viewer of Engelman's photos from the knowledge that the couch is not present to the belief that it was.

The critical eye knows what it sees is a photograph, and yet, in memory and fantasy, the absence (of the couch) is substituted by a presence.

As Freud defines them, both fetishism and melancholia involve a *perceptual* problem. The fetishist sees that the woman has no penis but disavows that threatening vision. With melancholia, loss is also unrecognized. As Freud writes, "[The melancholic] cannot *see* clearly what it is that has been lost" (my emphasis).[96] Because the lost object is unrecognizable, the melancholic cannot admit loss and thereby relinquish the love object. Both fetishism and melancholia revolt against emptiness. Whereas fetishism inserts a fantasmatic substitute to occupy the space of absence, melancholia preserves its emptiness. Because the couch itself cannot be fetishized as it can be in London, the Vienna Museum turns to Engelman's photos to fill its internal emptiness. The Museum's adaptation is to present the Engelman photos as fetishistic compensation for its loss, perpetuating a melancholia that works to preserve the past.

In a brief memoir published in conjunction with his photographs in 1976, Engelman recalls returning to Vienna after the apartments at Berggasse 19 had been vacated. Overwhelmed by the emptiness that so opposed his memory of its once crowded interiors, he noticed the outline of the couch on the floor. Returning a week later, he states: "The ghost of the couch had disappeared."[97] In a 1977 newspaper interview, Engelman says that he discerned a white mark on the floor where the couch had been, and he photographed it. He remembers that he returned three days later to photograph it again but workmen had sanded it over.[98] Then, almost two decades later, Marinelli recounts a conversation with Engelman in which he describes a dark shadow on the floor left by the couch, which he had not been able to capture on film.[99] Since these accounts differ, it remains unclear whether the mark of this loss was resistant to photographic capture; that is, whether it was unrepresentable, or whether it was Engelman's unconscious that was resistant to making accessible the image of loss. Freud identifies the shadow of the lost love object cast upon the melancholic ego, which retains its mark.[100] In the empty room at Berggasse 19, the unseen shadow of the absent couch is cast upon the space, rendering the Museum melancholic, in perpetual mourning over its father's expropriation.

In lieu of the lost couch, which can only be fetishized at the Vienna Museum by way of Engelman's photos, a little-known object may have assumed the role of the Museum's fetish. Marinelli tells the story of a literal lost object that embodies the Museum's struggle with Freud's compulsory displacement and the feeling of melancholic abandonment that remained in the absence of all his loved objects. Among the items that Anna Freud

Figure 17. Freud's consulting room, Sigmund Freud Vienna, 2013. Photograph by Lin + Lam.

donated to the Sigmund Freud Museum was her father's tweed cap. When it arrived at Berggasse 19, the cap was returned to its former position on Freud's coat rack, frequently hanging alongside museum visitors' apparel. Marinelli observes: "The cap is part of a small scene in the psychoanalyst's entrance hall that the museum founders thought would evoke both the presence and the enforced absence of the office's former occupant."[101] As an object that is worn and used so intimately, like a prosthesis, a cap might be construed as absorbing some of the qualities of its owner. This proved an irresistible temptation to one of the Museum's U.S. visitors, who exited the Museum with the cap. One can only imagine the anxious triumph of the thief who successfully enacted the fantasy of incorporating a partial object of his psychoanalytic father, and, in turn, the Museum's grief over the disappearance of its own good object. The cap that had hung freely in the hallway was the very one Freud wore as he undertook his flight into exile, and can be seen in photographs taken after he had safely arrived in France and was relaxing with Marie Bonaparte.

In her essay "About Losing and Being Lost," Anna Freud makes the connection between our embodiment and the material objects we own: "Our material possessions may represent for us parts of our own body, in which case we cathect them narcissistically; or they may represent human

Figure 18. Freud's cap, entrance of Sigmund Freud Museum Vienna, circa 1975. Photograph by Fred Prager.

love objects, in which case they are cathected with object libido."[102] She explains the process of identification with the lost object, and gives as an example a story about a lost cap. A young girl takes a hike through the Alps and forgets her cap. The girl is at first unfazed because she regards the cap as somewhat insignificant and without much value. But by nightfall her attitude has changed, and she cannot sleep for the misery of thinking of the lost cap "exposed and deserted in the dark solitude."[103] In her identification with the lost cap Anna Freud's own sense of abandonment is palpable. We might conjecture that this lost cap was Anna Freud's own or that it appeared in one of her dreams. Based on Anna Freud's recordings of her dreams, Elisabeth Young-Bruehl interprets this brief 1967 case study as Anna Freud's effort to work through her mourning over her father's death, noting that she took on her father's trait of using "disguised self-presentations" to illustrate theory.[104]

According to Marinelli's account, it would not have been long after Anna Freud lost her own cap—if we are to presume that the cap she writes about was indeed hers—that she gave her father's tweed cap to the Museum. Some time after the Museum's terrible loss, a package arrived containing the purloined headgear. A letter explained that the criminal had been tormented by "disquieting sensations . . . [that he was] getting all too close to Freud in a bodily sense."[105] In other words, his identification with Freud was so powerful that it was impinging upon his own autonomy. Naturally, he consulted a psychoanalyst, who advised him to return the stolen property. Having regained the lost object, the Museum set about to deter others from succumbing to the same urge and has now installed the cap in a vitrine, shielding it behind glass. Marinelli relates the cap's comings and goings to Freud's *fort/da* mythology. Upon Freud's exile the hat was banished from its home, then returned to its domicile by Anna Freud, then abducted by the thief, and consequently returned. The cap's trajectory fittingly reenacts Freud's absence and desired-for return. With this restitution narrative it fulfills its task as a reparative object and, like the collected objects in the London Freud Museum, can be interpreted as psychically and symbolically overcoming Freud's death. But the Vienna Museum can no longer claim ownership of the hat. When it was stolen, the insurance company compensated the Museum a modest sum, which the Museum has since been unable to repay. The cap therefore belongs to the insurance company,

Figure 19. Freud's couch, Freud Museum London, 2015. Photograph by Karolina Urbaniak.

saddling the Museum with the unhappy knowledge that it cannot guarantee the safety of its objects and that they, like us, are forever vulnerable to loss.

Just as during Engelman's momentous visit, to this day one cannot photograph with a flash in Freud's former home and offices at Berggasse 19. But at the London Freud Museum visitors cannot photograph at all. The Freud Museum, London prohibits any unofficial photography anywhere on its premises. The result of this is that all of the images of the London Museum are carefully constructed representations depicting the *official* image of contemporary psychoanalysis. The effort at repairing the image of psychoanalysis, which has lost some ground with modern psychologies, manifests itself in crafted images that depict the Freudian scene at Maresfield Gardens as unequivocally complete or replete. With dim lighting and velvet ropes putting distance between the carelessness of tourists and the cherished artifacts, ironically at the site that boasts Freud's authentic objects, visitors may feel closer to Freud's fetishes through representations—the replica of Freud's sphinx or postcards of his couch—that they can find in the gift shop. The souvenir, according to Susan Stewart, "is by definition always incomplete."[106] Its incompletion works on the metonymic level. One might say it is a kind of part-object. But is the representation of the couch a part of the whole scene of psychoanalysis in London or in Vienna? This question fails to recognize that the dual Freud Museums show there is no whole of psychoanalysis. The Freudian archive may be nothing but a collection of part-objects.

The two Freud Museums might together make a semblance of a whole, but independently they each signify that something is missing. The physical split in the contemporary Freudian archive calls for a mental reconstruction to perform the impossible task of repairing what war has torn asunder. The strongest desire that may emerge in the aftermath of devastation and ruin is to reconstruct in an attempt to restore the past. But, as Freud teaches us, the goal of psychoanalysis is to *construct*, which is not an end in itself but only the beginning of an ongoing engagement. In a lecture given at the Freud Museum, London, Derrida reminds us that the archive itself is a construction, and furthermore, turning to the Greek, is a commencement.[107] If Freud suffered from *mal d'archive*, as Derrida maintains, his illness conjoins his cancerous body with the fractured body of psychoanalysis. Derrida locates the archive fever that continues to afflict contemporary culture from the most trivial neuroses to the harshest historical tragedies "at the unstable limit between public and private, between the family, the society, and the State, between the family and an intimacy even more private than the family, between oneself and oneself."[108] Derrida's diagnosis of the archival malady coincides with the disunities that cancer spawns, in particular the discord between self and self. The disassembled Freudian archive, like the subjectivities-in-dissolution upon which this book has focused, shows how the work of integration is tethered to persistent discontinuities. Freud labored with his cancerous illness of the archive, the archive that is a body and a house, and specifically the Freudian houses, which lies between public and private, between family, society, and State. He spent the many years of this effort, first at Berggasse 19 and then at 20 Maresfield Gardens, troubled by, as Derrida describes the Freudian archive itself, the unstable and destabilizing divisions between himself and himself.

Conclusion
Last Objects

The goal of this conclusion is not to *complete* this book, to make it whole. Rather, I want to share some of the stories that I have collected over the course of its formation that have continued to resonate with me and with the ideas I have sought to convey. These stories indicate what has been a claim of *Freud's Jaw*: that our narratives, our bodies, and our lives consist of discontinuous parts that are loosely held together and that may not add up to a coherent, self-contained whole. We are held together by something that is not quite ourselves, or not only ourselves. We are held together by our desires to connect to and be connected with others, perhaps by the love we feel for and from objects. I found this to be true in my own experience with cancer, and in the many autopathographies I have encountered over the past number of years.

The last thing I did at the Sigmund Freud Museum in Vienna was to buy a snow globe containing a miniature bust of Freud. Given my ambivalent relationship to the ownership of things I did not expect to purchase anything at either of the gift shops in London or Vienna, but in the end I succumbed to the wish to carry home with me a metonymic part-object of my experience at Berggasse 19. My partner convinced me that the snow globe transcended run-of-the-mill kitsch, and it is true that I had seen nothing like it before. It was frankly hilarious. How would it occur to someone to design a snow globe of Freud? I am now working from memory as I try to recall the tiny Freud figurine that would collect artificial flakes until it looked like a lumpy mound. But just as Freud's grandson discovered the magic of loss and recovery in the *fort und da* scenario, the "lost" Freudian figure could be miraculously uncovered and recovered by a simple shake of the hand. There was something eminently satisfying in that, and I was finally able to realize that infantile pleasure of repetition compulsion in a way that I had not fully or consciously internalized before.

Packing up to head home to New York from London, my partner and I decided to put all our fragile items in our carry-on luggage. We were prepared to be stopped and searched by Heathrow's scrupulous security officers because our many hard drives, cameras, and other technical equipment always called for more examination than the cursory scan of the X-ray machine on the conveyer belt. We were, however, not prepared for the painstaking attention given to every single item of our well-packed luggage as each was assiduously unpacked and swabbed and put aside. At least half an hour later, my partner's backpack was put through the scanner one last time, and the attendant asked what was the bulky, padded item that was resting on the bottom. Out came the snow globe still in its box. It was removed and studied and then determined that it exceeded the liquid limit and could not be carried on board. We stood in stunned dismay, knowing that it would not behoove us to protest, but I couldn't help thinking, what, are you seriously worried that we're going to blow up this plane with a Freud snow globe?

I dwell upon this episode because it recapitulates some of the themes I have investigated throughout this book, namely, how one comes to terms with the loss of a loved object, and what the possibilities are for repairing the wounds produced through loss. Additionally, this incident hints that despite the apparent quiescence of contemporary psychoanalysis, its presence in material form might still arouse suspicion. Psychoanalysis historically and at present is often deemed suspect because it does not align with the prevailing social practices of the day. In the aftermath of my loss, I comforted myself that I would return to Vienna to restore my lost object some day, but I have since heard that not only does the gift shop not carry them, but they are no longer even manufactured.

One might say that a snow globe's essential feature is that it presents a worldview. In the conclusion of one of his last lectures, Freud admitted to psychoanalysis's incompletion as a reason it could not and did not need to produce a worldview: "Psycho-analysis, in my opinion, is incapable of creating a *Weltanschauung* of its own. It does not need one . . . it is too incomplete."[1] For Freud, psychoanalysis has no need and is not able to be preserved in a capsule; its very incompletion is what exempts and excludes it from presenting itself as having a complete worldview. It is this sense of completion that I have been arguing that cancer deprives the cancer patient of. A cancer diagnosis disturbs the kind of security that a snow globe grants, that of an intact vision of oneself and one's world. Marita Sturken confirms that a snow globe provides comfort because of the "expectation that it returns each time to its orginary state."[2] But *Freud's Jaw* has shown that some objects cannot be returned to, reconstructed, or repaired. In her personal and anthropological investigation of the modern cancer complex, S. Lochlann Jain is sensitive to the materiality of cancer and its aftermath, likening the storm of envelopes from the insurance company post cancer treatment to being trapped in a snow globe.[3] Jain has the sensation of being unable to escape the storm that continues to hail upon her, despite the calm between torrents. This form of repetition is not felt as comforting but as a threat of recurrence that dominates the psychic landscape of the person who has cancer.

As I discovered with my Freud snow globe, the material object is inseparable from the psychic object that attaches to it. That material object is seemingly lost to me, and yet my psyche finds a way of refuting loss, counterintuitively turning loss around and putting me into the position of the object. This is how loss can be described as melancholic, as the subject refuses to detach from the lost object, identifying with it, becoming it. The loss borne through the attrition of cancer seems to bring the subject closer to material objects, burying and entrapping her, as Jain describes, within the confines of materiality. Freud is overtaken by his prostheses; Lorde sees herself as nothing more than a gurney cart; and Sedgwick is haunted by IVs in her dreams.

Sedgwick recounts a story that highlights how loss is felt through an identification or misidentification with material objects. When Sedgwick was a child her mother explained to her if she were ever to get lost, she should ask someone to take her to the lost and found.[4] When the young Sedgwick did, in fact, get lost in a department store she asked to be taken to the lost and found, and the salesperson looked at her quizzically. The salesperson then told her that the lost and found was a drawer, which contained glasses and gloves that people had left behind. Sedgwick's experience of confusion and fear provokes the question that *Freud's Jaw* has raised in different terms: How is one to come to terms with loss when the conditions for recovery prove unavailable? Sedgwick's encounter with the lost and found drawer concludes with her sense of abandonment. She identifies with the forgotten glasses and gloves, as Anna Freud did with the lonely cap left in the Alps. Sedgwick's childhood feelings of loss are left unresolved.

Barthes, on the other hand, whose autobiographical excerpt begins this book, finds at least a temporary resolution concerning his drawer of lost love objects. Following an operation for his recurrent tuberculosis, Barthes kept a piece of his rib in a drawer along with treasured objects from his childhood. When he eventually resolves himself to what he calls the "death of objects," he is able to relinquish his part-object and fling it out the window. Barthes's curious tale seems to say that in order to accept one's mortality, one must surrender a part of oneself. But at the same time, by holding onto his childhood souvenirs, he verifies that the loved objects that we collect and sanctify are necessary to our continued existence, and perhaps even enable us not only to suffer our losses, but also to distribute parts of ourselves out into the world. Dual psychic movements—of retention and loosening—allow him to accept mortality while persisting in living. This is the psychic mode of coping with loss that Sedgwick learns to employ during her cancer experience, which she comes to understand as mastering the "art of loosing," that is, letting her life and her loves rest loosely upon her open hand.[5]

Freud enjoyed a German folktale that also dealt with mastering the "art of loosing," or in this case, literally losing. *Hans in Luck* (*Hans im Glück*) tells the story of young Hans who, having finished his apprenticeship, is sent home with a lump of gold as payment.[6] As he journeys home, he feels weighed down by the gold and barters it for a horse. He trots homeward, but the horse throws him, and he decides that a pork dinner would be more fulfilling than an unruly beast. He swaps the horse for a pig that also proves unmanageable, and the "diminishing exchanges" continue until he is left with only two stones that accidentally fall into a well. Freed from the burden of his possessions, Hans happily runs home. Freud's identification with this chronicle of material loss is evident when he exclaimed on receiving his emigration papers and facing exile without his treasured belongings: "Now I'm Hans im Glück!" But before this culminating event, the Grimm tale showed itself to be pertinent to psychoanalysis and Freud's conception of death. Freud wrote to Sandor Ferenczi: "Our therapeutic gain is a barter, as in the 'Hans im Glück' story. The last piece falls into the well only with death itself."[7]

Freud explains the practice of psychoanalysis as a process whereby the patient discards infantile complexes like "shed skin" or chips of necrotic bone.[8] Describing the psychoanalytic endeavor in these terms relates it to the process of degeneration Freud experienced with his cancer. But Hans experiences his accumulated losses as gains. This view of death aligns with the attitude Freud expressed in "On Transience." In his 1916 essay, the beauty of life is predicated upon its very ephemerality.[9] Yet the transience of life, and the foreknowledge that we all die, obstructs some people's enjoyment of it. Freud attributes this lack of appreciation to an inability to mourn. He adds that the traumatic destruction effected by world events such as war contributes to the refusal to mourn and to thus accept loss and separation from love objects.

If we follow Freud's logic, something has meaning *because* it dies. Illness and even war give life value because they threaten life with transience. Illness invests life with value, but we can only know it if we mourn its loss. When we mourn an object's transience, its significance is brought to keen attention. That an object's vulnerability to destruction is the very feature that renders it precious was made clear in January 2014, when thieves broke into Golders Green Crematorium in North London and destroyed the Greek urn where Freud's and his wife's ashes were stored.[10] Recalling the cap that was stolen from the Sigmund Freud Museum, for at least the second time since Freud's death, his objects have been the targets of theft. The urn had been a gift of Marie Bonaparte, among the countless antiquities she had given him during his lifetime, and can be discerned in Edmund Engelman's photographs standing behind Freud's desk. Dating from 300 BCE, the urn, like Freud's cap, is of inestimable value. It is unknown whether attempts at reconstructing the vase are underway, but some losses, as I have endeavored to show, are irreparable. After sixteen years of forestalling the intrusions of cancer, Freud endured a final intrusion even after his death.

Edward Said prefaces his memoir, *Out of Place*, by acknowledging that it was written in response to a fatal diagnosis of leukemia. He calls it "a record of an essentially lost or forgotten world" and a "subjective account" of his formative years.[11] Said confirms what I have argued, that cancer or the threat of death impels people to take account of their lives, and awakens a desire to make reparation. He writes: "I have set about reconstructing a remote time and experience."[12] I read the afflicted person's impulse to reconstruct as an effort to repair something that cannot be repaired; such reparation is always indirect, always mediated because the object that needs to be repaired cannot be recovered. This is why the reparative labors I have examined do not necessarily speak directly to illness or recovery. It is as if the debilitated person says, since I cannot do anything about the fact that I am dying, I must make something of my remaining life. Or, since I cannot do anything about the fact that I have cancer, I must do something else, I must write. Or, since I cannot do anything about the fact that my home and my ways of being are endangered, I must undertake some other kind of action, I can remember.

Said wants to make a bridge between his current moment and his past. Illness ignites this yearning to make a connection between parts of himself that are divided. He recalls returning to the houses where he grew up in West Jerusalem forty-five years after his and his family's exile, and not being able to enter the buildings, for they all had new occupants.[13] Said's house in former Palestine and Freud's house in Vienna stand as testaments to exile, as witnesses to trauma. If the possessions inside a house—the knick-knacks, caps, and drawers of souvenirs—are like parts of a body, the house is like the body itself. When new occupants or possessions fill these spaces, they feel like a foreign intrusion, as cancer does to the body, and death to life. At the end of his memoir, Said talks about sleep as death. He understands the kinship between the bardo of sleep and the bardo of dying. For him, the night and sleep bring a loss that the morning repairs as he wakes, "resuming what [he] might have lost completely a few hours earlier."[14] The snow globe presents a world akin to the one Said imagines of sleep. Esther Leslie points out that the German name given to snow globes is *Traumkugel*, which translates as dream bullets.[15] The *Traumkugel* offers dreams that wound. And this is perhaps why Said spurns sleep, even prior to the malady that often induces the ill to fear it.

When I was writing this book, my dentist found what he thought was a suspicious white lesion on the underside of my tongue. It turned out not to be cancer, which leaves me wondering if, rather, it marks my over identification with Freud, whose cancerous lesions were on the right side of his mouth as are my benign patches. But perhaps I should say I also *disidentify* with Freud, with psychoanalysis, and with my own cancer, which is in remission. After all, Freud's name is often associated with a conservatism that goes against the grain of my interests as a queer woman of color. Diagnosed with cancer at the same age that Audre Lorde was when her malignant tumor was discovered, and like her having had my right breast removed, at times I have felt, as she did, that I was never meant to survive. But I am reminded that Lorde addresses the problem of survival in the plural, intoning that *we* were never meant to survive. Her inclusive mode of address hails me, and it calls me to deploy disidentification in the manner José Esteban Muñoz has proposed, as a strategy of survival and communal mourning. Muñoz recognizes that a disidentifying subject will not simply give up her lost object but "works to hold on to this object and invest it with new life."[16] It may be through disidentification that those objects that were never meant to survive might be reanimated. Those identities that Said has called "besieged" may yet be reconstructed.[17] Disidentification, Muñoz tells us, offers "a mechanism that helps us (re)construct identity and take our dead with us to the various battles we must wage in their names—and in our names."[18]

Muñoz urges transporting fallen loved ones to accompany us toward futurity. Christina Crosby's dilemma is how to reckon with the future when our lost objects include cherished body parts and once familiar selves. Paralyzed from the waist down in an accident a month after her fiftieth birthday, Crosby narrates how her former body has for all intents and purposes passed away. She lives in a different kind of exile, unhoused from her broken body, deprived of the once-dependable comforts and strengths that made her body a home.[19] Referencing the house as the container of our bodies, possessions, ambitions, fears and dreams, a structure that protects and is at risk of damage, Rosi Braidotti remarks that "we build our house on the crack."[20] I presume that Braidotti means that we are situated on the crack between life and death, and may as well accept its instability and uncertainty. If Crosby's house was once secure, surely now it rests upon a fault line that continually puts her in peril. She describes the memories of her preaccident body as transfixed in golden amber and ponders with trepidation whether she will seal herself inside the resin's protective yet dangerous preservation.[21] This amber with its "small, ancient bit of life suspended inside" resembles a snow globe, whose flakes are likewise caught outside the chronology of time, courting the future but forever returning to the quietude of the past.[22]

Crosby refuses psychoanalyst Otto Kernberg's assertion, which echoes Freud's views on transience, that one can understand what one has secured only after its loss, for she maintains that she well knew what she had loved and lost. But Kernberg's words ring true in his judgment of mourning as creative. Mourning can be a creative form of care, and the work of mourning a labor of care. Saidiya Hartman recognizes such care as the basis of relation. Echoing Lorde's resonant refrain, she observes that although the fugitive black woman who toils in the cracks, or on the crack, was never meant to, nonetheless she persists in surviving. The care she delivers, "coerced and freely given, is the black heart of our social poesis, of making and relation."[23] This black heart, I imagine, pulses in the bardo of dying, making possible the prospect of productive relation.

The figures that haunt the bardo of dying have taught me that the destruction of grief and the creation of mourning are imbricated, that dis-identification and identification are interdependent, and that paradoxically and painfully some losses might be defiantly claimed as gains. While the snow globe's illusion of idyllic wholeness is seductive, none of us can escape disturbance and disrepair. Reconciling ourselves to this contradiction might entail a collaborative project of survival in which we as incomplete and fragile beings equip ourselves to provisionally repair the irreparable and contend with an ever-uncertain future.

ACKNOWLEDGMENTS

This book evolved, quite frankly, out of a breast cancer diagnosis that came during my second year of pursuing my doctorate. It was a life-altering event that followed a different set of life-altering events, one in which I left a job where I had just been approved for tenure, and another, several years later, when I returned to school, not as a professor but as a student. In the meantime, I continued to make films and art, and I trained as a psychoanalyst for three years. I found a deep affinity between making art and psychoanalytic practice. What has enraptured me about both fields of inquiry is the striving toward coherence of fragmentary pieces of our lives and worlds. These seemingly silent part-objects wish to speak themselves, ourselves, into sustained existence. Audre Lorde made the definitive statement about this transformation of silence into language as a means of survival. *Freud's Jaw* is probably the culmination of speaking out my fears and desires, of transforming silence into a language that loosely holds me together. And the words that collect me are themselves suspended and held together through a network of relations to which I remain indebted.

Ann Pellegrini encouraged me to send my manuscript to Richard Morrison with the conviction that he would be receptive. I may never have ventured into the intimidating realm of academic publishing had it not been for her support. Ann's acumen has been invaluable, and I continue to benefit from her wisdom and generosity. I could not have asked for a more careful and incisive intellectual interlocutor than Marita Sturken, and I am grateful for her rigor and ongoing support. Conversations with Ben Kafka were extremely generative from this project's inception and have contributed vitally to its fruition. This book is profoundly marked by his influence. I was also privileged to receive insightful commentary from Patricia Clough, Gayle Salamon, Emily Apter, Mara Mills, and Lauren Berlant. I also thank Marquard Smith for his generous reading and for listening to my thoughts and anxieties so attentively.

Many scholars have contributed to my education, and directly or indirectly to this book. Thank you to Lisa Gitelman, Martin Scherzinger,

Rayna Rapp, Jonathan Kahana, Orit Halpern, Arjun Appadurai, Alexander Galloway, Arvind Rajagopal, Nicholas Mirzoeff, Erica Robles-Anderson, Joanne Morra, Katie Gentile, Dina Georgis, Sara Matthews, and James Penney. Thank you to the small but actively engaged audience at Society for Cinema and Media Studies where I presented a fragment of my chapter on Eve Sedgwick, and special thanks to Judith Rodenbeck for moderating, Marie Shurkus for chairing the panel with me, and Jeannine Tang for joining us in discussion.

Funding from the Jacob K. Javits Foundation greatly facilitated this project. Research assistance from The New School has been very helpful in its development. I thank Dean Mary Watson for approving the course release that enabled me to devote the attention required to complete it. My colleagues in the School of Media Studies at The New School have provided a truly interdisciplinary environment, as Barthes defines it, where I can fashion what I hope to be "a new object that belongs to no one." I especially thank former Dean Anne Balsamo, current Dean Carol Wilder, friend, colleague, and now Dean Melissa Friedling, Eugene Thacker, Michelle Materre, Shannon Mattern, and Barry Salman. Thank you also to my research assistants, Livia Sá Dos Santos and Elvira Blanco.

A sympathetic audience at Vermont College of Fine Arts, where for over a decade I found more of an intellectual and creative home than I ever expected to, encouraged the initial murmurings of what became *Freud's Jaw*. I have learned much from my VCFA comrades, including (but certainly not limited to!) the late Janet Kaplan, David Deitcher, Moyra Davey, Sharon Hayes, Ashley Hunt, Michael Minelli, Marie Shurkus, Cauleen Smith, and Faith Wilding. Thank you to Danielle Dahline for easing my transition to the intensity of the residency environment following my treatment.

Friends who have helped me knowingly or unknowingly in ways large and small, I thank you: Jenny Bass, Matthew Buckingham, Cynthia Chris, Una Chung, Julie Felner, Jacob Gaboury, Andrea Geyer, Jackie Goss, Nguyen Tan Hoang, Toby Lee, Lize Mogel, Cara O'Connor, Polly Thistlethwaite, Carlin Wing, Shari Wolk, Kristine Woods, Hannah Zeavin, and, as Eve Kosofsky Sedgewick writes, "and, and, and the big spreading field of intimacy where love just grows wild."

Many thanks to the archives and archivists who made this project possible and so enthralling: Bryony Davies, assistant curator at the Freud Museum, London; Peter Nömaier, chairman of the board, and Simone Faxa, archivist, at the Sigmund Freud Museum, Vienna; Margaret McAleer, senior archives specialist in the Manuscript Division, Library of Congress,

Washington, D.C.; Holly A. Smith, college archivist in the Women's Research & Resource Center, Spelman College, Atlanta; and Saskia Scheffer, the Lesbian Herstory Archives, Brooklyn.

I am very grateful to Ralph Engelman for sharing his stories about his father and for helping me connect with his brother. Thank you to Thomas Engelman for granting me permission to reprint the inimitable photographs of Edmund Engelman. I thank David Kazanjian for graciously allowing me access to his family archives and for giving his permission to reprint his grandfather's remarkable sketch. This book has afforded me the distinct pleasure of meeting and spending time with Hal Sedgwick. I am moved by his honoring of Eve Kosofsky Sedgwick's legacy, and thank him for his tremendous generosity. Thank you also to Sarah McCarry for helping me with Eve's archive.

I count myself as incredibly fortunate to have had the opportunity to work with Fordham University Press and am grateful for the critical response of two anonymous reviewers that spurred my revisions. I cannot thank Richard Morrison enough for believing in this project. I greatly appreciate his guidance and support, and the assistance of the Fordham team, including Will Cerbone, Eric Newman, Ann-Christine Racette, Katie Sweeney, and John Garza. Much appreciation to Gregory McNamee for improving the readability of this text.

I am thankful for my family, especially my sister Ju-Pong, who was the first to teach me to value words and art and not to taken any of it for granted. Finally, I dedicate this book to H. Lan Thao Lam, without whom it and I would never have survived, at least not in desirable form. These words can only gesture at my unceasing love and gratitude to them for sharing and inspiring our collaborative project of living together.

Portions of Chapters 2 and 4 were developed in earlier articles, "Something and Nothing: On the Psychopolitics of Breasts and Breastlessness," *Studies in Gender and Sexuality* 17, no. 1 (2016), and "Lost Objects: Berggasse 19 and Absence in the Space of Psychoanalysis," *The Freudian Legacy Today*, ed. Dina Georgis, Sara Matthews, and James Penney, The Canadian Network for Psychoanalysis and Culture https://cnpcrcpc.com/cnpc-1-the-freudian-legacy-today-2015.

Poem to the Survival of Roaches". Copyright © 1974 by Audre Lorde, "Blackstudies" from *The Collected Poems of Audre Lorde*. Copyright © 1997 by The Audre Lorde Estate. Used by permission of W. W. Norton & Company, Inc. Excerpts from *A Burst of Light: Essays* Ithaca, N.Y.: Firebrand Books, 1988), Sister Outsider: Essays and Speeches (Berkeley: Crossing Press, 2007), *The Cancer Journals* (Argyle, N.Y.: Spinsters, Ink, 1980), and *Zami: A New Spelling of My Name* (New York: Crossing Press, 1982) used herewith by permission of the Charlotte Sheedy Literary Agency.

Lines from "A Woman Dead in Her Forties." Copyright © 2002 by Adrienne Rich. Copyright © 1978 by W. W. Norton & Company, Inc., from *The Fact of a Doorframe: Selected Poems 1950–2001* by Adrienne Rich. Used by permission of W. W. Norton & Company, Inc.

Notes

INTRODUCTION

1. Roland Barthes, *Roland Barthes* (New York: Hill and Wang, 2010), 61.
2. Ibid., 184. "A life: studies, diseases, appointments."
3. Ibid., 61.
4. I thank Ann Pellegrini for this precise articulation.
5. Audre Lorde, *The Marvelous Arithmetics of Distance: Poems 1987–1992* (New York: Norton, 1993), 52. African American women are all too familiar with cancer death, having "the highest rate of breast cancer mortality in the US, the highest incidence and mortality due to colorectal cancer, and are twice as likely to die from cervical cancer than Caucasian women." Black Women's Health Study, Office of Minority Health & Health Disparities Research (https://goo.gl/ojjSog).
6. David L. Eng and Shinhee Han, "A Dialogue on Racial Melancholia," in *Loss: The Politics of Mourning*, ed. David L. Eng and David Kazanjian (Berkeley: University of California Press, 2003), 365.
7. Judith Butler, *The Psychic Life of Power: Theories in Subjection* (Stanford: Stanford University Press, 1997); Ben Kafka, *The Demon of Writing: Powers and Failures of Paperwork* (New York: Zone Books, 2012).
8. Ernest Jones, *The Life and Work of Sigmund Freud, Volume Three: The Last Phase 1919–1939* (London: Hogarth Press, 1957), 260; Arthur W. Frank, *The Wounded Storyteller: Body, Illness, and Ethics* (Chicago: University of Chicago Press, 1995), 8.
9. Frank, *The Wounded Storyteller*, 8.
10. Eric Cazdyn, *The Already Dead: The New Time of Politics, Culture, and Illness* (Durham, N.C.: Duke University Press, 2012).
11. Audre Lorde, *A Burst of Light: Essays* (Ithaca, N.Y.: Firebrand Books, 1988), 112.
12. Mavis Himes, "Cancer and the Body: Reflections from a Lacanian Perspective," *European Journal of Psychotherapy, Counselling and Health* 7, no. 4 (December 2005): 239.
13. Avital Ronell, *The ÜberReader: Selected Works of Avital Ronell*, ed. Diane Davis (Urbana: University of Illinois Press, 2008), 146.

14. Siddhartha Mukherjee, *The Emperor of All Maladies: A Biography of Cancer* (New York: Scribner, 2010).

15. Susan Sontag, *Illness as Metaphor* (New York: Farrar, Straus & Giroux, 1988); S. Lochlann Jain, *Malignant: How Cancer Becomes Us* (Berkeley: University of California Press, 2013).

16. Sherwin Nuland, *How We Die: Reflections on Life's Final Chapter* (New York: Vintage Books, 1995), 210–212.

17. Sigmund Freud, *Civilization and Its Discontents*, ed. James Strachey (New York: Norton, 1961), 11–12.

18. Ibid.

19. Ibid., 13.

20. Jean Laplanche and J. B. Pontalis, *The Language of Psycho-Analysis*, trans. Donald Nicholson-Smith (New York: Norton, 1973), 152.

21. Jean-Luc Nancy, *Corpus* (New York: Fordham University Press, 2008), 164.

22. Ibid., 168–169.

23. Felix Deutsch, "Reflections on the 10th Anniversary of Freud's Death," ca 1949, 7, Box 116 Interviews+Recollections, Folder 17, Freud Papers, Library of Congress; Sharon Romm, *The Unwelcome Intruder: Freud's Struggle with Cancer* (New York: Praeger, 1983).

24. Sigmund Freud, "The 'Uncanny,'" in *The Standard Edition of the Complete Psychological Works of Sigmund Freud (SE)*, ed. James Strachey (London: Hogarth Press and the Institute of Psycho-analysis, 1919), 17:248.

25. Cancer's uncanny intrusion mirrors Freud's unconscious conflict with his own Jewish identity. If to be Jewish in twentieth-century Europe was to be an already split subject, cancer's fragmenting effect must have amplified this divided psychic condition. Freud most explicitly wrestles with his Jewish identity in Sigmund Freud, *Moses and Monotheism*, trans. Katherine Jones (Letchworth: Hogarth Press and the Institute of Psycho-Analysis, 1939). Also see Daniel Boyarin, "Freud's Baby, Fliess's Maybe; Or, Male Hysteria, Homophobia, and the Invention of the Jewish Man," in *Unheroic Conduct: The Rise of Heterosexuality and the Invention of the Jewish Man* (Berkeley: University of California Press, 1997), 189–220; Jacques Derrida, *Archive Fever: A Freudian Impression* (Chicago: University of Chicago Press, 1996); Jay Geller, *On Freud's Jewish Body: Mitigating Circumcisions* (New York: Fordham University Press, 2007); Sander L. Gilman, *Freud, Race, and Gender* (Princeton: Princeton University Press, 1993); Ann Pellegrini, *Performance Anxieties: Staging Psychoanalysis, Staging Race* (New York: Routledge, 1997); Eliza Slavet, *Racial Fever: Freud and the Jewish Question* (New York: Fordham University Press, 2009); Yosef Hayim Yerushalmi, *Freud's Moses: Judaism Terminable and Interminable* (New Haven: Yale University Press, 1991).

26. Jacques-Alain Miller, "Teachings of the Case Presentation," in *Returning to Freud: Clinical Psychoanalysis in the School of Lacan*, ed. Stuart Schneiderman (New Haven: Yale University Press, 1980), 49.

27. Julia Kristeva, *Powers of Horror: An Essay on Abjection* (New York: Columbia University Press, 1982), 11.

28. Ernst Simmel, *Anti-Semitism, A Social Disease* (New York: International Universities Press, 1946), 34.

29. Erich Fromm, *The Heart of Man: Its Genius for Good and Evil* (New York: Harper & Row, Publishers, 1964); Michael Balint, *The Basic Fault: Therapeutic Aspects of Regression* (London: Tavistock Publications, 1968).

30. Deutsch, "Reflections on the 10th Anniversary of Freud's Death," 9.

31. Paul Schilder, "On Rotting," *Psychoanalytic Review* 29 (1942): 49.

32. Melanie Klein, "A Contribution to the Psychogenesis of Manic-Depressive States," *International Journal of Psychoanalysis* 16 (1935): 157.

33. Ibid., 156.

34. Joyce Wadler, "My Breast: One Woman's Cancer Story," *New York Magazine*, accessed April 25, 2014, https://goo.gl/QiW3DP.

35. Jain, *Malignant*, 19.

36. Rebecca Skloot, *The Immortal Life of Henrietta Lacks* (New York: Broadway Books, 2011).

37. Mukherjee, *The Emperor of All Maladies*.

38. Sigmund Freud, "Beyond the Pleasure Principle," in *SE*, 18:50.

39. Ibid., 45.

40. Razinsky argues that the death drive and psychoanalysis as a whole actively denies death. See Liran Razinsky, *Freud, Psychoanalysis and Death* (Cambridge: Cambridge University Press, 2013).

41. See Jerry Adler, "Freud Is (Not) Dead," *Newsweek*, March 27, 2006; "Is Freud Dead?" *Time Magazine*, November 29, 1993; Elisabeth Roudinesco, "Freud Is Dead in America," in *Why Psychoanalysis?* (New York: Columbia University Press, 2001); Jamieson Webster, *The Life and Death of Psychoanalysis: On Unconscious Desire and Its Sublimation* (London: Karnac Books, 2011).

42. For more on this, see Edward Timms and Naomi Segal, eds., *Freud in Exile: Psychoanalysis and Its Vicissitudes* (New Haven: Yale University Press, 1988). For a recent treatment of the impact of the Holocaust on psychoanalysis see Emily A. Kuriloff, *Contemporary Psychoanalysis and the Legacy of the Third Reich: History, Memory, Tradition* (New York: Routledge, 2014). For psychoanalytic engagements of trauma, see Cathy Caruth, *Unclaimed Experience: Trauma, Narrative, and History* (Baltimore: John Hopkins University Press, 1996), and Shoshana Felman and Dori Laub, *Testimony: Crises of Witnessing in Literature, Psychoanalysis, and History* (New York: Routledge, 1991).

43. H.D., *Tribute to Freud* (New York: New Directions, 1974), 141.

44. Malcolm's assessment follows Freud's in "Analysis Terminable and Interminable," in *SE*, 23:248.

45. Janet Malcolm, *Psychoanalysis: The Impossible Profession* (New York: Vintage Books, 1982), 102.

46. Freud, "Beyond the Pleasure Principle," 39.

47. Max Schur, *Freud: Living and Dying* (New York: International Universities Press, 1972), 529.

48. Lorde, *A Burst of Light*, 132.

49. Audre Lorde, *The Cancer Journals* (Argyle, N.Y.: Spinsters, Ink, 1980), 13.

50. Lisa Diedrich, *Treatments: Language, Politics, and the Culture of Illness* (Minneapolis: University of Minnesota Press, 2007), 76.

51. Much has been made of James Strachey's translation of both the psychical *Trieb* and the biological *Instinkt* as "instinct." See Jean Laplanche and J. B. Pontalis, *The Language of Psycho-Analysis* (New York: Norton, 1973), and Mark Solms, "Controversies in Freud Translation," *Psychoanalysis and History* 1 (1999): 28–43. Further, a new translation of the first edition of *Three Essays* (1905) by Philippe Van Haute, Ulrike Kistner, and Herman Westerink argues that even the "sexual" aspect of "sexual instinct" may not be satisfactorily translated. I accept the translation of the *Standard Edition* for the sake of convention. Since nowhere in *Freud's Jaw* do I refer to instinct in the purely biological, species-specific sense, I use "instinct" and "drive" interchangeably.

52. Sigmund Freud, "Three Essays on the Theory of Sexuality," in *SE*, 7:135–136.

53. Sigmund Freud, "Instincts and Their Vicissitudes," in *SE*, 14:121–122.

54. Ibid., 122.

55. Unconscious phantasy is another concept that could take considerable time and space to unpack. Suffice it to say that for Klein it is "the mental representation of those somatic events in the body which comprise the instincts, and are physical sensations interpreted as relationships with objects that cause those sensations," such that objects can be understood to be exterior and interior to the self. R. D. Hinshelwood, *A Dictionary of Kleinian Thought*, 2nd ed. (Northvale, N.J.: Jason Aronson, 1991), 32.

56. Ibid., 378.

57. Ibid., 237.

58. Ibid.

59. Nancy, *Corpus*, 170; Eve Kosofsky Sedgwick, "Off My Chest. Advanced Degree: School Yourself in Resilience to Beat Depression," *MAMM* (September 2000), 24.

60. W. R. Bion, "Differentiation of the Psychotic from the Non-Psychotic Personalities," *The International Journal of Psychoanalysis* 38 (1957): 266–275.

61. Romm, *The Unwelcome Intruder*, 90.

62. Eve Kosofsky Sedgwick, *Tendencies* (Durham, N.C.: Duke University Press, 1993), 263.

63. Nancy, *Corpus*, 162.

64. Laplanche and Pontalis, *The Language of Psycho-Analysis*, 29–31.

65. Sigmund Freud, "Mourning and Melancholia," in *SE*, 14:237–258.

66. Freud, "Three Essays on the Theory of Sexuality," 222.

67. David L. Eng and David Kazanjian, eds., *Loss: The Politics of Mourning* (Berkeley: University of California Press, 2003), 2.

68. Ibid., 5.

69. Sigmund Freud, "Fetishism," in *SE*, 21:152.

70. Contra Freud, I do not believe that only men can be fetishists. But even Freud unsurprisingly contradicted his 1927 claim in his previously unpublished paper, "On the Genesis of Fetishism," which was recorded in the minutes of the Vienna Psychoanalytic Society, February 24, 1909. See Louis Rose, "Freud and Fetishism: Previously Unpublished Minutes of the Vienna Psychoanalytic Society," *Psychoanalytic Quarterly* 57 (1988): 147–166. For scholars who have discussed female fetishism, see Emily S. Apter, *Feminizing the Fetish: Psychoanalysis and Narrative Obsession in Turn-of-the-Century France* (Ithaca, N.Y.: Cornell University Press, 1991); Elizabeth Grosz, "Lesbian Fetishism?" in *Fetishism as Cultural Discourse*, ed. William Pietz and Emily Apter (Ithaca, N.Y.: Cornell University Press, 1993); Ann Pellegrini, *Performance Anxieties: Staging Psychoanalysis, Staging Race* (New York: Routledge, 1997); Naomi Schor, "Female Fetishism: The Case of George Sand," *Poetics Today* 6, nos. 1–2 (1985): 301–310.

71. Bill Brown, "Object Relations in an Expanded Field," *Differences: A Journal of Feminist Cultural Studies* 17, no. 3 (2006): 88–106.

72. Geoff Gilbert, *Before Modernism Was: Modern History and the Constituency of Writing* (New York: Palgrave Macmillan, 2004), 137.

73. Ibid.

74. Donald Woods Winnicott, *Playing and Reality* (Harmondsworth: Penguin Books, 1982).

75. Diana Fuss, *The Sense of an Interior: Four Writers and the Rooms That Shaped Them* (New York: Routledge, 2004), 6.

76. Lynn Gamwell, "A Collector Analyses Collecting: Sigmund Freud on the Passion to Possess," in *Excavations and Their Objects: Freud's Collection of Antiquity*, ed. Stephen Barker (Albany: State University of New York Press, 1996), 30 n. 15.

77. Richard A. Grusin, *The Nonhuman Turn* (Minneapolis: University of Minnesota Press, 2015).

78. Influential texts in this arena include Arjun Appadurai, *The Social Life of Things: Commodities in Cultural Perspective* (Cambridge: Cambridge University Press, 1986); Karen Barad, *Meeting the Universe Halfway: Quantum Physics and the Entanglement of Matter and Meaning* (Durham, N.C.: Duke University Press, 2007); Jane Bennett, *Vibrant Matter: A Political Ecology of Things* (Durham, N.C.: Duke University Press, 2010); Rosi Braidotti, *The Posthuman* (Cambridge: Polity Press, 2015); Donna J. Haraway, *Simians, Cyborgs, and Women: The Reinvention of Nature* (New York: Routledge, 1991); Bruno Latour, *We Have Never Been Modern* (Cambridge, Mass.: Harvard University Press, 1993); Steven Shaviro, *The Universe of Things: On Speculative Realism* (Minneapolis: University of Minnesota Press, 2014). Useful anthologies that contain overviews of sectors of this discursive terrain include: Levi R. Bryant, Nick Srnicek, and Graham Harman, eds., *The Speculative Turn: Continental Materialism and Realism* (Melbourne: re.press, 2011); Fiona Candlin and Raiford Guins, eds., *The Object Reader* (New York: Routledge, 2009); Diana Coole and Samantha Frost, *New Materialisms: Ontology, Agency, and Politics* (Durham, N.C.: Duke University Press, 2010); Melissa Gregg and Gregory J. Seigworth, eds., *The Affect Theory Reader* (Durham, N.C.: Duke University Press, 2010); Grusin, *The Nonhuman Turn*; Marquard Smith and Joanne Morra, *The Prosthetic Impulse: From a Posthuman Present to a Biocultural Future* (Cambridge, Mass.: MIT Press, 2006).

79. Graham Harman, *Tool-Being: Heidegger and the Metaphysics of Objects* (Chicago: Open Court, 2002).

80. Shaviro, *The Universe of Things*, 50.

81. Sara Ahmed, *Queer Phenomenology: Orientations, Objects, Others* (Durham, N.C.: Duke University Press, 2006).

82. Bennett, *Vibrant Matter*, ix.

83. Freud, "Mourning and Melancholia."

84. Adam Phillips, *Darwin's Worms* (London: Faber and Faber, 1999).

85. Haraway, *Simians, Cyborgs, and Women*, 174.

86. Ibid., 175.

87. Rosi Braidotti, "Posthuman, All Too Human: Towards a New Process Ontology," *Theory, Culture & Society* 23, no. 7–8 (2006): 201. The Onco-Mouse™ is a patented transgenic techno-body manufactured to be predisposed to breast cancer.

88. Braidotti, *The Posthuman*, 102.

89. Barbara Johnson, *Persons and Things* (Cambridge, Mass.: Harvard University Press, 2008), 2. Ben Kafka repeats this question in *The Demon of Writing*, 14.

90. Johnson, *Persons and Things*, 229.

91. Eve Kosofsky Sedgwick, *Epistemology of the Closet* (Berkeley: University of California Press, 1990), 23.

92. Eve Kosofsky Sedgwick, "Melanie Klein and the Difference Affect Makes," *South Atlantic Quarterly* 106, no. 3 (2007): 625–42; Eve Kosofsky Sedgwick, *The Weather in Proust*, ed. Jonathan Goldberg (Durham, N.C.: Duke University Press, 2011).

93. Sedgwick confirms Tomkins's conviction that any affect may have any object. Eve Kosofsky Sedgwick and Adam Frank, *Shame and Its Sisters: A Silvan Tomkins Reader* (Durham, N.C.: Duke University Press, 1995), 7.

94. Ibid., 12–13.

95. Elizabeth A. Wilson, *Affect and Artificial Intelligence* (Seattle: University of Washington Press, 2010), 25.

96. Sedgwick and Frank, *Shame and Its Sisters*, 179, 219.

97. Ibid., 212.

98. "Pathography," *Oxford English Dictionary Online* (Oxford: Oxford University Press, 2005).

99. Anne Hunsaker Hawkins, *Reconstructing Illness: Studies in Pathography* (West Lafayette, Ind.: Purdue University Press, 1999), 1.

100. G. Thomas Couser, *Recovering Bodies: Illness, Disability, and Life-Writing* (Madison: University of Wisconsin Press, 1997), 37.

101. Jacques Derrida, *The Post Card: From Socrates to Freud and Beyond* (Chicago: University of Chicago Press, 1987), 273.

102. Mel Y. Chen, *Animacies: Biopolitics, Racial Mattering, and Queer Affect* (Durham, N.C.: Duke University Press, 2012).

103. Ibid., 199.

104. Ibid., 217–218.

105. Ibid., 204.

106. Sigmund Freud, "Findings, Ideas, Problems," in *SE*, 23:300.

107. Chen, *Animacies*, 210.

108. Ibid., 236.

109. Eve Kosofsky Sedgwick, "Off My Chest. I Got It Good . . . and That Ain't Bad," *MAMM* (1998), 40.

110. Mary K. DeShazer, *Mammographies* (Ann Arbor: University of Michigan Press, 2013), 20.

111. Ibid., 150.

112. Eli Clare, *Exile and Pride: Disability, Queerness, and Liberation* (Durham, N.C.: Duke University Press, 2015), xix.

113. Ibid.

114. Chen, *Animacies*, 18–19; Chen is referring to Sharon Snyder and David Mitchell's discussion of compulsory feral-ization, a term borrowed

from Bruce Henderson, in *Cultural Locations of Disability* (Chicago: University of Chicago Press, 2006), 185–195.

115. Freud, *Civilization and Its Discontents*, 1961, 39.

116. Uwe Henrik Peters, *Anna Freud: A Life Dedicated to Children* (New York: Schocken Books, 1985), 56.

117. Lorde, *The Cancer Journals*, 55–77.

118. Audre Lorde, *Sister Outsider: Essays and Speeches* (Berkeley, Calif.: Crossing Press, 2007), 147.

119. Sedgwick, *Tendencies*, 257.

120. Sigmund Freud, "Constructions in Analysis," in *SE*, 23:259–260.

121. I thank an anonymous reviewer for this insight.

122. Lauren Berlant, *Cruel Optimism* (Durham, N.C.: Duke University Press, 2011), 9. See also Johanna Hedva, "Sick Woman Theory," *Mask Magazine*, January 2016, https://goo.gl/PJVC5E.

1. PROSTHETIC OBJECTS: ON SIGMUND FREUD'S AMBIVALENT ATTACHMENTS

1. I am indebted to Lauren Berlant's discussion of genre as it pertains to the persistent adjustments required to maintain oneself in life. See Lauren Berlant, *Cruel Optimism* (Durham, N.C.: Duke University Press, 2011).

2. Ernst L. Freud, *The Letters of Sigmund Freud and Arnold Zweig* (New York: Harcourt Brace Jovanovich, 1970), 178.

3. David Wills, *Dorsality: Thinking Back through Technology and Politics* (Minneapolis: University of Minnesota Press, 2008).

4. Ibid., 7.

5. Ibid.

6. Rosi Braidotti, *The Posthuman* (Cambridge: Polity Press, 2015), 113, 109.

7. Jacques Derrida, *Dissemination*, trans. Barbara Johnson (Chicago: University of Chicago Press, 1981), 70.

8. Jacques Derrida, *The Post Card: From Socrates to Freud and Beyond* (Chicago: University of Chicago Press, 1987), 273.

9. Sharon Romm, *The Unwelcome Intruder: Freud's Struggle with Cancer* (New York: Praeger, 1983), 38.

10. J. C. Davenport, "The Prosthetic Care of Sigmund Freud," *Dental History*, March 7, 1992, 205.

11. Ibid., 206; John C. Davenport, "Sigmund Freud's Illness—The Ultimate Approach to Head and Neck Cancer?" *Facial Plastic Surgery* 9, no. 2 (April 1993): 130.

12. Ernest Jones, "Letter to Max Schur," February 21, 1956, Box 2 Correspondence Jones, Ernest and Katherine 1953–61, Max Schur Papers, Library of Congress.

13. Ernest Jones, *The Life and Work of Sigmund Freud, Volume Three: The Last Phase 1919–1939* (London: Hogarth Press, 1957), 100.

14. Christina Crosby, *A Body, Undone: Living On After Great Pain* (New York: New York University Press, 2016), 189.

15. Hans Pichler and Anna Freud, "Sigmund Freud Illness Record," 1923–1939, 1927, 11, Box 159 Folder 2 Miscellany Freud Family, Anna Freud Papers, Library of Congress.

16. Jones, *The Life and Work of Sigmund Freud, Volume Three*, 499.

17. Ibid., 500.

18. Jacques Lacan, "The Mirror Stage as Formative of the Function of the I as Revealed in Psychoanalytic Experience," in *Écrits*, trans. Alan Sheridan (New York: Norton, 1977).

19. Melanie Klein, "Notes on Some Schizoid Mechanisms," *International Journal of Psycho-Analysis* 27 (1946): 99–110.

20. Vivian Carol Sobchack, *Carnal Thoughts: Embodiment and Moving Image Culture* (Berkeley: University of California Press, 2004); David Wills, *Prosthesis* (Stanford: Stanford University Press, 1995).

21. "The Double Amputee Who Designs Better Limbs," interview by Terry Gross, NPR, August 10, 2011, http://www.npr.org.

22. Donald Woods Winnicott, "Transitional Objects and Transitional Phenomena—A Study of the First Not-Me Possession," *International Journal of Psycho-Analysis* 34 (1953): 89–97.

23. Romm, *The Unwelcome Intruder*, 62.

24. Davenport, "The Prosthetic Care of Sigmund Freud," 206.

25. Pichler and Freud, "Sigmund Freud Illness Record," 1927, 13–14.

26. Davenport, "The Prosthetic Care of Sigmund Freud," 207.

27. Romm, *The Unwelcome Intruder*, 23.

28. John Tully, "A Victorian Ecological Disaster: Imperialism, the Telegraph, and Gutta-Percha," *Journal of World History* 20, no. 4 (2009): 559–579.

29. Ibid., 571–572.

30. Daniel R. Headrick, "Gutta-Percha: A Case of Resource Depletion and International Rivalry," *IEEE Technology and Society Magazine*, December 1987, 12–16.

31. John M. Picker, "Atlantic Cable," *Victorian Review* 34, no. 1 (Spring 2008): 34–38.

32. Sigmund Freud, "Civilization and Its Discontents," in *SE*, 21:120.

33. Pichler and Freud, "Sigmund Freud Illness Record," 1935, 10–11.

34. Ibid., 1925, 36.

35. Ibid., 1925, 45.

36. Ibid., 1926, 53.

37. Ibid., 1931, 34.

38. S. H. Foulkes, Interviews + Recollections: Foulkes, S. H., interview by K. R. Eissler, September 7, 1969, 4, Box 116 Interviews+Recollections, Folder 20, Freud Papers, Library of Congress.

39. Pichler and Freud, "Sigmund Freud Illness Record," 1927, 18.

40. Ibid., 1928, 3.

41. Ibid., 1938, 4.

42. Ibid., 1927, 4.

43. Ibid., 1936, 2.

44. Derrida, *Dissemination*.

45. Romm, *The Unwelcome Intruder*, 90.

46. Honoré Balzac, *The Magic Skin* (New York: Charles Scribner's Sons, 1915), 182.

47. Sigmund Freud, *Civilization and Its Discontents*, ed. James Strachey (New York: Norton, 1961), 39.

48. Sarah S. Jain, "The Prosthetic Imagination: Enabling and Disabling the Prosthesis Trope," *Science, Technology, and Human Values* 24, no. 1 (Winter 1999): 32.

49. Smith and Morra, *The Prosthetic Impulse*, 6.

50. Wills, *Dorsality*, 105.

51. Harold Searles, *The Nonhuman Environment* (New York: International Universities Press, 1960), 7.

52. Max Schur, *Freud: Living and Dying* (New York: International Universities Press, 1972), 32.

53. Ibid., 523.

54. Balzac, *The Magic Skin*, 181.

55. Freud, "Beyond the Pleasure Principle," 21.

56. Martin Heidegger, *The Question Concerning Technology*, trans. William Lovitt (New York: Harper & Row, 1977).

57. Anatole Broyard, *Intoxicated by My Illness* (New York: Clarkson N. Potter, 1992), 20.

58. Bion, "Differentiation of the Psychotic from the Non-Psychotic Personalities."

59. Sigmund Freud, "The 'Uncanny,'" in *SE*, 17:217–256; Ernst Jentsch, "On the Psychology of the Uncanny (1906)," trans. Roy Sellars, *Angelaki* 2, no. 1 (1997): 7–16.

60. Melanie Klein, *The Psycho-Analysis of Children* (London: Hogarth Press, 1932), 212.

61. Melanie Klein, "The Importance of Symbol-Formation in the Development of the Ego," *International Journal of Psycho-Analysis* 11 (1930): 26.

62. Searles, *The Nonhuman Environment*, 29–30.

63. Winnicott admits that the transitional object can be the mother herself, but it is noteworthy that in such cases the transitional object does not

appear to be as effective in performing one of its primary tasks, which is to facilitate an adaptation to and acceptance of internal subjective reality and external reality. Winnicott, *Playing and Reality*, 5.

64. Searles, *The Nonhuman Environment*, 39.

65. Freud, "Three Essays on the Theory of Sexuality."

66. Sigmund Freud, "Findings, Ideas, Problems," in *SE*, 23:300.

67. Schur, *Freud: Living and Dying*, 524.

68. Paul Schilder, *The Image and Appearance of the Human Body* (New York: International Universities Press, 1950).

69. Paul Schilder, "Psycho-Analysis of Space," *International Journal of Psycho-Analysis* 16 (1935): 295; Schur, *Freud: Living and Dying*, 524.

70. Nancy, *Corpus*, 166.

71. Schur, *Freud: Living and Dying*, 519.

72. Laplanche and Pontalis, *The Language of Psycho-Analysis*, 29.

73. Sigmund Freud, "On Narcissism: An Introduction," in *SE*, 14:87.

74. Wills, *Prosthesis*, 218.

75. Laplanche and Pontalis, *The Language of Psycho-Analysis*, 29.

76. Romm, *The Unwelcome Intruder*, 54.

77. Freud, "Three Essays on the Theory of Sexuality," 198.

78. Sigmund Freud, "An Outline of Psycho-Analysis," in *SE*, 23:153.

79. Freud, "Three Essays on the Theory of Sexuality," 135.

80. Sigmund Freud, "Letter 79 Extracts from the Fliess Papers," in *SE*, 1:272.

81. Avital Ronell, *Crack Wars: Lizterature, Addiction, Mania* (Urbana: University of Illinois Press, 2004), 59.

82. Jones, *The Life and Work of Sigmund Freud, Volume Three*, 423.

83. Scott Wilson, "Dying for a Smoke: Freudian Addiction and the Joy of Consumption," *Angelaki* 7, no. 2 (August 2002): 164–165.

84. Freud goes on to include in his list of irresolvable contradictions that despite his frugality he has spent much of his savings on his antiquities collection and that he has read more archaeology than psychology. Schur, *Freud: Living and Dying*, 9.

85. Ronell, *Crack Wars*, 50.

86. Pichler and Freud, "Sigmund Freud Illness Record," 1926, 56.

87. Ibid., 1926, 57.

88. Ibid., 1928, 11.

89. Ibid., 1931, 33–34.

90. Kazanjian, Interview with Dr. V. Kasanjian [*sic*], 3.

91. V. H. Kazanjian, Recollection by V. H. Kazanjian, February 18, 1959, 2, Box OV15 Centenary of Freud's Birth. Miscellany, Freud Papers, Library of Congress.

92. Ibid., 3.

93. Pichler and Freud, "Sigmund Freud Illness Record," 1931, 38.

94. Romm, *The Unwelcome Intruder*, 71.

95. Schur, *Freud: Living and Dying*, 430.

96. Ronell, *Crack Wars*, 59.

97. Wilson, "Dying for a Smoke," 164.

98. Schur, *Freud: Living and Dying*, 62.

99. Derrida, *The Post Card*; Wilson, "Dying for a Smoke."

100. From an uncredited film at the Library of Congress Motion Picture Reading Room.

101. Philip R. Lehrman, *Sigmund Freud, His Family and Colleagues, 1928– 1947*, 16mm film transferred to VHS, 1986; Lydia Marinelli discusses this scene in "Smoking, Laughing and the Compulsion to Film: On the Beginnings of Psychoanalytic Documentaries," *American Imago* 61, no. 1 (Spring 2004): 35–58.

102. Wilhelm Stekel, "On the History of the Analytical Movement," *Psychoanalysis and History* 7 (2005): 104.

103. Schur, *Freud: Living and Dying*, 62.

104. Ibid.

105. Peter Gay, *Freud: A Life for Our Time* (New York: Norton, 2006), 39.

106. Freud, "Beyond the Pleasure Principle," 38.

107. Havi Carel, *Life and Death in Freud and Heidegger* (Amsterdam: Editions Rodopi, 2006).

108. Laplanche and Pontalis, *The Language of Psycho-Analysis*, 97.

109. Freud, "Beyond the Pleasure Principle," 47.

110. Carel, *Life and Death in Freud and Heidegger*; Derrida, *The Post Card*; Jean Laplanche, *Life and Death in Psychoanalysis* (Baltimore: Johns Hopkins University Press, 1985); Phillips, *Darwin's Worms*; Razinsky, *Freud, Psychoanalysis and Death*; Samuel Weber, *The Legend of Freud* (Stanford: Stanford University Press, 2000).

111. Freud, "Beyond the Pleasure Principle," 36.

112. Ibid., 38.

113. Ibid., 45–46.

114. Ibid., 50.

115. Ibid.

116. Freud, "On Narcissism: An Introduction," 82.

117. Siddhartha Mukherjee, *The Emperor of All Maladies: A Biography of Cancer* (New York: Scribner, 2010); Sherwin Nuland, *How We Die: Reflections on Life's Final Chapter* (New York: Vintage Books, 1995); Rebecca Skloot, *The Immortal Life of Henrietta Lacks* (New York: Broadway Books, 2011).

118. Freud, "Beyond the Pleasure Principle," 45.

119. William Saroyan, *Obituaries* (Berkeley: Creative Arts Book Co., 1979).

120. Sigmund Freud, "Thoughts for the Times on War and Death," in *SE*, 14:289.

121. Sigmund Freud, "Analysis Terminable and Interminable," in *SE*, 23:229.

122. Carel, *Life and Death in Freud and Heidegger*.

123. Schur, *Freud: Living and Dying*; Derrida, *The Post Card*.

124. Sigmund Freud, "Negation," in *SE*, 19:235.

125. Freud, "Beyond the Pleasure Principle," 55.

126. Freud, "Civilization and Its Discontents," 1930, 122.

127. Derrida, *The Post Card*, 272.

128. Ibid., 272–337.

129. Ibid., 283.

130. Felix Deutsch called Freud's cancer "an uninvited, unwished intruder." Deutsch, "Reflections on the 10th Anniversary of Freud's Death," 7.

131. See, for instance, Slavoj Žižek, *The Metastases of Enjoyment: Six Essays on Woman and Causality* (New York: Verso, 1994).

132. Schur, *Freud: Living and Dying*, 193.

133. I thank an anonymous reviewer for pointing out the relation between Freud's prostheses, fort/da, and the uncanny. It is not by chance that "The 'Uncanny'" and Beyond the Pleasure Principle were written at the same time. See Nicholas Royle, *The Uncanny* (Manchester: Manchester University Press, 2003), 84–106.

134. Caruth and Pellegrini, following Caruth, both link this literary depiction of traumatic wounding to history and the social, to the historical trace of the pain of others. See Cathy Caruth, *Unclaimed Experience: Trauma, Narrative, and History* (Baltimore: Johns Hopkins University Press, 1996) and Ann Pellegrini, "The Dogs of War and the Dogs at Home: Thresholds of Loss," *American Imago* 66, no. 2 (Summer 2009): 231–251. Novak criticizes Caruth for forgetting racial wounding at the expense of gender. See Amy Novak, "Who Speaks? Who Listens? The Problem of Address in Two Nigerian Trauma Novels," *Studies in the Novel* 40, nos. 1–2 (Spring–Summer 2008): 31–51.

135. Derrida, *The Post Card*; Alan Bass, *Interpretation and Difference: The Strangeness of Care* (Stanford: Stanford University Press, 2006).

136. Steven Miller, *War After Death: On Violence and Its Limits* (New York: Fordham University Press, 2014), 9.

137. Ibid., 10.

138. Ibid.

139. Liran Razinsky, *Freud, Psychoanalysis and Death* (Cambridge: Cambridge University Press, 2013), 273.

140. Louis Breger, *Freud: Darkness in the Midst of Vision* (New York: John Wiley & Sons, 2000), 362; Ernest Jones, "Letter to Max Schur," March 13,

1956, Box 2 Correspondence Jones, Ernest and Katherine 1953–61, Max Schur Papers, Library of Congress.

141. Elisabeth Young-Bruehl, *Anna Freud: A Biography*, 2nd ed. (New Haven: Yale University Press, 2008), 117.

142. Jones, *The Life and Work of Sigmund Freud, Volume Three*, 491.

143. See information card at the Freud Museum in London.

144. Miller, *War After Death*, 5.

145. Peters, *Anna Freud*, 56.

146. Donna Greene, "Films Honor a Writer's Father, and Freud," *New York Times*, January 2, 2000, sec. 14WC, 3; Marinelli, "Smoking, Laughing and the Compulsion to Film: On the Beginnings of Psychoanalytic Documentaries," 41.

147. Greene, "Films Honor a Writer's Father, and Freud," 3.

148. Anna Freud, "Beating Fantasies and Daydreams," in *The Writings of Anna Freud, Vol. 1: Introduction to Psychoanalysis, Lectures for Child Analysts and Teachers 1922–1935* (New York: International Universities Press, 1922), 137–157.

149. Sigmund Freud, "'A Child Is Being Beaten' A Contribution to the Study of the Origin of Sexual Perversions," in *SE*, vol. 17: 175–204.

150. Max Schur, "Letter to Jones," September 30, 1955, 3, Box 59 Folder 6 Freud Medical History: Correspondence between Jones, Schur, and Anna Freud, Freud Papers, Library of Congress.

151. Michael Molnar, "Of Dogs and Doggerel," *American Imago* 53 (1996): 272.

152. Ibid.; Pellegrini, "The Dogs of War and the Dogs at Home"; Lynn Whisnant Reiser, "Topsy—Living and Dying: A Footnote to History," *Psychoanalytic Quarterly* 56 (1987): 667–688.

153. Molnar, "Of Dogs and Doggerel," 275, 276.

154. Ibid., 275.

155. H.D., *Tribute to Freud*.

156. Reiser, "Topsy," 679; Marie Bonaparte and Gary Genosko, *Topsy: The Story of a Golden-Haired Chow* (New Brunswick, N.J.: Transaction Publishers, 1994).

157. Pellegrini, "The Dogs of War and the Dogs at Home," 244.

2. KEEN FOR THE FIRST OBJECT: A KLEINIAN READING OF AUDRE LORDE'S LIFE WRITING

1. Alexis De Veaux, *Warrior Poet: A Biography of Audre Lorde* (New York: Norton, 2004), 189–190.

2. Melanie Klein, "A Contribution to the Psychogenesis of Manic-Depressive States," *International Journal of Psychoanalysis* 16 (1935): 145–174, at 145.

3. Criticisms against Klein were led by Anna Freud and her followers, raising questions as to which daughter was the "proper" heir to psychoanalysis upon Freud's death. For exhaustive documentation, see Pearl King and Riccardo Steiner, eds., *The Freud-Klein Controversies 1941–45* (London: Tavistock/Routledge, 1991). For particularly insightful commentary, see Jacqueline Rose, *Why War? Psychoanalysis, Politics, and the Return to Melanie Klein* (Cambridge, Mass.: Blackwell, 1993).

4. Audre Lorde, *Sister Outsider: Essays and Speeches* (Berkeley: Crossing Press, 2007), 173. For an extensive analysis of this concept, see Alexis Pauline Gumbs, "We Can Learn to Mother Ourselves: The Queer Survival of Black Feminism 1968–1996" (Duke University, 2010), ProQuest, UMI Dissertations Publishing, 3398433.

5. De Veaux, *Warrior Poet*, 230.

6. Audre Lorde, *The Cancer Journals* (Argyle, N.Y.: Spinsters, Ink, 1980), 29.

7. Freud, "An Outline of Psycho-Analysis," 188.

8. Sigmund Freud, "Three Essays on the Theory of Sexuality," in *The Standard Edition of the Complete Psychological Works of Sigmund Freud (SE)*, ed. James Strachey (London: Hogarth Press and the Institute of Psycho-Analysis, 1937), 23:222.

9. Melanie Klein, "Envy and Gratitude (1957)," in *Envy and Gratitude and Other Works 1946–1963*, ed. M. Masud R. Khan (London: Hogarth Press and the Institute of Psycho-Analysis, 1975), 179.

10. Meira Likierman, *Melanie Klein: Her Work in Context* (London: Continuum, 2001), 140.

11. Klein, "Envy and Gratitude (1957)," 180.

12. Klein, "A Contribution to the Psychogenesis of Manic-Depressive States," 145.

13. W. R. Bion, "The Psycho-Analytic Study of Thinking," *International Journal of Psycho-Analysis* 43 (1962): 307.

14. Ada Gay Griffin and Michelle Parkerson, *A Litany for Survival: The Life and Work of Audre Lorde* (Third World Newsreel, 1995).

15. De Veaux, *Warrior Poet*, 230.

16. Deborah Rhodes, "Deborah Rhodes: A Tool That Finds 3x More Breast Tumors, and Why It's Not Available to You," *TED.com*, December 2010, https://goo.gl/XpbDtp.

17. Lorde, *The Cancer Journals*, 66.

18. Intersectionality refers to the multidimensionality of experience, in particular the black woman's experience, which is marginalized and often erased through single-axis frameworks that treat complex and interrelated impacts of identity as if they were mutually exclusive categories. See Kimberlé Crenshaw, "Demarginalizing the Intersection of Race and Sex: A Black

Feminist Critique of Antidiscrimination Doctrine, Feminist Theory and Antiracist Politics," *University of Chicago Legal Forum* 1989, no. 8 (1989): 139–167; Kimberlé Crenshaw, "Mapping the Margins: Intersectionality, Identity Politics, and Violence against Women of Color," *Stanford Law Review* 43, no. 6 (July 1991): 1241–1299.

19. The premature deaths of two prominent black female cultural figures just this year—journalist Gwen Ifill at sixty-one and singer Sharon Jones at sixty—underscore the persistence of cancer's disproportionate effect on African Americans. The U.S. Department of Health and Human Services Office of Minority Health puts this in no uncertain terms: "African Americans have the highest mortality rate of any racial and ethnic group for all cancers combined and for most major cancers" (https://goo.gl/9t57Rh). For a history of the intertwined relationship between race, ethnicity, and cancer, see Keith Wailoo, *How Cancer Crossed the Color Line* (New York: Oxford University Press, 2011).

20. Frantz Fanon, *Black Skin, White Masks*, trans. Charles Lam Markmann (New York: Grove Weidenfeld, 1967), 112.

21. Audre Lorde, *A Burst of Light: Essays* (Ithaca, N.Y.: Firebrand Books, 1988), 61.

22. Lorde, *Sister Outsider*, 156.

23. Rudolph P. Byrd, Johnnetta Betsch Cole, and Beverly Guy-Sheftall, eds., *I Am Your Sister* (Oxford: Oxford University Press, 2009), 184.

24. Lorde, *Sister Outsider*, 37.

25. Likierman, *Melanie Klein*, 143.

26. Audre Lorde, *Zami: A New Spelling of My Name* (New York: Crossing Press, 1982), 226.

27. Klein, "A Contribution to the Psychogenesis of Manic-Depressive States," 153.

28. See especially Mary Ann Doane, "Dark Continents: Epistemologies of Racial and Sexual Difference in Psychoanalysis and the Cinema," in *Femmes Fatales: Feminism, Film Theory, and Psychoanalysis* (New York: Routledge, 1991), 209–248; Ann Pellegrini, *Performance Anxieties: Staging Psychoanalysis, Staging Race*; Jean Walton, *Fair Sex, Savage Dreams: Race, Psychoanalysis, Sexual Difference* (Durham, N.C.: Duke University Press, 2001).

29. Audre Lorde, *Chosen Poems Old and New* (New York: Norton, 1982), 92.

30. Ibid., 92–93.

31. Ibid., 93.

32. Lorde, *Sister Outsider*, 147.

33. Lorde, *The Cancer Journals*, 36.

34. Max Schur, *Freud: Living and Dying* (New York: International Universities Press, 1972), 524; Lorde, *The Cancer Journals*, 30.

35. Audre Lorde, "Of Generators and Survival—Hugo Letter," *Callaloo* 14, no. 1 (Winter 1991): 75.

36. Ibid., 80.

37. Ibid.

38. Audre Lorde, *The Black Unicorn* (New York: Norton, 1978), 32.

39. Lorde, *The Cancer Journals*, 21.

40. Ibid., 55.

41. Ibid., 21.

42. Sigmund Freud, "Group Psychology and the Analysis of the Ego," in *SE*, 18:105.

43. Freud, "Negation," 237.

44. Lorde, *The Cancer Journals*, 21.

45. Lorde, *Sister Outsider*, 97.

46. Lorde, *Chosen Poems Old and New*, 95.

47. Ibid., 95.

48. Ibid., 97.

49. Ibid.

50. Ibid., 98.

51. Lorde, *Sister Outsider*, 41.

52. Lorde, *Zami*, 70.

53. Lauren Berlant uses Lorde's noxious trip to Washington as an entry into outlining her theory of infantile citizenship. Lorde's family's dogged political faith in the face of systemic racism exposes the contradictions of political subjectivity, identification, and patriotic performance. Lauren Berlant, *The Queen of America Goes to Washington City: Essays on Sex and Citizenship* (Durham, N.C.: Duke University Press, 1997), 25–26.

54. Lorde, *Sister Outsider*, 146.

55. Ibid., 129.

56. Ibid., 152.

57. Maria Torok, Barbro Sylwan, and Adèle Covello, "Melanie Mell by Herself," in *Reading Melanie Klein*, ed. Lyndsey Stonebridge and John Phillips (London: Routledge, 1998), 52.

58. Klein's paper "What does death represent to the individual?" can be found in the Melanie Klein archive at the Wellcome Library in London. It is discussed in Lyndsey Stonebridge, "Anxiety in Klein: The Missing Witch's Letter," in ibid., 185–197.

59. Lorde, *Zami*, 34.

60. Ibid., 71–72.

61. Melanie Klein, "Weaning (1936)," in *Love, Guilt and Reparation and Other Works (1921–1945)* (New York: Free Press, 1975), 295.

62. Lorde, *Zami*, 30.

63. Ibid., 190.

64. Ibid.

65. Lorde, *Sister Outsider*, 120.

66. Lorde, *A Burst of Light*, 111–112.

67. Rosemarie Garland Thomson, *Extraordinary Bodies: Figuring Physical Disability in American Culture and Literature* (New York: Columbia University Press, 1997).

68. Lorde, *Zami*, 7.

69. That "zami" is a pejorative term in the Caribbean underscores Lorde's intention of empowering herself by re-signifying and claiming her own name. See Jennifer Abod, *The Edge of Each Other's Battles: The Vision of Audre Lorde* (Women Make Movies, 2002).

70. Lorde, *Zami*, 15.

71. Melanie Klein, *The Psycho-Analysis of Children* (London: Hogarth Press, 1932), 190.

72. See, for example, Judith Butler, *The Psychic Life of Power: Theories in Subjection* (Stanford: Stanford University Press, 1997); Esther Sanchez-Pardo, *Cultures of the Death Drive: Melanie Klein and Modernist Melancholia* (Durham, N.C.: Duke University Press, 2003); Stonebridge, "Anxiety in Klein: The Missing Witch's Letter," in Stonebridge and Phillips, *Reading Melanie Klein*, 185–197.

73. Eve Kosofsky Sedgwick, *Tendencies* (Durham, N.C.: Duke University Press, 1993), 262.

74. Ibid.

75. Gayle Salamon, *Assuming a Body: Transgender and Rhetorics of Materiality* (New York: Columbia University Press, 2010), 188.

76. Lorde, *The Cancer Journals*, 65.

77. Ibid., 55.

78. Freud, "Findings, Ideas, Problems," in *SE*, 23:299.

79. Freud, "Fetishism," in *SE*, 21:152–153.

80. Klein, "The Importance of Symbol-Formation in the Development of the Ego," 26.

81. Lorde, *The Cancer Journals*, 42.

82. Anne Anlin Cheng, "Josephine Baker: Psychoanalysis and the Colonial Fetish," *Psychoanalytic Quarterly* 75 (2006): 103.

83. Lorde, *The Cancer Journals*, 55.

84. Ibid., 68.

85. Angelina Jolie, "My Medical Choice," *New York Times*, May 14, 2013. Those who are BRCA+ have a genetic mutation that puts them at high risk for cancer.

86. I do not mean to critique the justification for preventative mastectomy in cases of genetic predisposition.

87. J. Kluger and A. Park, "The Angelina Effect," *Time*, May 27, 2013; M. Puente, D. Freydkin, and A. Mandell, "Her Mastectomy Could Change Women's Lives," *USA Today*, May 15, 2013.

88. American Society of Plastic Surgeons, "State Laws on Breast Reconstruction," accessed May 10, 2014, https://goo.gl/p1RNZj.

89. Judith Butler, *Bodies That Matter: On the Discursive Limits of Sex* (New York: Routledge, 1993), 3.

90. Lorde, *The Cancer Journals*, 16.

91. Martha Teichner, "The Model and the Mastectomy: Baring Scars Then and Now—CBS News," *CBSNews.com*, September 23, 2013.

92. I thank Ann Pellegrini for this insight.

93. Homi K. Bhabha, "The Other Question: Stereotype, Discrimination and the Discourse of Colonialism," in *The Location of Culture* (London: Routledge, 1994), 66–84.

94. Sigmund Freud, "The Question of Lay Analysis," in *SE*, 20:212.

95. Bhabha, "The Other Question," 74.

96. Fanon, *Black Skin, White Masks*, 151.

97. Doane, "Dark Continents," 225.

98. Fanon, *Black Skin, White Masks*, 129.

99. Lorde, *The Cancer Journals*, 57.

100. Darian Leader, *The New Black: Mourning, Melancholia, and Depression* (London: Hamish Hamilton, 2008), 199.

101. Ibid., 208.

102. Melanie Klein, "Mourning and Its Relation to Manic-Depressive States," *International Journal of Psycho-Analysis* 21 (1940): 126.

103. Klein, "A Contribution to the Psychogenesis of Manic-Depressive States," 147.

104. Ibid.

105. Klein, "Envy and Gratitude (1957)," 201.

106. Donald Woods Winnicott, "Transitional Objects and Transitional Phenomena—A Study of the First Not-Me Possession," *International Journal of Psycho-Analysis* 34 (1953): 89–97, at 95.

107. Freud, "Three Essays on the Theory of Sexuality," 222.

108. Lorde, *The Cancer Journals*, 61.

109. Lorde, *Sister Outsider*, 173.

110. Lorde, *The Black Unicorn*, 6.

111. Klein, "A Contribution to the Psychogenesis of Manic-Depressive States," 164.

112. She also interprets the kidney burning in the hot oil as the patient's father's penis.

113. Lorde, *Sister Outsider*, 86.

114. Lorde, *The Black Unicorn*, 108.

115. Ibid.

116. Thomson, *Extraordinary Bodies*, 105.

117. Lorde, *The Cancer Journals*, 12–13.

118. Lorde, *Sister Outsider*, 112.

119. Ibid., 147.

120. Winnicott, "Transitional Objects and Transitional Phenomena."

121. At least two community organizations in New York take Lorde's name, Callen-Lorde Community Health Center and the Audre Lorde Project, which advocates for Lesbian, Gay, Bisexual, Two Spirit, Trans and Gender Non Conforming People of Color.

122. Ada Gay Griffin and Michelle Parkerson, *A Litany for Survival: The Life and Work of Audre Lorde* (Third World Newsreel, 1995).

123. William Pietz, "The Problem of the Fetish, I," *RES: Anthropology and Aesthetics* 9 (Spring 1985): 11.

124. Sigmund Freud, "The 'Uncanny,'" in *SE*, 17:217–256, at 245.

125. Audre Lorde, *Our Dead Behind Us: Poems* (New York: Norton, 1986), 59.

126. Klein, "Mourning and Its Relation to Manic-Depressive States," 130.

127. Adrienne Rich, *The Fact of a Doorframe: Selected Poems 1950–2001* (New York: Norton, 2002), 159.

3 · OBJECT-LOVE IN THE LATER WRITINGS OF EVE KOSOFSKY SEDGWICK

1. Eve Kosofsky Sedgwick, "Living with Advanced Cancer: The ABCs," *MAMM*, May 2001, 30.

2. Sedgwick wrote poetry throughout her life, some of which deals with her cancer. To my mind, however, she did not embark on poetry as a specific response to illness in the manner in which she undertook the record of her therapy and her "cancer journalism." Her passion for arts and crafts, which coincided with her illness, is treated, for example, in Katy Hawkins, "Woven Spaces: Eve Kosofsky Sedgwick's Dialogue on Love," *Women & Performance: A Journal of Feminist Theory* 16, no. 2 (July 2006): 251–267, and Eve Kosofsky Sedgwick, *The Weather in Proust*, ed. Jonathan Goldberg (Durham, N.C.: Duke University Press, 2011).

3. Eve Kosofsky Sedgwick, *Touching Feeling: Affect, Pedagogy, Performativity* (Durham, N.C.: Duke University Press, 2003), 3.

4. Cynthia Ryan, "Struggling to Survive: A Study of Editorial Decision-Making Strategies at MAMM Magazine," *Journal of Business and Technical Communication* 19, no. 3 (July 2005): 357.

5. Although I would not want to read into this too heavily, the fate of the two publications concisely illustrates the economic power of a predomi-

nantly gay male population in comparison to a community focused on women as well as the effectiveness of AIDS research in relation to cancer research.

6. Sandy M. Fernandez, "Pretty in Pink," *MAMM Magazine* (1998), http://thinkbeforeyoupink.org.

7. Gayle A. Sulik, *Pink Ribbon Blues: How Breast Cancer Culture Undermines Women's Health* (New York: Oxford University Press, 2011), 22.

8. Barbara Ehrenreich, "Welcome to Cancerland," *Harper's Magazine* (November 1, 2001), 46–47.

9. Marita Sturken, *Tourists of History: Memory, Kitsch, and Consumerism from Oklahoma City to Ground Zero* (Durham, N.C.: Duke University Press, 2007).

10. Barbara Ehrenreich, *Bright-Sided: How the Relentless Promotion of Positive Thinking Has Undermined America* (New York: Metropolitan Books, 2009), 4; Breast Cancer Action, "Think Before You Buy Pink," accessed October 7, 2014, http://thinkbeforeyoupink.org.

11. Gayle A. Sulik, *Pink Ribbon Blues: How Breast Cancer Culture Undermines Women's Health* (New York: Oxford University Press, 2011), 318.

12. Ehrenreich, "Welcome to Cancerland," 48; Ryan, "Struggling to Survive," 366.

13. Ryan, "Struggling to Survive," 354.

14. Eve Kosofsky Sedgwick, "Breast Cancer: Issues and Resources," *Lesbian and Gay Studies Newsletter*, Fall 1995, 15.

15. Sigmund Freud, "Recommendations to Physicians Practising Psycho-Analysis," in *The Standard Edition of the Complete Psychological Works of Sigmund Freud (SE)*, ed. James Strachey, 12:115.

16. Stephen M. Barber and David L. Clark, eds., *Regarding Sedgwick: Essays on Queer Culture and Critical Theory* (New York: Routledge, 2002), 255.

17. Cynthia G. Franklin, *Academic Lives: Memoir, Cultural Theory, and the University Today* (Athens: University of Georgia Press, 2009), 260.

18. Eve Kosofsky Sedgwick, *Tendencies* (Durham, N.C.: Duke University Press, 1993), 261.

19. Eve Kosofsky Sedgwick, *A Dialogue On Love* (Boston: Beacon Press, 1999), 165.

20. Freud, "Group Psychology and the Analysis of the Ego," 136.

21. Ibid., 105, 107.

22. Sigmund Freud, "The Ego and the Id," in *SE*, 19:58.

23. Ibid., 28–29; Deborah Britzman, *Freud and Education* (New York: Routledge, 2011), 111.

24. Freud, "The Ego and the Id," 30.

25. Eve Kosofsky Sedgwick, "Off My Chest. A Scar Is Just A Scar: Approaching That First Postmastectomy Tryst," *MAMM*, 1998, 27.

26. Here and elsewhere I use the gender neutral pronouns "they" and "their" when gender is indeterminable.

27. Eve Kosofsky Sedgwick, "Off My Chest. World of Confusion: What Should We Make of the Mammography Controversy?" *MAMM*, February 2003, 20.

28. Sedgwick, *Tendencies*, 256.

29. Sigmund Freud, "Jokes and Their Relation to the Unconscious," in *SE*, 8:1–247.

30. Sigmund Freud, "Humour," in *SE*, 21:159–166.

31. S. Lochlann Jain, *Malignant: How Cancer Becomes Us* (Berkeley: University of California Press, 2013), 9.

32. Sedgwick, "Living with Advanced Cancer," 30–31.

33. Jasbir K. Puar, "Prognosis Time: Towards a Geopolitics of Affect, Debility and Capacity," *Women & Performance: A Journal of Feminist Theory* 19, no. 2 (July 2009): 161–172.

34. Lauren Berlant, "Slow Death (Sovereignty, Obesity, Lateral Agency)," *Critical Inquiry* 33, no. 4 (Summer 2007): 759.

35. Ibid., 758.

36. Ibid., 760.

37. Eve Kosofsky Sedgwick, "Off My Chest. Fat or Thin? Can't Win: What to Do and How to Do It," *MAMM*, Summer 2002, 11.

38. Lauren Berlant, *Cruel Optimism* (Durham, N.C.: Duke University Press, 2011), 16.

39. Ibid., 23.

40. Ibid., 24.

41. Ibid.

42. Rosemarie Garland Thomson, *Extraordinary Bodies: Figuring Physical Disability in American Culture and Literature* (New York: Columbia University Press, 1997).

43. Sedgwick, "Living with Advanced Cancer," 28.

44. Ibid., 27.

45. Ibid.

46. Eve Kosofsky Sedgwick, "Off My Chest. The Guy Factor in BC Support Groups," *MAMM*, 2000.

47. Ibid., 21.

48. Ann Pellegrini, *Performance Anxieties: Staging Psychoanalysis, Staging Race* (New York: Routledge, 1997), 67–68.

49. Sigmund Freud, "The Interpretation of Dreams," in *SE*, 4:149.

50. Ibid., 150.

51. Sedgwick, *A Dialogue On Love*, 168.

52. Cynthia G. Franklin, *Academic Lives: Memoir, Cultural Theory, and the University Today* (Athens: University of Georgia Press, 2009), 250.

53. Sedgwick, *A Dialogue On Love*, 1.

54. Franklin, *Academic Lives*, 253.

55. Ibid., 254.

56. Eve Kosofsky Sedgwick, "Teaching/Depression," *The Scholar & Feminist Online: Writing a Feminist's Life: The Legacy of Carolyn G. Heilbrun* 4, no. 2 (Spring 2006), https:// goo.gl/ohf9H5.

57. Sedgwick, *Tendencies*, xiv.

58. Michael Moon, "Psychosomatic? Mental and Physical Pain in Eve Sedgwick's Writing," *Criticism* 52, no. 2 (Spring 2010): 211.

59. Sedgwick, *A Dialogue On Love*, 207.

60. Ibid., 67.

61. Sedgwick, "Teaching/Depression"; Sedgwick, *A Dialogue On Love*, 117.

62. Sedgwick, *A Dialogue On Love*, 123.

63. Ibid., 106.

64. Ibid., 83.

65. J. L. Austin, *How to Do Things with Words* (Cambridge, Mass.: Harvard University Press, 1978); Judith Butler, *Gender Trouble: Feminism and the Subversion of Identity* (New York: Routledge, 1999).

66. Philomila Tsoukala, "Reading 'A Poem Is Being Written': A Tribute to Eve Kosofsky Sedgwick," *Harvard Journal of Law & Gender* 33 (2010): 340.

67. Ibid., 347.

68. Jonathan A. Allan, for instance, evidences this transference dynamic in his "Falling in Love with Eve Kosofsky Sedgwick," *Mosaic: A Journal for the Interdisciplinary Study of Literature* 48, no. 1 (March 2015): 1–16.

69. Sedgwick, *A Dialogue On Love*, 116.

70. Published in 1999, *Dialogue* covers the time period from 1992 to 1996 or 1997. Sedgwick and Frank's anthology of Silvan Tompkins was published in 1995: Eve Kosofsky Sedgwick and Adam Frank. *Shame and Its Sisters: A Silvan Tomkins Reader* (Durham, N.C.: Duke University Press, 1995), 23.

71. Deborah Britzman, *Freud and Education* (New York: Routledge, 2011), 89.

72. Sedgwick, *A Dialogue On Love*, 115.

73. Sigmund Freud, "Remembering, Repeating and Working-Through (Further Recommendations on the Technique of Psycho-Analysis II)," in *SE*, 12:154.

74. Sedgwick and Frank, *Shame and Its Sisters*, 23.

75. Diana Fuss, *Identification Papers* (New York: Routledge, 1995).

76. Sulik, *Pink Ribbon Blues*, 45.

77. Sedgwick, *Tendencies*, 262.

78. Ibid., 257.

79. Fuss, *Identification Papers*, 2.

80. Sedgwick, *Tendencies*, 262.

81. Ibid., 263.

82. Audre Lorde, *The Cancer Journals* (Argyle, N.Y.: Spinsters, Ink, 1980), 42.

83. Sedgwick, *Tendencies*, 263–264.

84. Ibid., 209.

85. Gary Fisher, *Gary In Your Pocket*, ed. Eve Kosofsky Sedgwick (Durham, N.C.: Duke University Press, 1996), 291.

86. Lorde, as we have seen, came to this understanding by recognizing that her compatriots in race, class, and sex gained strength not through their similarities but through their differences.

87. Sedgwick, *Tendencies*, 253.

88. Stephen M. Barber and David L. Clark, *Regarding Sedgwick: Essays on Queer Culture and Critical Theory* (New York: Routledge, 2002), 14.

89. Donald Woods Winnicott, *Playing and Reality* (Harmondsworth: Penguin Books, 1982), 105.

90. Ibid.

91. Ibid., 111.

92. Sedgwick, *A Dialogue On Love*, 47.

93. Ibid., 90.

94. Christopher Bollas, *The Shadow of the Object: Psychoanalysis of the Unthought Known* (New York: Columbia University Press, 1987), 14.

95. I believe Bollas means "sacred" in its less familiar usages as "devoted to some purpose, not to be lightly intruded upon or handled," or "regarded with or entitled to respect or reverence similar to that which attaches to holy things," or even more rarely "accursed." "Sacred," *Oxford English Dictionary Online*.

96. Lauren Berlant and Lee Edelman, *Sex, Or The Unbearable* (Durham, N.C.: Duke University Press, 2014), 61.

97. Sedgwick, *A Dialogue On Love*, 199; Sedgwick gleefully describes her "Martian-looking neck brace" that she decorated with panda medallions, flowers and skeletons in Sedgwick, "Caregivers Do's & Don'ts," MAMM Magazine, February 2000, 29; and "Making Things, Practicing Emptiness," in *The Weather in Proust*, ed. Jonathan Goldberg (Durham, N.C.: Duke University Press, 2011), 119.

98. Sedgwick, "Teaching/Depression."

99. Sedgwick, *A Dialogue On Love*, 165.

100. Sedgwick, "Teaching/Depression."

101. Sedgwick, "Melanie Klein and the Difference Affect Makes," 640.

102. Lauren Berlant et al., "After Eve, In Honor of Eve Kosofsky Sedgwick," *Supervalent Thought*, March 18, 2010, https://goo.gl/7bQOlJ.

103. Sedgwick, *Touching Feeling*, 176.

104. Ibid.

105. Sedgwick, "Off My Chest. I Got It Good . . . and That Ain't Bad," 40.

106. Sedgwick, "Living with Advanced Cancer: The ABCs," 27.

107. Sedgwick, "Off My Chest. I Got It Good . . . and That Ain't Bad," 40.

108. Ibid.

109. In conversation February 7, 2014.

110. Sedgwick, "Off My Chest. Advanced Degree: School Yourself in Resilience to Beat Depression," 24.

111. Sedgwick, *Touching Feeling*, 177.

112. Donald S. Lopez, ed., *Critical Terms of the Study of Buddhism* (Chicago: University of Chicago Press, 2005).

113. Sedgwick, *Touching Feeling*, 157.

114. Ibid., 159.

115. Ibid.

116. Ibid., 160.

117. Ibid., 167.

118. Sedgwick, "Living with Advanced Cancer," 29.

119. Sedgwick, *Touching Feeling*, 3.

120. Sedgwick, *A Dialogue On Love*, 214.

121. Sedgwick, *Tendencies*, 261.

122. Sedgwick, *A Dialogue On Love*, 116.

123. Ibid., 208.

124. Ibid., 78.

125. Ibid., 57.

126. Ibid., 95.

127. Ibid., 91.

128. Berlant and Edelman, *Sex, Or The Unbearable*, 47.

129. Ibid.

130. As psychoanalysts would have it, it would still be experiencing mother and self as one.

131. Bollas, *The Shadow of the Object*, 41–63.

132. Ibid., 42.

133. This essay was composed for the introduction to *Novel Gazing: Queer Readings in Fiction* (Durham, N.C.: Duke University Press, 1997) and was later anthologized in *Touching Feeling* as "Paranoid Reading and Reparative Reading, or, You're So Paranoid, You Probably Think This Essay Is About You." Aside from introductions to the essays collected in *Novel Gazing*, the differences between the two versions are relatively minor. I will cite from the essay in *Touching Feeling*, 128.

134. Meira Likierman, *Melanie Klein: Her Work in Context* (London: Continuum, 2001), 100.

135. Berlant, *Cruel Optimism*, 24.

136. Lorde, *The Cancer Journals*, 21.

137. Sedgwick, *Touching Feeling*, 150–151.

138. Ibid., 219.

139. Sedgwick, *A Dialogue On Love*, 220.

140. Ibid.

141. Sedgwick, "Melanie Klein and the Difference Affect Makes."

142. Likierman, *Melanie Klein*, 127.

143. Freud, "Group Psychology and the Analysis of the Ego," 90.

144. Ibid., 92.

145. Sedgwick, "Living with Advanced Cancer," 32.

146. *Bar* means "in between" and *do* "suspended or thrown." Sedgwick, "Reality and Realization," in *The Weather in Proust*, 210.

147. Ibid., 213.

148. Ibid.

149. Barber and Clark, *Regarding Sedgwick*, 256.

150. Fisher, *Gary In Your Pocket*, 281.

151. Ibid.

152. Sedgwick, "Reality and Realization," 215.

153. Sedgwick, *Touching Feeling*, 173.

154. Rosi Braidotti, *The Posthuman* (Cambridge: Polity Press, 2015), 132.

155. Ibid.

156. Ellis Hanson, "The Future's Eve: Reparative Reading after Sedgwick," *The South Atlantic Quarterly* 110, no. 1 (Winter 2011): 113.

157. Eve Kosofsky Sedgwick, *Epistemology of the Closet* (Berkeley: University of California Press, 1990), 22.

158. Fisher, *Gary In Your Pocket*, 286.

159. Sigmund Freud, "Fragment of an Analysis of a Case of Hysteria," in *SE*, 7:116. For an interpretation of transference as literature, see Steven Marcus, "Freud and Dora: Story, History, Case History," in *In Dora's Case: Freud/Hysteria/Feminism*, ed. Charles Bernheimer and Claire Kahane, 2nd ed. (New York: Columbia University Press, 1990), 56–91.

4. REPARATIVE OBJECTS IN THE FREUDIAN ARCHIVES

1. Christina Crosby, *A Body, Undone: Living on after Great Pain* (New York: New York University Press, 2016).

2. Sigmund Freud, "Constructions in Analysis," in *The Standard Edition of the Complete Psychological Works of Sigmund Freud (SE)*, ed. James Strachey (London: Hogarth Press and the Institute of Psycho-Analysis, 1937), 23:259–260.

3. David L. Eng and David Kazanjian, eds., *Loss: The Politics of Mourning* (Berkeley: University of California Press, 2003), 365.

4. Lynn Gamwell and Richard Wells, eds., *Sigmund Freud and Art: His Personal Collection of Antiquities* (New York: State University of New York; Freud Museum in association with Harry N. Abrams, 1989), 123.

5. Theodor W. Adorno, "Valéry Proust Museum," in *Prisms*, trans. Samuel and Shierry Weber (Cambridge, Mass.: MIT Press, 1981), 175.

6. Ibid., 182.

7. Hal Foster, "Archives of Modern Art," *October* 99 (Winter 2002): 86.

8. For a definition of aura, see Walter Benjamin, "The Work of Art in the Age of Mechanical Reproduction," in *Illuminations: Essays and Reflections*, ed. Hannah Arendt (New York: Schocken Books, 1969), 217–251. In brief, Benjamin argues that the aura of originality that is associated with unique forms of art such as painting is undercut by techniques of mechanical reproduction, exemplified, for instance, by photography.

9. Douglas Crimp, "On the Museum's Ruins," in *The Anti-Aesthetic: Essays on Postmodern Culture*, ed. Hal Foster (Seattle: Bay Press, 1982), 48.

10. Sigmund Freud, "Letter from Sigmund Freud to Max Eitingon, June 6, 1938," in *Letters of Sigmund Freud 1873–1939* (London: Hogarth Press, 1961), 444–446.

11. See, for example, Mark Gerald, "In the Shadow of Freud's Couch," accessed July 21, 2014, https://goo.gl/YVyVp6; Mignon Nixon, "On the Couch," *October* 113 (Summer 2005): 39–76.

12. David Newlands, "The Significance of the Freud Museum," in *Freud in Exile: Psychoanalysis and Its Vicissitudes*, ed. Edward Timms and Naomi Segal (New Haven: Yale University Press, 1988), 295.

13. The Freud Museum, *20 Maresfield Gardens: A Guide to the Freud Museum* (London: Serpent's Tail, 1998), 50.

14. Peter Gay, *Freud: A Life for Our Time* (New York: Norton, 2006), 635.

15. I mean "plush" in the sense that Benjamin means when he notes that "plush" is material in which traces remain visible. Walter Benjamin, *The Arcades Project* (Cambridge, Mass.: Harvard University Press, 2003), 20.

16. Newlands, "The Significance of the Freud Museum," 297.

17. Ibid.

18. H.D., *Tribute to Freud* (New York: New Directions, 1974), 116.

19. Benjamin, *The Arcades Project*, 208.

20. Lynn Gamwell, "The Origins of Freud's Antiquities Collection," in Gamwell and Wells, *Sigmund Freud and Art*.

21. Sigmund Freud, "Letter from Sigmund Freud to Martha Bernays, October 19, 1885," in *Letters of Sigmund Freud 1873–1939*, 174.

22. Gamwell and Wells, *Sigmund Freud and Art*, 103.

23. Rubén Gallo, *Freud's Mexico: Into the Wilds of Psychoanalysis* (Cambridge, Mass.: MIT Press, 2010), 262–266. Freud grew interested in Chinese

art in his later years, and he also acquired relics from India, North Africa, and South America.

24. Jean Baudrillard, *The System of Objects* (London: Verso, 1996), 91.

25. Ibid., 96.

26. Ibid., 96–97.

27. Ibid., 97.

28. Ibid., 106.

29. Benjamin, *The Arcades Project*, 204.

30. Ibid., 211.

31. Walter Benjamin, "Unpacking My Library," in *Illuminations*, 61.

32. Ibid., 66.

33. John Forrester, *Dispatches from the Freud Wars: Psychoanalysis and Its Passions* (Cambridge, Mass.: Harvard University Press, 1997), 111.

34. Ibid., 113.

35. Ibid., 115.

36. Donald Kuspit, "A Mighty Metaphor: The Analogy of Archaeology and Psychoanalysis," in Gamwell and Wells, *Sigmund Freud and Art*, 134.

37. Freud, "Fragment of an Analysis of a Case of Hysteria," 12.

38. Kuspit, "A Mighty Metaphor," 142.

39. Sigmund Freud, "Letter from Freud to Fliess, August 1, 1899," in *The Complete Letters of Sigmund Freud to Wilhelm Fliess, 1887–1904* (Cambridge, Mass.: Belknap Press of Harvard University Press, 1985), 363.

40. H.D., *Tribute to Freud*, 14.

41. Ibid., 68.

42. Ibid., 35.

43. Gamwell, "The Origins of Freud's Antiquities Collection," 27; Michael Molnar, "Half-Way Region," in *Freud's Sculpture* (Leeds: Henry Moore Institute, 2006); Jon Wood, "Re-Staging Freud's Sculpture," in *Freud's Sculpture* (Leeds: Henry Moore Institute, 2006), 6–18.

44. See Gallo, *Freud's Mexico*, 263; Griselda Pollock, "The Image in Psychoanalysis and the Archaeological Metaphor," in *Psychoanalysis and the Image*, ed. Griselda Pollock (Malden, Mass.: Blackwell, 2006), cover and 1.

45. Forrester, *Dispatches from the Freud Wars*, 119.

46. Lynn Gamwell, "A Collector Analyses Collecting," in *Excavations and Their Objects: Freud's Collection of Antiquity*, ed. Stephen Barker (Albany: State University of New York Press, 1996), 6.

47. Judith Bernays Heller, "Freud's Voice," 1953, 3, Box 116 Interviews+Recollections, Folder 36, Freud Papers, Library of Congress.

48. Gamwell, "The Origins of Freud's Antiquities Collection," 24–25.

49. Ibid., 30 n. 15.

50. Ernest Jones, *Sigmund Freud: Life and Work, Volume One: The Young Freud 1856–1900* (London: Hogarth Press, 1972), 363; Jones, *The Life and*

Work of Sigmund Freud, Volume Three: The Last Phase 1919–1939 (London: Hogarth Press, 1957), 340.

51. Gay, *Freud*, 171.

52. Sigmund Freud and Michael Molnar, *The Diary of Sigmund Freud, 1929–1939: A Record of the Final Decade* (New York: Scribner's, 1992), 70–75.

53. Helga Jobst, "Freud and Archaeology," *Sigmund Freud House Bulletin* 2, no. 1 (1978): 47.

54. Helen Dudar, "The Unexpected Private Passion of Sigmund Freud," *Smithsonian* 21, no. 5 (August 1990): 100.

55. Freud and Molnar, *The Diary of Sigmund Freud, 1929–1939*, 70.

56. Louise Bourgeois, *Freud's Toys* (London: Freud Museum, 1989, republished 2012).

57. Freud and Molnar, *The Diary of Sigmund Freud, 1929–1939*.

58. Ibid., 239.

59. Jones, *The Life and Work of Sigmund Freud, Volume Three*, 340–341.

60. Benjamin, "Unpacking My Library," 67.

61. Jobst, "Freud and Archaeology," 49.

62. A copy of this script is located in the Anna Freud Papers at the Library of Congress, Box X1 Folder 10 Correspondence 2010 Eissler, K.R, 1970, and is on display at the Freud Museum in London.

63. For a seminal essay on collecting as cultural appropriation, see James Clifford, "On Collecting Art and Culture," in *The Predicament of Culture: Twentieth-Century Ethnography, Literature, and Art* (Cambridge, Mass.: Harvard University Press, 1988), 215–251.

64. Peter Ucko, "Unprovenanced Material Culture and Freud's Collection of Antiquities," *Journal of Material Culture* 6, no. 3 (2001): 270.

65. W. H. Auden, "In Memory of Sigmund Freud," in *Collected Poems* (London: Faber and Faber, 1994), 276.

66. Benjamin, "Unpacking My Library," 64.

67. Chris Marker, "The Statues Also Die (transcript of 1953 film)," trans. Lauren Ashby, *Art in Translation* 5, no. 4 (2013): 431.

68. Edmund Engelman, *Berggasse 19: Sigmund Freud's Home and Offices, Vienna 1938* (New York: Basic Books, 1976), 136.

69. Arnold Werner, "Edmund Engelman: Photographer of Sigmund Freud's Home and Offices," *International Journal of Psychoanalysis* 83 (2002): 447.

70. Yomtov Ludwig Bato, Evelyn Adunka, and Israel O. Lehman, "Vienna," *Encyclopaedia Judaica*, ed. Michael Berenbaum and Fred Skolnik (Detroit: Macmillan Reference USA, 2007), 522.

71. Tamara Nosenko, "Path of Memory: A Walking Tour Honoring Jewish Residents of Vienna's 2nd District Who Died at the Hands of the Nazis," March 1, 2008, https://goo.gl/onyM5T.

72. Bato, Adunka, and Lehman, "Vienna," 522.

73. John Merriman and Jay Winter, eds., "Vienna," *Europe Since 1914: Encyclopedia of the Age of War and Reconstruction* (Detroit: Charles Scribner's Sons, 2006), 2646.

74. Edward Timms and Naomi Segal, *Freud in Exile: Psychoanalysis and Its Vicissitudes* (New Haven: Yale University Press, 1988).

75. This wish to repair is explicitly enacted by, for instance, Stones of Remembrance, a project by Elisabeth Ben David-Hindler that commemorates Jews who had lived in Vienna's Second District. As of 2008, 350 plaques have been placed with the names, birthdates, and deportation dates of Jews from the neighborhood. David-Hindler says her motivation was to give the residents of Leopoldstadt "a bit of their life back." Nosenko, "Path of Memory."

76. According to the Board of the Sigmund Freud Foundation, the Sigmund Freud Museum Vienna receives 70,000 visitors per year. According to Carol Seigel, director of the Freud Museum, the London Museum receives 20,000 visitors per year. The Board of the Sigmund Freud Foundation et al., *The Project: Sigmund Freud Museum Vienna*, accessed April 24, 2013, https://goo.gl/zy1Sog; Julie Mollins, "Freud Museum London Celebrates 25th Anniversary," Reuters, July 28, 2011.

77. Lydia Marinelli, "'Body Missing' at Berggasse 19," trans. Joy Titheridge, *American Imago* 66, no. 2 (Summer 2009): 165.

78. Andreas Mayer, "Shadow of a Couch," *American Imago* 66, no. 2 (Summer 2009): 137, 140.

79. Ibid., 140.

80. Marinelli, "'Body Missing' at Berggasse 19," 164.

81. André Green, *The Work of the Negative*, trans. Andrew Weller (New York: Free Association Books, 1999), 232.

82. Pollock, "The Image in Psychoanalysis and the Archaeological Metaphor," 2.

83. Harold Leupold-Löwenthal, Hans Lobner, and Inge Scholz-Strasser, eds., *Sigmund Freud Museum Berggasse 19 Vienna Catalogue* (Corte Madera, Calif.: Gingko Press, 1995), 7.

84. Forrester, *Dispatches from the Freud Wars*, 132.

85. Sigmund Freud, "On Beginning the Treatment (Further Recommendations on the Technique of Psycho-Analysis I)," in *SE*, 12:135.

86. Joanne Morra, "Seemingly Empty: Freud at Berggasse 19, A Conceptual Museum in Vienna," *Journal of Visual Culture* 12, no. 1 (2013): 100.

87. H.D., *Tribute to Freud*, 9.

88. Ruth Leys, *Trauma: A Genealogy* (Chicago: University of Chicago Press, 2000), 21.

89. This would be to exploit the creative and political potential of melancholia, as Muñoz, Eng, and Kazanjian have discussed. See Eng and Kazanjian,

Loss; José Esteban Muñoz, *Disidentifications: Queers of Color and the Performance of Politics* (Minneapolis: University of Minnesota Press, 1999).

90. Harold Leupold-Löwenthal and Hans Lobner, *Sigmund Freud-House Catalogue* (Vienna: Löcker & Wögenstein, 1975), 2.

91. Engelman, *Berggasse 19*, 73.

92. Edmund Engelman, *Sigmund Freud: Wien IX. Berggasse 19—Photographien und Rückblick* (Vienna: Verlag Christian Brandstätter, 1993), 23.

93. I thank an anonymous reviewer for the Canadian Network for Psychoanalysis for this comment.

94. Marinelli, "'Body Missing' at Berggasse 19," 164.

95. Victor Burgin, *The End of Art Theory: Criticism and Postmodernity* (Atlantic Highlands, N.J.: Humanities Press International, 1986), 19.

96. Freud, "Mourning and Melancholia," 245.

97. Engelman, *Berggasse 19*, 143.

98. Ellen Edwards, "Photo Exhibit Gives A Penetrating Look At World of Freud," *Miami Herald*, November 1977, Box 158, Folder 18 Miscellany Freud Family Freud, Sigmund General, 1938–82, Anna Freud Papers, Library of Congress.

99. Marinelli, "'Body Missing' at Berggasse 19," 163.

100. Freud, "Mourning and Melancholia," 249.

101. Lydia Marinelli, "Fort, Da: The Cap in the Museum," *Psychoanalysis and History* 11, no. 1 (2009): 118.

102. Anna Freud, "About Losing and Being Lost," *The Psychoanalytic Study of the Child* 22 (1967): 10.

103. Ibid., 14.

104. Elisabeth Young-Bruehl, *Anna Freud: A Biography*, 2nd ed. (New Haven: Yale University Press, 2008), 295; Anna Freud similarly referred to concealed autobiographical material in her "Beating Fantasies and Daydreams," *The Writings of Anna Freud, Vol. 1: Introduction to Psychoanalysis, Lectures for Child Analysts and Teachers 1922–1935* (New York: International Universities Press, 1922), 137–157.

105. Marinelli, "Fort, Da," 119.

106. Susan Stewart, *On Longing: Narratives of the Miniature, the Gigantic, the Souvenir, the Collection* (Durham, N.C.: Duke University Press, 1993), 136.

107. Jacques Derrida, *Archive Fever: A Freudian Impression* (Chicago: University of Chicago Press, 1996), 1.

108. Ibid., 90.

CONCLUSION: LAST OBJECTS

1. Freud, "New Introductory Lectures on Psycho-Analysis," 181–182.

2. Marita Sturken, *Tourists of History: Memory, Kitsch, and Consumerism from Oklahoma City to Ground Zero* (Durham, N.C.: Duke University Press, 2007), 3.

3. S. Lochlann Jain, *Malignant: How Cancer Becomes Us* (Berkeley: University of California Press, 2013), 11.

4. Eve Kosofsky Sedgwick, *A Dialogue on Love* (Boston: Beacon Press, 1999), 27–28.

5. Eve Kosofsky Sedgwick, *Touching Feeling: Affect, Pedagogy, Performativity* (Durham, N.C.: Duke University Press, 2003), 3.

6. Sigmund Freud and Michael Molnar, *The Diary of Sigmund Freud, 1929–1939: A Record of the Final Decade* (New York: Scribner's, 1992), xxiv.

7. Ibid. This corroborates Freud's belief that at the end of analysis the person is dead.

8. Ibid.; Freud, "Analysis Terminable and Interminable," in *The Standard Edition of the Complete Psychological Works of Sigmund Freud (SE)*, ed. James Strachey, 23:209–54. 218.

9. Sigmund Freud, "On Transience," in *SE*, 14:303–7.

10. Maev Kennedy, "Thieves Smash Urn Holding Freud's Ashes," *The Guardian*, January 16, 2014.

11. Edward W. Said, *Out of Place: A Memoir* (New York: Knopf, 1999), xi.

12. Ibid., xiv.

13. Ibid., xii.

14. Ibid., 295.

15. Esther Leslie, "Snow Shaker," in *The Object Reader*, ed. Fiona Candlin and Raiford Guins (New York: Routledge, 2009), 518.

16. José Esteban Muñoz, *Disidentifications: Queers of Color and the Performance of Politics* (Minneapolis: University of Minnesota Press, 1999), 12.

17. Edward W. Said and Jacqueline Rose, *Freud and the Non-European* (London: Verso, 2003), 54.

18. Muñoz, *Disidentifications*, 74.

19. In a salon honoring Crosby, Gayle Salamon refers to Crosby's body as "unhoused" after the accident. Barnard Center for Research on Women and the Center for the Study of Gender and Sexuality at NYU, *Body Undone: A Salon in Honor of Christina Crosby* (Barnard College, 2015), https://goo.gl/dkqoxt.

20. Rosi Braidotti, *The Posthuman* (Cambridge: Polity Press, 2015), 132.

21. Christina Crosby, *A Body, Undone: Living on after Great Pain* (New York: New York University Press, 2016), 195.

22. Ibid., 201.

23. Saidiya Hartman, "The Belly of the World: A Note on Black Women's Labors," *Souls* 18, no. 1 (2016): 171.

BIBLIOGRAPHY

Abod, Jennifer. *The Edge of Each Other's Battles: The Vision of Audre Lorde.* Women Make Movies, 2002.

Adler, Jerry. "Freud Is (Not) Dead." *Newsweek*, March 27, 2006.

Adorno, Theodor W. "Valéry Proust Museum." In *Prisms*, translated by Samuel and Shierry Weber, 173–186. Cambridge, Mass.: MIT Press, 1981.

Ahmed, Sara. *Queer Phenomenology: Orientations, Objects, Others.* Durham, N.C.: Duke University Press, 2006.

Allan, Jonathan A. "Falling in Love with Eve Kosofsky Sedgwick." *Mosaic: A Journal for the Interdisciplinary Study of Literature* 48, no. 1 (March 2015): 1–16.

American Society of Plastic Surgeons. "State Laws on Breast Reconstruction." Accessed May 10, 2014. https://goo.gl/p1RNZj.

Appadurai, Arjun. *The Social Life of Things: Commodities in Cultural Perspective.* Cambridge: Cambridge University Press, 1986.

Apter, Emily S. *Feminizing the Fetish: Psychoanalysis and Narrative Obsession in Turn-of-the-Century France.* Ithaca, N.Y.: Cornell University Press, 1991.

Auden, W. H. "In Memory of Sigmund Freud." In *Collected Poems*. London: Faber and Faber, 1994.

Austin, J. L. *How to Do Things with Words.* Cambridge, Mass.: Harvard University Press, 1978.

Balint, Michael. *The Basic Fault: Therapeutic Aspects of Regression.* London: Tavistock, 1968.

Balzac, Honoré. *The Magic Skin.* New York: Charles Scribner's Sons, 1915.

Barad, Karen. *Meeting the Universe Halfway: Quantum Physics and the Entanglement of Matter and Meaning.* Durham, N.C.: Duke University Press, 2007.

Barber, Stephen M., and David L. Clark, eds. *Regarding Sedgwick: Essays on Queer Culture and Critical Theory.* New York: Routledge, 2002.

Barnard Center for Research on Women and the Center for the Study of Gender and Sexuality at N.Y.U. *Body Undone: A Salon in Honor of Christina Crosby.* Barnard College, New York, 2015. https://goo.gl/dkqoxt.

Barthes, Roland. *Roland Barthes.* New York: Hill and Wang, 2010.

Bass, Alan. *Interpretation and Difference: The Strangeness of Care*. Stanford: Stanford University Press, 2006.

Bato, Yomtov Ludwig, Evelyn Adunka, and Israel O. Lehman. "Vienna." Edited by Michael Berenbaum and Fred Skolnik. *Encyclopaedia Judaica*. Detroit: Macmillan Reference USA, 2007.

Benjamin, Walter. *The Arcades Project*. Cambridge, Mass.: Harvard University Press, 2003.

———. *Illuminations: Essays and Reflections*. Edited by Hannah Arendt. New York: Schocken Books, 1969.

Bennett, Jane. *Vibrant Matter: A Political Ecology of Things*. Durham, N.C.: Duke University Press, 2010.

Berlant, Lauren. *Cruel Optimism*. Durham, N.C.: Duke University Press, 2011.

———. *The Queen of America Goes to Washington City: Essays on Sex and Citizenship*. Durham, N.C.: Duke University Press, 1997.

———. "Slow Death (Sovereignty, Obesity, Lateral Agency)." *Critical Inquiry* 33, no. 4 (Summer 2007): 754–780.

Berlant, Lauren, Tyler Curtain, Maurice Wallace, and Robyn Wiegman. "After Eve, In Honor of Eve Kosofsky Sedgwick." *Supervalent Thought*, March 18, 2010. https://goo.gl/7bQOlJ.

Berlant, Lauren, and Lee Edelman. *Sex, or The Unbearable*. Durham, N.C.: Duke University Press, 2014.

Bhabha, Homi K. "The Other Question: Stereotype, Discrimination and the Discourse of Colonialism." In *The Location of Culture*, 66–84. London: Routledge, 1994.

Bion, W.R. "Differentiation of the Psychotic from the Non-Psychotic Personalities." *The International Journal of Psychoanalysis* 38 (1957): 266–275.

———. "The Psycho-Analytic Study of Thinking." *International Journal of Psycho-Analysis* 43 (1962): 306–310.

Black Women's Health Study, Office of Minority Health & Health Disparities Research, Georgetown University. Accessed November 30, 2016. https://goo.gl/ojjSog.

Board of the Sigmund Freud Foundation, Inge Scholz-Strasser, Rudolf Dirisamer, and Herbert Allram. "The Project: Sigmund Freud Museum Vienna." Accessed April 24, 2013. https://goo.gl/zy1Sog.

Bollas, Christopher. *The Shadow of the Object: Psychoanalysis of the Unthought Known*. New York: Columbia University Press, 1987.

Bonaparte, Marie, and Gary Genosko. *Topsy: The Story of a Golden-Haired Chow*. New Brunswick, N.J.: Transaction Publishers, 1994.

Bourgeois, Louise. "Freud's Toys." London: Freud Museum, 1989/2012.

Boyarin, Daniel. "Freud's Baby, Fliess's Maybe; Or, Male Hysteria, Homophobia, and the Invention of the Jewish Man." In *Unheroic Conduct: The Rise of Heterosexuality and the Invention of the Jewish Man*, 189–220. Berkeley: University of California Press, 1997.

Braidotti, Rosi. *The Posthuman*. Cambridge: Polity Press, 2015.

——. "Posthuman, All Too Human: Towards a New Process Ontology." *Theory, Culture & Society* 23, nos. 7–8 (2006): 197–208.

Breast Cancer Action. "Think Before You Pink." Accessed October 7, 2014. http://thinkbeforeyoupink.org.

Breger, Louis. *Freud: Darkness in the Midst of Vision*. New York: John Wiley & Sons, 2000.

Britzman, Deborah. *Freud and Education*. New York: Routledge, 2011.

Brown, Bill. "Object Relations in an Expanded Field." *Differences: A Journal of Feminist Cultural Studies* 17, no. 3 (2006): 88–106.

Broyard, Anatole. *Intoxicated by My Illness*. New York: Clarkson N. Potter, 1992.

Bryant, Levi R., Nick Srnicek, and Graham Harman, eds. *The Speculative Turn: Continental Materialism and Realism*. Melbourne: re.press, 2011.

Burgin, Victor. *The End of Art Theory: Criticism and Postmodernity*. Atlantic Highlands, N.J.: Humanities Press International, 1986.

Butler, Judith. *Bodies That Matter: On the Discursive Limits of Sex*. New York: Routledge, 1993.

——. *Gender Trouble: Feminism and the Subversion of Identity*. New York: Routledge, 1999.

——. *The Psychic Life of Power: Theories in Subjection*. Stanford: Stanford University Press, 1997.

Byrd, Rudolph P., Johnnetta Betsch Cole, and Beverly Guy-Sheftall, eds. *I Am Your Sister*. Oxford: Oxford University Press, 2009.

Candlin, Fiona, and Raiford Guins, eds. *The Object Reader*. New York: Routledge, 2009.

Carel, Havi. *Life and Death in Freud and Heidegger*. Contemporary Psychoanalytic Studies. Amsterdam: Editions Rodopi, 2006.

Caruth, Cathy. *Unclaimed Experience: Trauma, Narrative, and History*. Baltimore: Johns Hopkins University Press, 1996.

Cazdyn, Eric. *The Already Dead: The New Time of Politics, Culture, and Illness*. Durham, N.C.: Duke University Press, 2012.

Chen, Mel Y. *Animacies: Biopolitics, Racial Mattering, and Queer Affect*. Durham, N.C.: Duke University Press, 2012.

Cheng, Anne Anlin. "Josephine Baker: Psychoanalysis and the Colonial Fetish." *Psychoanalytic Quarterly* 75 (2006): 95–129.

Clare, Eli. *Exile and Pride: Disability, Queerness, and Liberation*. Durham, N.C.: Duke University Press, 2015.

Clifford, James. "On Collecting Art and Culture." In *The Predicament of Culture: Twentieth-Century Ethnography, Literature, and Art*, 215–251. Cambridge, Mass.: Harvard University Press, 1988.

Coole, Diana, and Samantha Frost. *New Materialisms: Ontology, Agency, and Politics*. Durham, N.C.: Duke University Press, 2010.

Couser, G. Thomas. *Recovering Bodies: Illness, Disability, and Life-Writing*. Madison: University of Wisconsin Press, 1997.

Crenshaw, Kimberlé. "Demarginalizing the Intersection of Race and Sex: A Black Feminist Critique of Antidiscrimination Doctrine, Feminist Theory and Antiracist Politics." *University of Chicago Legal Forum* 1989, no. 8 (1989): 139–167.

———. "Mapping the Margins: Intersectionality, Identity Politics, and Violence against Women of Color." *Stanford Law Review* 43, no. 6 (July 1991): 1241–1299.

Crimp, Douglas. "On the Museum's Ruins." In *The Anti-Aesthetic: Essays on Postmodern Culture*, edited by Hal Foster, 43–56. Seattle: Bay Press, 1982.

Crosby, Christina. *A Body, Undone: Living on after Great Pain*. New York: New York University Press, 2016.

Davenport, John C. "The Prosthetic Care of Sigmund Freud." *Dental History*, March 7, 1992.

———. "Sigmund Freud's Illness—The Ultimate Approach to Head and Neck Cancer?" *Facial Plastic Surgery* 9, no. 2 (April 1993): 125–132.

De Veaux, Alexis. *Warrior Poet: A Biography of Audre Lorde*. New York: Norton, 2004.

Derrida, Jacques. *Archive Fever: A Freudian Impression*. Chicago: University of Chicago Press, 1996.

———. *Dissemination*. Translated by Barbara Johnson. Chicago: University of Chicago Press, 1981.

———. *The Post Card: From Socrates to Freud and Beyond*. Chicago: University of Chicago Press, 1987.

DeShazer, Mary K. *Mammographies*. Ann Arbor: University of Michigan Press, 2013.

Deutsch, Felix. "Reflections on the 10th Anniversary of Freud's Death," ca 1949. Box 116 Interviews+Recollections, Folder 17. Freud Papers, Library of Congress.

Diedrich, Lisa. *Treatments: Language, Politics, and the Culture of Illness*. Minneapolis: University of Minnesota Press, 2007.

Doane, Mary Ann. "Dark Continents: Epistemologies of Racial and Sexual Difference in Psychoanalysis and the Cinema." In *Femmes Fatales: Feminism, Film Theory, and Psychoanalysis*, 209–248. New York: Routledge, 1991.

Dudar, Helen. "The Unexpected Private Passion of Sigmund Freud." *Smithsonian* 21, no. 5 (August 1990): 100.

Edwards, Ellen. "Photo Exhibit Gives A Penetrating Look At World of Freud." *Miami Herald*, November 1977. Box 158, Folder 18 Miscellany Freud Family Freud, Sigmund General, 1938–82. Anna Freud Papers, Library of Congress.

Ehrenreich, Barbara. *Bright-Sided: How the Relentless Promotion of Positive Thinking Has Undermined America*. New York: Metropolitan Books, 2009.
———. "Welcome to Cancerland." *Harper's Magazine*, November 1, 2001.
Eng, David L., and David Kazanjian, eds. *Loss: The Politics of Mourning*. Berkeley: University of California Press, 2003.
Engelman, Edmund. *Sigmund Freud: Wien IX. Berggasse 19—Photographien und Rückblick*. Vienna: Verlag Christian Brandstätter, 1993.
Fanon, Frantz. *Black Skin, White Masks*. Translated by Charles Lam Markmann. New York: Grove Weidenfeld, 1967.
Felman, Shoshana, and Dori Laub. *Testimony: Crises of Witnessing in Literature, Psychoanalysis, and History*. New York: Routledge, 1991.
Fernandez, Sandy M. "Pretty in Pink." *MAMM Magazine*, 1998. http://thinkbeforeyoupink.org.
Fisher, Gary. *Gary in Your Pocket*. Edited by Eve Kosofsky Sedgwick. Durham, N.C.: Duke University Press, 1996.
Forrester, John. *Dispatches from the Freud Wars: Psychoanalysis and Its Passions*. Cambridge, Mass.: Harvard University Press, 1997.
Foster, Hal. "Archives of Modern Art." *October* 99 (Winter 2002): 81–95.
Foulkes, S. H. Interviews + Recollections: Foulkes, S. H. Interview by K. R. Eissler, September 7, 1969. Box 116 Interviews+Recollections, Folder 20. Freud Papers, Library of Congress.
Frank, Arthur W. *The Wounded Storyteller: Body, Illness, and Ethics*. Chicago: University of Chicago Press, 1995.
Franklin, Cynthia G. *Academic Lives: Memoir, Cultural Theory, and the University Today*. Athens: University of Georgia Press, 2009.
Freud, Anna. "About Losing and Being Lost." *The Psychoanalytic Study of the Child* 22 (1967): 9–19.
———. "Beating Fantasies and Daydreams." In *The Writings of Anna Freud, Vol. 1: Introduction to Psychoanalysis, Lectures for Child Analysts and Teachers 1922–1935*, 137–157. New York: International Universities Press, 1922.
Freud, Ernst L. *The Letters of Sigmund Freud and Arnold Zweig*. New York: Harcourt Brace Jovanovich, 1970.
Freud, Sigmund. "Analysis Terminable and Interminable." In *The Standard Edition of the Complete Psychological Works of Sigmund Freud (SE)*, edited by James Strachey, 23:209–254. London: Hogarth Press and the Institute of Psycho-Analysis, 1937.
———. "Beyond the Pleasure Principle." In *SE*, 18:1–64.
———. "'A Child Is Being Beaten': A Contribution to the Study of the Origin of Sexual Perversions." In *SE*, 17:175–204.
———. "Civilization and Its Discontents." In *SE*, 21:57–146.
———. *Civilization and Its Discontents*. Edited by James Strachey. New York and London: Norton, 1961.

———. "Constructions in Analysis." In *SE*, 23:255–270.

———. "The Ego and the Id." In *SE*, 19:1–66.

———. "Fetishism." In *SE*, 21:147–158.

———. "Findings, Ideas, Problems." In *SE*, 23:299–300.

———. "Fragment of an Analysis of a Case of Hysteria." In *SE*, 7:1–122.

———. "Group Psychology and the Analysis of the Ego." In *SE*, 18:65–144.

———. "Humour." In *SE*, 21:159–166.

———. "Instincts and Their Vicissitudes." In *SE*, 14:109–140.

———. "The Interpretation of Dreams (First Part)." In *SE*, 4:ix–627.

———. "Jokes and Their Relation to the Unconscious." In *SE*, 8:1–247.

———. "Letter 79 Extracts From The Fliess Papers." In *SE*, 1:272–273.

———. "Letter from Freud to Fliess, August 1, 1899." In *The Complete Letters of Sigmund Freud to Wilhelm Fliess, 1887–1904*, 363–364. Cambridge, Mass.: Belknap Press of Harvard University Press, 1985.

———. "Letter from Sigmund Freud to Martha Bernays, October 19, 1885." In *Letters of Sigmund Freud 1873–1939*, 171–174. London: Hogarth Press, 1961.

———. "Letter from Sigmund Freud to Max Eitingon, June 6, 1938." In *Letters of Sigmund Freud 1873–1939*, 444–446.

———. *Moses and Monotheism*. Translated by Katherine Jones. Letchworth: Hogarth Press and the Institute of Psycho-Analysis, 1939.

———. "Mourning and Melancholia." In *SE*, 14:237–258.

———. "Negation." In *SE*, 19:233–240.

———. "New Introductory Lectures on Psycho-Analysis." In *SE*, 22:1–182.

———. "On Beginning the Treatment (Further Recommendations on the Technique of Psycho-Analysis I)." In *SE*, 12:121–144.

———. "On Narcissism: An Introduction." In *SE*, 14:67–102.

———. "An Outline of Psycho-Analysis." In *SE*, 23:139–208.

———. "The Question of Lay Analysis." In *SE*, 20:177–258.

———. "Recommendations to Physicians Practising Psycho-Analysis." In *SE*, 12:106–120.

———. "Remembering, Repeating and Working-Through (Further Recommendations on the Technique of Psycho-Analysis II)." In *SE*, 12:145–156.

———. "Thoughts for the Times on War and Death." In *SE*, 14:273–300.

———. "Three Essays on the Theory of Sexuality." In *SE*, 7:123–246.

———. *Three Essays on the Theory of Sexuality: The 1905 Edition*. Translated by Ulrike Kistner. New York: Verso, 2017.

———. "The 'Uncanny.'" In *SE*, 17:217–256.

Freud, Sigmund, and Michael Molnar. *The Diary of Sigmund Freud, 1929–1939: A Record of the Final Decade*. New York: Scribner's, 1992.

Freud Museum. *20 Maresfield Gardens: A Guide to the Freud Museum*. London: Serpent's Tail, 1998.

Fromm, Erich. *The Heart of Man: Its Genius for Good and Evil*. New York: Harper & Row, 1964.

Fuss, Diana. *Identification Papers*. New York: Routledge, 1995.

———. *The Sense of an Interior: Four Writers and the Rooms That Shaped Them*. New York: Routledge, 2004.

Gallo, Rubén. *Freud's Mexico: Into the Wilds of Psychoanalysis*. Cambridge, Mass.: MIT Press, 2010.

Gamwell, Lynn. "A Collector Analyses Collecting: Sigmund Freud on the Passion to Possess." In *Excavations and Their Objects: Freud's Collection of Antiquity*, edited by Stephen Barker. Albany: State University of New York Press, 1996.

Gamwell, Lynn, and Richard Wells, eds. *Sigmund Freud and Art: His Personal Collection of Antiquities*. New York and London: State University of New York and Freud Museum, in association with Harry N. Abrams, 1989.

Garland Thomson, Rosemarie. *Extraordinary Bodies: Figuring Physical Disability in American Culture and Literature*. New York: Columbia University Press, 1997.

Gay, Peter. *Freud: A Life for Our Time*. New York: Norton, 2006.

Geller, Jay. *On Freud's Jewish Body: Mitigating Circumcisions*. New York: Fordham University Press, 2007.

Gerald, Mark. "In the Shadow of Freud's Couch." Accessed July 21, 2014. https://goo.gl/YVyVp6.

Gilbert, Geoff. *Before Modernism Was: Modern History and the Constituency of Writing*. New York: Palgrave Macmillan, 2004.

Gilman, Sander L. *Freud, Race, and Gender*. Princeton: Princeton University Press, 1993.

Green, André. *The Work of the Negative*. Translated by Andrew Weller. New York: Free Association Books, 1999.

Greene, Donna. "Films Honor a Writer's Father, and Freud." *New York Times*, January 2, 2000.

Gregg, Melissa, and Gregory J. Seigworth, eds. *The Affect Theory Reader*. Durham, N.C.: Duke University Press, 2010.

Griffin, Ada Gay, and Michelle Parkerson. *A Litany for Survival: The Life and Work of Audre Lorde*. Third World Newsreel, 1995.

Grosz, Elizabeth. "Lesbian Fetishism?" In *Fetishism as Cultural Discourse*, edited by William Pietz and Emily Apter. Ithaca, N.Y.: Cornell University Press, 1993.

Grusin, Richard A. *The Nonhuman Turn*. Minneapolis: University of Minnesota Press, 2015.

Gumbs, Alexis Pauline. "We Can Learn to Mother Ourselves: The Queer Survival of Black Feminism 1968–1996." Duke University, 2010. ProQuest, UMI Dissertations Publishing. 3398433.

Hanson, Ellis. "The Future's Eve: Reparative Reading after Sedgwick." *The South Atlantic Quarterly* 110, no. 1 (Winter 2011): 101–119.

Haraway, Donna J. *Simians, Cyborgs, and Women: The Reinvention of Nature.* New York: Routledge, 1991.

Harman, Graham. *Tool-Being: Heidegger and the Metaphysics of Objects.* Chicago: Open Court, 2002.

Hartman, Saidiya. "The Belly of the World: A Note on Black Women's Labors." *Souls* 18, no. 1 (2016): 166–173.

Hawkins, Anne Hunsaker. *Reconstructing Illness: Studies in Pathography.* West Lafayette, Ind.: Purdue University Press, 1999.

Hawkins, Katy. "Woven Spaces: Eve Kosofsky Sedgwick's Dialogue on Love." *Women & Performance: A Journal of Feminist Theory* 16, no. 2 (July 2006): 251–267.

H.D. *Tribute to Freud.* New York: New Directions, 1974.

Headrick, Daniel R. "Gutta-Percha: A Case of Resource Depletion and International Rivalry." *IEEE Technology and Society Magazine*, December 1987, 12–16.

Hedva, Johanna. "Sick Woman Theory." *Mask Magazine*, January 2016. https://goo.gl/PJVC5E.

Heidegger, Martin. *The Question Concerning Technology.* Translated by William Lovitt. New York: Harper & Row, 1977.

Heller, Judith Bernays. "Freud's Voice," 1953. Box 116 Interviews+Recollections, Folder 36. Freud Papers, Library of Congress.

Herr, Hugh. "The Double Amputee Who Designs Better Limbs." Interview by Terry Gross. NPR, August 10, 2011. http://www.npr.org.

Himes, Mavis. "Cancer and the Body: Reflections from a Lacanian Perspective." *European Journal of Psychotherapy, Counselling and Health* 7, no. 4 (December 2005): 235–244.

Hinshelwood, R. D. *A Dictionary of Kleinian Thought.* 2nd edition. Northvale, N.J.: Jason Aronson, 1991.

"Is Freud Dead?" *Time Magazine*, November 29, 1993.

Jain, S. Lochlann. *Malignant: How Cancer Becomes Us.* Berkeley: University of California Press, 2013.

Jain, Sarah S. "The Prosthetic Imagination: Enabling and Disabling the Prosthesis Trope." *Science, Technology, and Human Values* 24, no. 1 (Winter 1999): 31–54.

Jentsch, Ernst. "On the Psychology of the Uncanny (1906)." Translated by Roy Sellars. *Angelaki* 2, no. 1 (1997): 7–16.

Jobst, Helga. "Freud and Archaeology." *Sigmund Freud House Bulletin* 2, no. 1 (1978): 46–51.

Johnson, Barbara. *Persons and Things.* Cambridge, Mass.: Harvard University Press, 2008.

Jolie, Angelina. "My Medical Choice." *New York Times*, May 14, 2013.

Jones, Ernest. "Letter to Max Schur," February 21, 1956. Box 2 Correspondence Jones, Ernest and Katherine 1953–61. Max Schur Papers, Library of Congress.

———. "Letter to Max Schur," March 13, 1956. Box 2 Correspondence Jones, Ernest and Katherine 1953–61. Max Schur Papers, Library of Congress.

———. *The Life and Work of Sigmund Freud, Volume Three: The Last Phase 1919–1939.* London: Hogarth Press, 1957.

———. *Sigmund Freud: Life and Work, Volume One: The Young Freud 1856–1900.* London: Hogarth Press, 1972.

Kafka, Ben. *The Demon of Writing: Powers and Failures of Paperwork.* New York: Zone Books, 2012.

Kazanjian, V. H. Interview with Dr. V. Kasanjian (sic), October 26, 1958. Box 112 Interview+Recollections, Folder 21. Freud Papers, Library of Congress.

———. Recollection by V. H. Kazanjian, February 18, 1959. Box OV15 Centenary of Freud's Birth. Miscellany. Freud Papers, Library of Congress.

Kennedy, Maev. "Thieves Smash Urn Holding Freud's Ashes." *The Guardian*, January 16, 2014.

King, Pearl, and Riccardo Steiner, eds. *The Freud-Klein Controversies 1941–45.* London: Tavistock/Routledge, 1991.

Klein, Melanie. "A Contribution to the Psychogenesis of Manic-Depressive States." *The International Journal of Psychoanalysis* 16 (1935): 145–174.

———. "Envy and Gratitude (1957)." In *Envy and Gratitude and Other Works 1946–1963*, edited by M. Masud R. Khan, 176–235. London: Hogarth Press and the Institute of Psycho-Analysis, 1975.

———. "The Importance of Symbol-Formation in the Development of the Ego." *International Journal of Psycho-Analysis* 11 (1930): 24–39.

———. "Mourning and Its Relation to Manic-Depressive States." *International Journal of Psycho-Analysis* 21 (1940): 125–153.

———. "Notes on Some Schizoid Mechanisms." *International Journal of Psycho-Analysis* 27 (1946): 99–110.

———. *The Psycho-Analysis of Children.* London: Hogarth Press, 1932.

———. "Weaning (1936)." In *Love, Guilt and Reparation and Other Works (1921–1945)*, 290–305. New York: Free Press, 1975.

Kluger, J., and A. Park. "The Angelina Effect." *Time*, May 27, 2013.

Kristeva, Julia. *Powers of Horror: An Essay on Abjection.* New York: Columbia University Press, 1982.

Kuriloff, Emily A. *Contemporary Psychoanalysis and the Legacy of the Third Reich: History, Memory, Tradition.* New York: Routledge, 2014.

Kuspit, Donald. "A Mighty Metaphor: The Analogy of Archaeology and Psychoanalysis." In Gamwell and Wells, *Sigmund Freud and Art.*

Lacan, Jacques. "The Mirror Stage as Formative of the Function of the I as Revealed in Psychoanalytic Experience." In *Écrits*, translated by Alan Sheridan. New York: Norton, 1977.

Laplanche, Jean. *Life and Death in Psychoanalysis*. Baltimore: Johns Hopkins University Press, 1985.

Laplanche, Jean, and J. B. Pontalis. *The Language of Psycho-Analysis*. Translated by Donald Nicholson-Smith. New York: Norton, 1973.

Latour, Bruno. *We Have Never Been Modern*. Cambridge, Mass.: Harvard University Press, 1993.

Leader, Darian. *The New Black: Mourning, Melancholia, and Depression*. London: Hamish Hamilton, 2008.

Lehrman, Philip R. *Sigmund Freud, His Family and Colleagues, 1928–1947*. 16mm film transferred to VHS, 1986.

Leslie, Esther. "Snow Shaker." In *The Object Reader*, edited by Fiona Candlin and Raiford Guins, 516–518. New York: Routledge, 2009.

Leupold-Löwenthal, Harold, and Hans Lobner. *Sigmund Freud-House Catalogue*. Vienna: Löcker & Wögenstein, 1975.

Leys, Ruth. *Trauma: A Genealogy*. Chicago: University of Chicago Press, 2000.

Likierman, Meira. *Melanie Klein: Her Work in Context*. London: Continuum, 2001.

Lopez, Donald S., ed. *Critical Terms of the Study of Buddhism*. Chicago: University of Chicago Press, 2005.

Lorde, Audre. *The Black Unicorn*. New York: Norton, 1978.

———. *A Burst of Light: Essays*. Ithaca, N.Y.: Firebrand Books, 1988.

———. *The Cancer Journals*. Argyle, N.Y.: Spinsters, Ink, 1980.

———. *Chosen Poems Old and New*. New York: Norton, 1982.

———. *The Marvelous Arithmetics of Distance: Poems 1987–1992*. New York: Norton, 1993.

———. "Of Generators and Survival—Hugo Letter." *Callaloo* 14, no. 1 (Winter 1991): 72–82.

———. *Our Dead Behind Us: Poems*. New York: Norton, 1986.

———. *Sister Outsider: Essays and Speeches*. Berkeley: Crossing Press, 2007.

———. *Zami: A New Spelling of My Name*. New York: Crossing Press, 1982.

Malcolm, Janet. *Psychoanalysis: The Impossible Profession*. New York: Vintage Books, 1982.

Marcus, Steven. "Freud and Dora: Story, History, Case History." In *In Dora's Case: Freud/Hysteria/Feminism*, edited by Charles Bernheimer and Claire Kahane, 2nd edition, 56–91. New York: Columbia University Press, 1990.

Marinelli, Lydia. "'Body Missing' at Berggasse 19." Translated by Joy Titheridge. *American Imago* 66, no. 2 (Summer 2009): 161–167.

———. "Fort, Da: The Cap in the Museum." *Psychoanalysis and History* 11, no. 1 (2009): 117–120.

———. "Smoking, Laughing and the Compulsion to Film: On the Beginnings of Psychoanalytic Documentaries." *American Imago* 61, no. 1 (Spring 2004): 35–58.

Marker, Chris. "The Statues Also Die (Transcript of 1953 Film)." Translated by Lauren Ashby. *Art in Translation* 5, no. 4 (2013): 429–438.

Marker, Chris, and Alain Resnais. *The Statues Also Die* (*Les Statues meurent aussi*). 35mm film. Paris: Présence Africaine, Tadié-Cinéma, 1953.

Mayer, Andreas. "Shadow of a Couch." *American Imago* 66, no. 2 (Summer 2009): 137–147.

Merriman, John, and Jay Winter, eds. "Vienna." *Europe Since 1914: Encyclopedia of the Age of War and Reconstruction*. Detroit: Charles Scribner's Sons, 2006.

Miller, Jacques-Alain. "Teachings of the Case Presentation." In *Returning to Freud: Clinical Psychoanalysis in the School of Lacan*, edited by Stuart Schneiderman. New Haven: Yale University Press, 1980.

Miller, Steven. *War After Death: On Violence and Its Limits*. New York: Fordham University Press, 2014.

Mollins, Julie. "Freud Museum London Celebrates 25th Anniversary." Reuters, July 28, 2011.

Molnar, Michael. "Half-Way Region." In *Freud's Sculpture*. Leeds: Henry Moore Institute, 2006.

———. "Of Dogs and Doggerel." *American Imago* 53 (1996): 269–280.

Moon, Michael. "Psychosomatic? Mental and Physical Pain in Eve Sedgwick's Writing." *Criticism* 52, no. 2 (Spring 2010): 203–213.

Morra, Joanne. "Seemingly Empty: Freud at Berggasse 19, A Conceptual Museum in Vienna." *Journal of Visual Culture* 12, no. 1 (2013): 89–127.

Mukherjee, Siddhartha. *The Emperor of All Maladies: A Biography of Cancer*. New York: Scribner, 2010.

Muñoz, José Esteban. *Disidentifications: Queers of Color and the Performance of Politics*. Minneapolis: University of Minnesota Press, 1999.

Nancy, Jean-Luc. *Corpus*. New York: Fordham University Press, 2008.

Newlands, David. "The Significance of the Freud Museum." In *Freud in Exile: Psychoanalysis and Its Vicissitudes*, edited by Edward Timms and Naomi Segal, 290–298. New Haven: Yale University Press, 1988.

Nixon, Mignon. "On the Couch." *October* 113 (Summer 2005): 39–76.

Nosenko, Tamara. "Path of Memory: A Walking Tour Honoring Jewish Residents of Vienna's 2nd District Who Died at the Hands of the Nazis." *Vienna Review*, March 1, 2008. https://goo.gl/onyM5T.

Novak, Amy. "Who Speaks? Who Listens? The Problem of Address in Two Nigerian Trauma Novels." *Studies in the Novel* 40, nos. 1–2 (Spring–Summer 2008): 31–51.

Nuland, Sherwin. *How We Die: Reflections on Life's Final Chapter*. New York: Vintage Books, 1995.

Pellegrini, Ann. "The Dogs of War and the Dogs at Home: Thresholds of Loss." *American Imago* 66, no. 2 (Summer 2009): 231–251.

———. *Performance Anxieties: Staging Psychoanalysis, Staging Race*. New York: Routledge, 1997.

Peters, Uwe Henrik. *Anna Freud: A Life Dedicated to Children*. New York: Schocken Books, 1985.

Phillips, Adam. *Darwin's Worms*. London: Faber and Faber, 1999.

Pichler, Hans, and Anna Freud. "Sigmund Freud Illness Record," 1939 1923. Box 159 Folder 2 Miscellany Freud Family. Anna Freud Papers, Library of Congress.

Picker, John M. "Atlantic Cable." *Victorian Review* 34, no. 1 (Spring 2008): 34–38.

Pietz, William. "The Problem of the Fetish, I." *RES: Anthropology and Aesthetics* 9 (Spring 1985): 5–17.

Pollock, Griselda, ed. *Psychoanalysis and the Image*. Malden, Mass.: Blackwell, 2006.

Puar, Jasbir K. "Prognosis Time: Towards a Geopolitics of Affect, Debility and Capacity." *Women & Performance: A Journal of Feminist Theory* 19, no. 2 (July 2009): 161–172.

Puente, M., D. Freydkin, and A. Mandell. "Her Mastectomy Could Change Women's Lives." *USA Today*, May 15, 2013.

Razinsky, Liran. *Freud, Psychoanalysis and Death*. Cambridge: Cambridge University Press, 2013.

Reiser, Lynn Whisnant. "Topsy—Living and Dying: A Footnote to History." *Psychoanalytic Quarterly* 56 (1987): 667–688.

Rhodes, Deborah. "Deborah Rhodes: A Tool That Finds 3x More Breast Tumors, and Why It's Not Available to You." *TED.com*, December 2010. https://goo.gl/XpbDtp.

Rich, Adrienne. *The Fact of a Doorframe: Selected Poems 1950–2001*. New York: Norton, 2002.

Romm, Sharon. *The Unwelcome Intruder: Freud's Struggle with Cancer*. New York: Praeger, 1983.

Ronell, Avital. *Crack Wars: Literature, Addiction, Mania*. Urbana: University of Illinois Press, 2004.

———. *The ÜberReader: Selected Works of Avital Ronell*. Edited by Diane Davis. Urbana: University of Illinois Press, 2008.

Rose, Jacqueline. *Why War? Psychoanalysis, Politics, and the Return to Melanie Klein*. Cambridge, Mass.: Blackwell, 1993.

Rose, Louis. "Freud and Fetishism: Previously Unpublished Minutes of the Vienna Psychoanalytic Society." *Psychoanalytic Quarterly* 57 (1988): 147–166.

Roudinesco, Elisabeth. *Why Psychoanalysis?* New York: Columbia University Press, 2001.

Royle, Nicholas. *The Uncanny*. Manchester: Manchester University Press, 2003.

Ryan, Cynthia. "Struggling to Survive: A Study of Editorial Decision-Making Strategies at MAMM Magazine." *Journal of Business and Technical Communication* 19, no. 3 (July 2005): 353–376.

Said, Edward W. *Out of Place: A Memoir*. New York: Knopf, 1999.

Said, Edward W., and Jacqueline Rose. *Freud and the Non-European*. London: Verso, 2003.

Salamon, Gayle. *Assuming a Body: Transgender and Rhetorics of Materiality*. New York: Columbia University Press, 2010.

Sanchez-Pardo, Esther. *Cultures of the Death Drive: Melanie Klein and Modernist Melancholia*. Durham, N.C.: Duke University Press, 2003.

Saroyan, William. *Obituaries*. Berkeley: Creative Arts Book Co., 1979.

Schilder, Paul. *The Image and Appearance of the Human Body*. New York: International Universities Press, 1950.

———. "On Rotting." *Psychoanalytic Review* 29 (1942): 46–49.

———. "Psycho-Analysis of Space." *International Journal of Psycho-Analysis* 16 (1935): 274–295.

Schor, Naomi. "Female Fetishism: The Case of George Sand." *Poetics Today* 6, nos. 1–2 (1985): 301–310.

Schur, Max. *Freud: Living and Dying*. New York: International Universities Press, 1972.

———. "Letter to Jones," September 30, 1955. Box 59 Folder 6 Freud Medical History: Correspondence between Jones, Schur, and Anna Freud. Freud Papers, Library of Congress.

Searles, Harold. *The Nonhuman Environment*. New York: International Universities Press, 1960.

Sedgwick, Eve Kosofsky. "Breast Cancer: Issues and Resources." *Lesbian and Gay Studies Newsletter*, Fall 1995.

———. "Caregivers Do's & Don'ts." *MAMM*, February 2000.

———. *A Dialogue on Love*. Boston: Beacon Press, 1999.

———. *Epistemology of the Closet*. Berkeley: University of California Press, 1990.

———. "Living with Advanced Cancer: The ABCs." *MAMM*, May 2001.

———. "Melanie Klein and the Difference Affect Makes." *South Atlantic Quarterly* 106, no. 3 (2007): 625–642.

———. "Off My Chest. Advanced Degree: School Yourself in Resilience to Beat Depression." *MAMM*, September 2000.

———. "Off My Chest. Fat or Thin? Can't Win: What to Do and How to Do It." *MAMM*, Summer 2002.

———. "Off My Chest. I Got It Good . . . and That Ain't Bad." *MAMM*, 1998.

———. "Off My Chest. The Guy Factor in BC Support Groups." *MAMM*, 2000.

———. "Off My Chest. A Scar Is Just a Scar: Approaching That First Post-mastectomy Tryst." *MAMM*, 1998.

———. "Off My Chest. World of Confusion: What Should We Make of the Mammography Controversy?" *MAMM*, February 2003.

———. "Teaching/Depression." *The Scholar & Feminist Online: Writing a Feminist's Life—The Legacy of Carolyn G. Heilbrun* 4, no. 2 (Spring 2006). https://goo.gl/ohf9H5.

———. *Tendencies.* Durham, N.C.: Duke University Press, 1993.

———. *Touching Feeling: Affect, Pedagogy, Performativity.* Durham, N.C.: Duke University Press, 2003.

———. *The Weather in Proust.* Edited by Jonathan Goldberg. Durham, N.C.: Duke University Press, 2011.

Sedgwick, Eve Kosofsky, ed. *Novel Gazing: Queer Readings in Fiction.* Durham, N.C.: Duke University Press, 1997.

Sedgwick, Eve Kosofsky, and Adam Frank. *Shame and Its Sisters: A Silvan Tomkins Reader.* Durham, N.C.: Duke University Press, 1995.

Shaviro, Steven. *The Universe of Things: On Speculative Realism.* Minneapolis: University of Minnesota Press, 2014.

Simmel, Ernst. *Anti-Semitism, A Social Disease.* New York: International Universities Press, 1946.

Skloot, Rebecca. *The Immortal Life of Henrietta Lacks.* New York: Broadway Books, 2011.

Slavet, Eliza. *Racial Fever: Freud and the Jewish Question.* New York: Fordham University Press, 2009.

Smith, Marquard, and Joanne Morra. *The Prosthetic Impulse: From a Posthuman Present to a Biocultural Future.* Cambridge, Mass.: MIT Press, 2006.

Snyder, Sharon L., and David T. Mitchell. *Cultural Locations of Disability.* Chicago: University of Chicago Press, 2006.

Sobchack, Vivian Carol. *Carnal Thoughts: Embodiment and Moving Image Culture.* Berkeley: University of California Press, 2004.

Solms, Mark. "Controversies in Freud Translation." *Psychoanalysis and History* 1 (1999): 28–43.

Sontag, Susan. *Illness as Metaphor.* New York: Farrar, Straus & Giroux, 1988.

Stekel, Wilhelm. "On the History of the Analytical Movement." *Psychoanalysis and History* 7 (2005): 99–130.

Stewart, Susan. *On Longing: Narratives of the Miniature, the Gigantic, the Souvenir, the Collection.* Durham, N.C.: Duke University Press, 1993.

Stonebridge, Lyndsey, and John Phillips, eds. *Reading Melanie Klein.* London: Routledge, 1998.

Sturken, Marita. *Tourists of History: Memory, Kitsch, and Consumerism from Oklahoma City to Ground Zero.* Durham, N.C.: Duke University Press, 2007.

Sulik, Gayle A. *Pink Ribbon Blues: How Breast Cancer Culture Undermines Women's Health.* New York: Oxford University Press, 2011.

Teichner, Martha. "The Model and the Mastectomy: Baring Scars Then and Now—CBS News." *CBSNews.com*, September 23, 2013.

Timms, Edward, and Naomi Segal, eds. *Freud in Exile: Psychoanalysis and Its Vicissitudes.* New Haven: Yale University Press, 1988.

Torok, Maria, Barbro Sylwan, and Adèle Covello. "Melanie Mell by Herself." In Stonebridge and Phillips, *Reading Melanie Klein*, 49–78.

Tsoukala, Philomila. "Reading 'A Poem Is Being Written': A Tribute to Eve Kosofsky Sedgwick." *Harvard Journal of Law & Gender* 33 (2010): 339–347.

Tully, John. "A Victorian Ecological Disaster: Imperialism, the Telegraph, and Gutta-Percha." *Journal of World History* 20, no. 4 (2009): 559–579.

Ucko, Peter. "Unprovenanced Material Culture and Freud's Collection of Antiquities." *Journal of Material Culture* 6, no. 3 (2001): 269–322.

U.S. Department of Health and Human Services Office of Minority Health. Accessed November 30, 2017. https://goo.gl/9t57Rh.

Wadler, Joyce. "My Breast: One Woman's Cancer Story." *New York Magazine.* Accessed April 25, 2014. https://goo.gl/QiW3DP.

Wailoo, Keith. *How Cancer Crossed the Color Line.* New York: Oxford University Press, 2011.

Walton, Jean. *Fair Sex, Savage Dreams: Race, Psychoanalysis, Sexual Difference.* Durham, N.C.: Duke University Press, 2001.

Weber, Samuel. *The Legend of Freud.* Stanford: Stanford University Press, 2000.

Webster, Jamieson. *The Life and Death of Psychoanalysis: On Unconscious Desire and Its Sublimation.* London: Karnac Books, 2011.

Werner, Arnold. "Edmund Engelman: Photographer of Sigmund Freud's Home and Offices." *The International Journal of Psychoanalysis* 83 (2002): 445–451.

Wills, David. *Dorsality: Thinking Back through Technology and Politics.* Minneapolis: University of Minnesota Press, 2008.

———. *Prosthesis.* Stanford: Stanford University Press, 1995.

Wilson, Elizabeth A. *Affect and Artificial Intelligence.* Seattle: University of Washington Press, 2010.

Wilson, Scott. "Dying for a Smoke: Freudian Addiction and the Joy of Consumption." *Angelaki* 7, no. 2 (August 2002): 161–173.

Winnicott, Donald Woods. *Playing and Reality.* Reprint. Harmondsworth: Penguin Books, 1982.

————. "Transitional Objects and Transitional Phenomena: A Study of the First Not-Me Possession." *International Journal of Psycho-Analysis* 34 (1953): 89–97.

Wood, Jon. "Re-Staging Freud's Sculpture." In *Freud's Sculpture*, 6–18. Leeds: Henry Moore Institute, 2006.

Yerushalmi, Yosef Hayim. *Freud's Moses: Judaism Terminable and Interminable*. New Haven: Yale University Press, 1991.

Young-Bruehl, Elisabeth. *Anna Freud: A Biography*. 2nd edition. New Haven: Yale University Press, 2008.

Žižek, Slavoj. *The Metastases of Enjoyment: Six Essays on Woman and Causality*. New York: Verso, 1994.

INDEX